A CONSPIRACY OF SILENCE

"Child abuse is just one of many frightening realities that it would be more comfortable to ignore. There is overwhelming proof of its pervasiveness, but many people work very hard at denying the seriousness of the problem. In this context, it is not surprising that few people would want to believe young children's bizarre stories of cannibalism and ritual murder. In looking at the documented cases of child exploitation that surround us, in observing the images of violence and dehumanized sexuality that are part of our everyday cultural landscape, it is not hard to believe that, conspiracy or no conspiracy, the satanists' goal could easily be achieved without much effort on their part."

—Kevin Marron, from *Ritual Abuse*

RITUAL ABUSE

Kevin Marron

SEAL BOOKS
McClelland-Bantam, Inc.
Toronto

RITUAL ABUSE

A Seal Book
Seal hardcover edition / April 1988
Seal paperback edition / February 1989

Canadian Cataloguing in Publication Data
Marron, Kevin
  Ritual Abuse

  ISBN 0-7704-2250-0

  1. Child abuse. 2. Satanism—Rituals. 3. Child
abuse—Ontario—Hamilton. Custody of
children—Ontario—Hamilton. I. Title.

HV6625.5.M37 1988   362.7'044   C87-094765-6

Seal Books are published by McClelland-Bantam, Inc. Its trademark,
consisting of the words "Seal Books" and the portrayal of a seal, is
the property of McClelland-Bantam, Inc., 105 Bond Street, Toronto,
Ontario M5B 1Y3, Canada. This trademark has been duly registered
in the Trademarks Office of Canada. The trademark consisting of
the words "Bantam Books" and the portrayal of a rooster is the property
of and is used with the consent of Bantam Books, 666 Fifth
Avenue, New York, New York 10103. This trademark has been duly
registered in the Trademarks Office of Canada and elsewhere

PRINTED IN CANADA

COVER PRINTED IN U.S.A.

U   0 9 8 7 6 5 4 3 2 1

Contents

INTRODUCTION

This book is about two young girls, who dared to tell their story of sexual abuse and savage rituals. It is a story that seemed beyond belief to the policemen who first investigated it. But the children's stories of sexual molestation, pornography, cannibalism and ritual murder were so detailed and consistent, contained so much knowledge inappropriate to children, and were accompanied by such clear symptoms of distress, that doctors, social workers and eventually the judge concluded that the children were not fantasizing or fabricating, but describing events from their own experience.

To these two sisters, whom I will call Janis and Linda, I dedicate this book. They were both less than eight years old when they first disclosed their history of abuse. A court order protecting their identity prevents me from disclosing their precise ages and some other details. I have never met them, but feel I have come to know them well, after covering the 18-month-long Crown wardship hearing that examined their story in painstaking detail. They are gentle, loving children, who have maintained a certain trust and innocence, in spite of having lived through horrors that are quite beyond the experience or even the imagination of almost any adult. They are now in the care of the state, and it is up to therapists and foster parents to help them cope with their bizarre and traumatic experiences, and, hopefully, grow up to lead normal lives.

Like almost everyone who attended the 150-day hearing in the Hamilton-Wentworth Unified Family Court, I was shocked and deeply distressed by what we heard of the children's graphic descriptions of horrendous degradation and abuse. I have not led a sheltered life, and as a working journalist I have frequently been exposed to quite horrible examples of human perversity, and have encountered many tragic victims. But I was quite unprepared for the gruesome and sordid details that we heard day after day in that small Hamilton courtroom. The horror of this material was rendered all the more intense by the knowledge that it represented a part of the life experience of two little girls, one of whom is barely out of kindergarten, and that the children's own parents were among the perpetrators of these shameful acts. The traumatic memories will stay with Janis and Linda for the rest of their lives. I, too, feel haunted by the image of their suffering, and can only hope that some good will come of it, as a result of the extraordinary level of publicity, which focused public attention on their case, and the issues that arose from it.

Besides providing some moving testimony on the emotional impact of extreme child abuse, the case raised important questions about the investigation of sexual abuse, and the rights of parents and children in the subsequent court process. The hearing also shed light on the new and frightening phenomenon of ritual abuse. This is the abuse of children as part of the rituals of a cult. It is different from other forms of child abuse in that it appears to be motivated not by passion or frustration, but by the pursuit of some perverse spiritual goal.

The children gave detailed descriptions of graveyard rituals, which suggested that they were the victims of a satanic cult. They described scenes that included cannibalism, pornography and the ritual murder of children and animals. Many elements of their descriptions were strikingly similar to disclosures made by children in various parts of the United States.

Such allegations have been taken seriously by many child abuse experts and police investigators in different communities across North America, while others have treated them with scorn and derision. No one has yet come up with any satisfactory explanation for the spate of more than 100 similar cases, which could point to the existence of organized or closely related groups engaging in cult activities, or using the trappings of satanism as a means of terrorizing and exploiting children. The Hamilton hearing represented the first attempt by a Canadian court to probe this new aberration, and was, perhaps, the most thorough investigation of such a case undertaken anywhere.

Janis and Linda began making disclosures about sexual abuse in February, 1985, after being placed in temporary foster care by their mother. The mother was herself a former victim of child abuse, who had suffered through a violent and tumultuous marriage to the children's father, an aggressive, hot-tempered man. At the time she put the children in care, the mother was experiencing difficulties in her relationship with her boyfriend, and was afraid she might harm the girls while in her depressed state. In a series of gradual and painful disclosures, the children accused their mother, her boyfriend, and their father of sexually abusing them. They then went on to describe in graphic detail pornographic video-making sessions at a television studio, macabre orgies of sex and violence and graveyard rituals involving cannibalism and the murder of other children.

Representatives of the Hamilton-Wentworth Children's Aid Society, who had concluded that the children were telling the truth, launched a court action under the *Ontario Child Welfare Act* seeking to have the children made wards of the Crown. This court action cited the children's forced participation in cannibalism and ritual murder as grounds for their being in need of protection from their parents. A police investigation, which child welfare workers believed was lax and haphazard, failed to find evidence to support criminal charges against the alleged perpetrators.

It was initially the bizarre allegations that attracted media interest. Child welfare hearings are not normally open to the public, and it was only after hearing submissions from media representatives that the case involved matters of public concern, that the presiding judge, District Court Judge Thomas Beckett, decided to allow reporters for six media organizations to attend the trial. As one of these reporters, representing the *Globe and Mail*, I had no idea, when I took my seat in the courtroom in October, 1985, that the hearing, which was scheduled for ten days, would extend for 18 months. I had no idea that I would hear a horrific and moving story that will probably haunt me for the rest of my life. I also had no idea then of the shocking pervasiveness of child sexual abuse in our society and the devastating impact it has on so many lives.

The hearing came at a time when the public was just becoming alerted to the significance of the problem of child sexual abuse, which has recently been discovered to be a disease of endemic proportions in North America. The extensive media coverage that the case received also fell in the context of a wider public debate on new federal legislation concerning the use of children's evidence in court. The sexual abuse of children presents peculiarly difficult problems for the legislators and the courts because it is a crime that usually takes place within the privacy of the home, and often leaves no physical scars on its victims. In most cases the victims have been molested by a family member, and the sometimes confused and intimidated victim is the only eyewitness to the crime.

The question of how to handle such cases in the courts is a new one, because it was not until the early 1980s that the sexual exploitation of children was recognized to be a widespread problem. Just a few years ago, hardly anyone was aware of its existence. Described by one expert in the field as "the best kept secret,"[1] this phenomenon, which has probably been with us for generations, has not been recognized for a number of reasons. It has remained hidden, first, because abused children are extremely reluctant to disclose that they have been victimized by family members or other trusted adults whom they fear and love; second, because adults have generally not been prepared to believe the few abused children who have attempted to disclose their painful secrets. Children were seldom considered to be credible witnesses and their allegations of abuse were often dismissed as fantasies.

In the 1950s the work of radiologists, who detected bone damage in a large number of young children, made the public aware of the problem of the physical abuse of children. Child protection services grew as a result of this, and psychiatrists began paying more attention to the problem of family violence. Out of this new concern grew an awareness of an even greater problem, as more and more reports of sexual abuse were investigated and found to be valid. The women's movement also helped to make the public more aware of sexual violence against women and children. By the mid-1980s, about two-thirds of the cases of child abuse reported to Canadian child protection agencies involved sexual molestation.

Many psychiatrists and social workers have come to believe that children rarely lie in making such allegations, particularly when they make them against their parents. However, until new legislation was passed in 1987, it remained extremely difficult for children to testify in Canadian criminal courts. No special arrangements were made to prevent young children from being frightened and intimidated by the ordeal of facing their alleged abuser in a formal court process. In order to be sworn to testify in court, children under 14 years of age had to pass a competency test to satisfy a judge that they understood the meaning of the oath. If they did not pass this test, which sometimes involved questions about their religious education, their evidence was heard by the court, but was not given the same credibility afforded to an adult witness.

In a package of measures designed to address the problem of child sexual abuse, the federal government amended the criminal code and the *Canada Evidence Act* in 1987. This legislation created three new offenses: sexual interference, invitation to sexual touching, and sexual exploitation. These will make it easier to prosecute child sexual abuse cases that were previously dealt with under the same sexual assault laws that applied to offenses against adults. The rules of evidence were changed so that it will now be possible for children's evidence to be given the same weight as that of adults, providing the child is found to be capable of communicating and can promise to tell the truth. The new law enables children to testify outside the courtroom, providing the accused is able to view the testimony on a closed-circuit television. Another important change allows for the use in court of videotaped statements made by the child on a prior occasion. If such statements are used, the child still has to be available for cross-examination in court, but does not necessarily have to undergo the ordeal of detailing all of the alleged abuse.

This new legislation was being formulated and debated during the 18 months that the Hamilton case was before the court. Child welfare advocates were pressuring the government to enact the changes, and opponents of the legislation were concerned that the rights of accused people would be compromised by the new laws. While supporters of the legislation drew attention to dramatic increases in the number of validated reports of child sexual abuse, other people expressed alarm about the preponderance of false allegations of abuse that were surfacing in divorce and custody cases.

The Crown wardship hearing that resulted from Janis's and Linda's allegations explored some of the crucial questions in this ongoing debate. How can the credibility of young children's statements be adequately assessed? Is it possible to do this without subjecting the children to the ordeal of testifying? Is it appropriate to use videotaped therapy sessions as evidence in court? The family court, which was not required to follow the same strict rules of evidence as a criminal trial, considered the hearsay testimony of foster parents and social workers, examined the children's credibility through the analyses of expert witnesses, and watched the children in videotaped therapy sessions, without ever forcing them to testify. Some of these novel procedures went further than anything proposed in the new federal laws, which will still require that children testify in some way before their evidence can be used in a criminal trial. But these procedures do involve new methods that some experts would like to see applied in a modified way to criminal proceedings. Even before the Hamilton hearing was over, lawyers, judges and psychiatrists had begun to consider the lessons that could be learned from it.

My initial reaction on hearing about the children's bizarre allegations was that they were preposterous and incredible. I thought they must have been either lying or fantasizing, and I wondered how the doctors and social workers who examined their stories could possibly have taken them seriously. But as I listened to the evidence, it became clear to me that the girls' horrible descriptions of sexual abuse could only have been based on experience, and that their accounts of ritual violence had the same ring of authenticity. Other evidence at the trial tended to strengthen the possibility that the children might have been involved in satanic cult activities.

Even if one dismisses the possibility that the children were describing actual murders that they witnessed, and assumes that they were confused or mistaken about this, their evidence still presents profoundly disturbing questions. Were these children used in rituals that featured sex, sadism and animal mutilation? Were they used in the making of pornographic movies, involving simulated violence and terror? Were they terrorized by the trappings of satanism and simulations of murder and cannibalism, in order to insure their compliance in sexual abuse? Or were they exposed to such traumatic sexual abuse and brutality in their home that their distorted memories of this came out as a lurid, but realistic, horror story? In pondering all these questions we have to think seriously about the level of protection that our society is providing to children, the resources it is allocating to the investigation of such abuse, and the underlying social conditions that have resulted in such perversions of human values.

The length of the case and the estimated $1 million that it cost the taxpayers was a subject of great public concern. Lawyers involved in the hearing became concerned that the children's right to a speedy determination about their future was being eroded by the process that was supposed to be protecting them. The rights of the children's parents to the same speedy determination were also compromised, and the process took a very heavy toll on the girls' emotionally unstable mother, who had to be hospitalized when she collapsed screaming and shaking on the courtroom floor while giving her evidence.

The case also posed broader questions of public policy on the issue of child sexual abuse. Evidence in the trial exposed inadequacies in the level of communication between doctors, day-care workers and child protection workers about the plight of the children before they were taken into care. If that communication had been better, it is possible that the abuse and neglect of these children might have been identified sooner, and they could have been saved from some of their horrifying ordeals. Does this therefore point to a need for more professional education and training in this field and better coordination of services? Did the police adequately investigate the children's allegations? Do they have the resources and the training to cope with the ever-increasing number of reported cases of child sexual abuse? Are they able to properly investigate ritual abuse or organized pornography rings?

Editors at the *Globe and Mail*, like those at the five other media organizations that obtained permission to attend the closed hearing, clearly believed that all these issues were important enough to merit daily coverage throughout the 18 months of the hearing. All were confronted with the problem of how to present the sordid and gruesome material that emerged from the trial in a way that would neither sensationalize nor offend, but at the same time reflect the gravity and the very specific nature of the children's allegations. This issue, which provoked anguish and considerable debate in newsrooms, was handled in different ways at different times: at some times the stories were shockingly graphic; at other times they were perhaps lacking in relevant detail. Judge Beckett did, however, several times express his belief that the media had done a responsible job in covering the trial. Other parties, including the Hamilton-Wentworth Children's Aid Society, emphasized the important role that this publicity was playing in focusing public attention on the issues involved.

What newspapers, radio and television could not do, because of the limitations of these media, was to present the full story of the case, explain its full context and explore the vital problems that it addressed. That is the role of this book, and again I am confronted with the dilemma of how to present the material in a way that does justice to the subject, without unnecessarily disturbing the reader with grossly offensive descriptions.

I do not believe it is possible to convey the truly horrendous quality of the children's allegations, or explain why so many people found them to be totally convincing, without including many lurid details, which most sensitive readers will find difficult and deeply disturbing. I was shocked both by the overall import of what the children disclosed and by their specific descriptions of extreme sexual abuse and sadistic violence. Psychiatrists, who have worked with many abused children throughout their professional careers, reported that they spent sleepless nights brooding over the particularly distressful disclosures that these children made. In his final judgement on the case, Judge Beckett referred to the girls' allegations as "a virtual flood of the most lurid, gruesome, bloodthirsty stories that any person could possibly imagine." But, he said, "as distasteful and as upsetting as it may be to have to repeat this material here, I consider it important to do so, because I believe that these allegations that the children made to a large extent form the basis of decision."

The reader will no doubt find some passages in the book extraordinarily disturbing to read. What I can promise, however, is that such passages are not included for any reason other than to inform the reader of the horrors of child sexual abuse, which must not be ignored. If we are aware of the physical and emotional pain that these children experienced, perhaps we can prevent other children from suffering a similar fate.

Doctors have long had to struggle with their personal sense of outrage as they dealt with the victims of what a 19th-century French physician described as "crimes of the home." Another French doctor from the same era said child abuse "is one of the most terrifying problems that can trouble the heart of man."[2]

In 1970 an American surgeon told the National Commission on Pornography and Obscenity: "Lately, I've been in gynecology and obstetrics. It's absolutely frightening to see what's going on. The wards and private rooms are filled with young girls. . . . Their insides are torn to pieces. It is impossible to describe the repair jobs we do. These girls suffer from every kind of sexual abuse."[3]

Yet the statistics suggest that the victims seen by doctors represent just a tiny fraction of the hundreds of thousands of children who endure their pain in a fearful and guilt-ridden silence, and whose scars cannot be detected by a physical examination. Psychiatrists and former victims have documented the crippling effects that the invisible internal injuries of sexual abuse usually have on the future lives of molested children.

"Statistics, for all the horror they imply, can be so vast that we shield ourselves from the individual lives they represent," wrote Ellen Bass, in an introduction to a book of writings by survivors of child sexual abuse. "It is not easy to open oneself to the knowledge that millions of children are raped. Our defenses rush to protect us from experiencing the pain. But we cannot close ourselves off and hope for the best. We are in danger. Our daughters are in danger. Even our sons are in danger. Behind each statistic, there is a child. She may be you. She may be your daughter. She may be your sister. She may be your friend. You cannot protect her until we can protect all children."[4]

In telling the story of Janis and Linda, I have attempted to explain its significance by drawing on material gleaned from interviews and research on child abuse and satanic cults. But the narrative itself is based entirely on court testimony. All the quotes from the children and adults involved in the case are taken directly from court testimony or documents filed as evidence at the hearing. Some details have been omitted to prevent the children from being identified, and for the same reason I have not used the real names of the children, their parents, their mother's boyfriend and other individuals whom the court ordered must not be identified.

In order to present the children's story and the issues raised at the hearing in a logical and readable sequence, I have not followed the order in which evidence was presented at the hearing. The first section, on the mother's background and the children's early lives, is drawn from the evidence of social workers, teachers, day-care staff and doctors, as well as from the mother's own testimony and statements she made to other people that were entered as evidence at the hearing. The section on the children's allegations is based largely on the foster mother's notes and testimony, with additional information that was supplied by other witnesses. The third section, which deals with the investigation of the case, recounts and analyzes the testimony of police, psychiatrists and social workers. The final section contains detailed accounts of the children's videotaped therapy sessions and the testimony of the three people they accused of abusing them—their mother, her boyfriend and their father.

Although this book documents an extreme example of human depravity, it also describes the love and idealism that fortunately survives in the face of all suffering. While the children's stories were shocking, they were also intensely moving. After hearing the girls' disclosures and seeing them in videotaped therapy sessions, I was left not only repulsed by the abuse they had suffered, but also inspired by the fact that these traumatic experiences have not broken the spirit of these children. I was also greatly impressed by the sincerity and commitment of the foster parents, social workers and doctors who have devoted much energy to helping them deal with their pain. I fervently hope that readers of this book will share these insights, address the overwhelming problem of child sexual abuse and help make some changes in our society.

RITUAL
ABUSE

PART ONE

A BACKGROUND OF ABUSE

CHAPTER 1
SETTING THE SCENE

A last-day-of-school atmosphere prevailed on January 22, 1987, as lawyers made their final submissions in Canada's longest-ever child welfare hearing. One of the lawyers, Michael O'Neail, a large, bald-headed fellow, whose conviviality always looked as if it was bursting to break out of his somber legal garb, brought a party noisemaker with him. He blew it, with the slightly surreptitious air of a schoolboy venturing a classroom prank, just after Judge Thomas Beckett, another large, affable man, adjourned the hearing to await his final judgment, and left the bench with an unaccustomedly sprightly gait.

For 17 months the court had been delving into the allegations of two very young children, whose tales of ritual violence, degradation and abuse contained more stark horror and brutality than almost anything anyone present had ever heard, seen, read or imagined. As they probed from the calm and security of a Hamilton, Ontario, courtroom into a grim and violent story of life in Canada's hidden slums, the judge and lawyers had heard about threats on their own lives, allegedly made by the girls' irate father. They had witnessed a dramatic courtroom scene in which the mother, herself a tragic victim of the cycle of deprivation and abuse, ran screaming from the witness stand and fell shaking into a fetal

3

ball on the courtroom floor, believing that the black-gowned lawyer, who was trying to comfort her, was her now-deceased father threatening to hit her again.

But, as the court adjourned to await a final judgment in the case, the talk was mostly about football. The Toronto lawyers, who had been taken to the cleaners when they bet against Hamilton in the 1986 Grey Cup, were now hoping to get their money back on the Giants in the Super Bowl. They were exchanging banter and pieces of paper with the court constable. This had become quite a ritual as the hearing had continued through two Super Bowls, two Grey Cups and two World Series, while two young children waited in foster homes for the court to determine their future.

It is not every day that lawyers specializing in child welfare issues get their pictures in the paper, and some of them were quite excited about the photographs that the *Toronto Star* reporter was taking to go with her wrap-up stories on the case. Michael Hartrick, a witty, urbane young man, who represented the children's notoriously violent and unsophisticated father, was very concerned about his hair. He had had his long red mane trimmed a little after the reporter had mentioned that, when it was blowing in the wind, it gave the impression that he was balding on top. O'Neail, who represented the mother's enigmatic boyfriend at the hearing, was taking great delight in an unreassuring show of mock sympathy for Hartrick's concerns.

John Harper, the lawyer for the Children's Aid Society, a dark-haired, serious man with a brusque but friendly manner, was listening with amusement to Hugh Atwood, the representative of the Ontario Official Guardian, express his pique when told that his assistant was more photogenic than he. He said he thought it must be because he had a few gray hairs, and he was hoping for better things from the sketch artist, who was there for the *Globe and Mail*.

Meanwhile, the *Star* reporter was cajoling the mother's lawyer, Arthur Brown, a slightly pudgy, red-haired man with a ruddy complexion, who, unlike the other lawyers, considered it beneath his dignity to pose for a photograph. He had just put on a large comical-looking fur hat, and the reporter was telling him he would look quite foolish if she had to resort to sneaking a shot of him in that ridiculous hat. His client, Sharon Wells, was taking great delight in this discussion. Though she had shown huge swings of emotion during the 150 days she had sat in the courtroom, she usually enjoyed a simple joke outside the court and often affectionately teased her lawyer, who, she said, was the only person she trusted in the whole world.

Some reporters and court staff watching this exchange were quietly speculating about a change they had noticed in Sharon during the last few weeks of the hearing. She was a small woman, whose shabby dress and disheveled appearance seemed to reflect the disintegration of her life. But she recently appeared to have acquired a new wardrobe, and had started to take more care of herself. She was now quite smartly dressed and was even wearing makeup—and this new guise coincided with a subtle change in her behavior. She suddenly appeared more distant and controlled, where before she had been casual and friendly outside the courtroom, though in a guarded and distracted way. This new image might have been a last-minute attempt to persuade the court that she was a competent and stable person, who would be capable of caring for her children. Perhaps it was an attempt to convince herself of that.

Nobody who followed the case could fail to feel great compassion for Sharon, after witnessing the young mother's courtroom breakdown and hearing her tell her story of the horrendous abuse she suffered as a child and in her tumultuous marriage. One could not help but feel that this slightly built woman, who somehow gave the impression of never having been given a chance to grow, was a victim of a harsh system that was now grinding her down with this relentless, interminable legal process. Everyone in the courtroom was touched when she would show off her Instamatic snapshots of her baby daughter, Melanie, who was born while the trial was already in progress, and then snatched away by the authorities within days of her birth.

Yet it was a sympathy that was mixed with horror and disgust. The court had also seen hours of videotaped play-therapy sessions in which Sharon's young children Janis and Linda screamed, hid in cupboards, played at being little babies who were being cooked in ovens and showed almost unbearable anguish and fear as they told their psychiatrists about grotesque forms of sexual abuse inflicted by their mother and her boyfriend Gary. The handful of observers permitted to attend the closed Crown wardship hearing had been shocked and repulsed by witnesses' accounts of the children's detailed graphic descriptions, not only of ugly, degrading abuse, but also of macabre scenes of violent ritual, including murders and cannibalistic acts, which the girls said their mother and Gary and their father involved them in.

Beyond belief these stories may have been, though the psychiatrists who examined them and many of the people who sat in the court eventually ceased to think so. But where did they come from? What perverse influences could have so warped the minds or life experience of two young girls who were barely out of kindergarten? Why did their mother, who reveled so much in her own role as victim, display no horror or sympathy for the dreadful things her children were relating?

These questions lingered in the minds of people who observed Sharon Wells as she sat in the courtroom, gasping and sighing, shaking her head and wringing her hands, her prominent lips open in a vacant expression, as her unexpectedly piercing eyes darted all around her. People wondered about her as she would rock back and forth in her chair, repeating a prayer that became almost a chant, "God give me strength," while she waited for the judge to decide if she would ever be allowed to see her children again.

Those who puzzled over their mixed and confusing responses to Sharon Wells had less opportunity to study the character of her former husband, Gordon, whose comparatively brief appearance nevertheless deeply impressed all who saw him testify. If ever there was someone whose reputation preceded him, it was Gordon Wells. For months the court had been hearing details of his alleged acts and threats of extreme violence, culminating in Sharon's claim that he had told her he was going to shut the court down and "bring his satanic friends to testify." Even his lawyer, Michael Hartrick, was not being entirely facetious when he said he was scared of him— in fact Hartrick had been one of the people in the court whom Gordon had, according to Sharon, threatened to "blow away."

When he did appear, this brusque, aggressive man exhibited a certain rough charm. He spoke softly most of the time, but in a rapid, clipped manner, seldom finishing a sentence. His long black hair appeared to be carefully brushed back and greased down and he wore a slightly threadbare black velvet jacket over his jeans and work boots. But his eyes glared threats and his brow furrowed menacingly with anger as his voice sometimes rose to a fierce, blustering tone.

Again the questions lingered. Was this man, who made

light of the fact that he carried a sawed-off shotgun in the trunk of his car, really just a "mush-ball" on the inside, as his lawyer claimed? Or could he have committed the grisly murders that his daughters alleged? Why could he say no more about his children's bizarre tales than "It's all B.S."? Did he have to give an explanation in the face of quite thin evidence against him? Was he a potential victim of a child-protection philosophy that assumes parents to be guilty solely on the basis of children's statements? Did the state have the right to take away this man's children because they were emotionally threatened by his violent lifestyle?

As Judge Beckett retired to consider his judgment, he was also confronted with the puzzle of what to make of Gary Evans, the young university graduate who had become the boyfriend of the unattractive, hostile and somewhat simple-minded Sharon Wells. Evans was the father of the new baby and the most prominent figure in the two older girls' detailed descriptions of sexual abuse. A soft-spoken, mild-mannered man of West Indian descent, he had told the court that he was not the "type of person" who would harm children in any way, and psychiatric reports had supported this claim. Was he a predatory pedophile who got involved with Sharon in order to molest her little girls, or was he an innocent who had become entangled in a legal web woven from children's fairy tales?

Another possibility that the judge would have to consider was that these small children had been somehow manipulated, that someone had planted strange ideas in their minds—ideas that had been elaborated and distorted through the promptings of prejudiced or gullible social workers and foster parents. Perhaps their foster mother, the grandmotherly Catherine McInnis, who was almost driven to distraction by the girls' fearsome horror stories, was, as their father suggested, "a nut case." Could the foster mother have encouraged their fantasies?

Judge Beckett would also have to think about what to make of the fiasco of the police investigation of the case, which seemed to have been founded on the assumption that the girls' stories were "beyond belief" and not worth taking seriously. The Hamilton-Wentworth Regional Police had found no tangible evidence to support the children's allegations. But what was the judge to make of that, when the officers assigned to the investigation had not even interviewed some of the key people involved the case. Also, they had cajoled the children with their aggressive skeptical interrogations and allowed plenty of time for evidence to be destroyed or removed before they went looking for it.

All these questions, and many more, confronted Thomas Beckett as he walked out of the court to begin the monumental task of sifting through the evidence contained in 142 exhibits and more than 15,000 pages of court transcripts in order to arrive at a judgment as to whether Janis, Linda and Melanie should be made wards of the Crown, and, if so, whether their parents should have any access to them.

When it began in September, 1985, the case of *the Children's Aid Society of Hamilton-Wentworth versus Children X and Y* had been scheduled to last ten days. However, it had soon become apparent that it would take considerably longer because of the detail and bizarre character of the children's allegations and the fact that they were too young to testify. Their statements had been made to a variety of people and been analyzed by a bevy of experts, all of whom would also have to testify.

At that point no one dreamed how much longer it would take. Certainly not the newspaper, television and radio reporters who gathered in an art deco style downtown office building that housed the Unified Family Court to cover what promised to be a weird and sensational case. Their very presence caused the first of many delays and legal wrangles, as lawyers argued about whether the media should have access to the proceedings, which were closed to the general public in order to protect the identity of the children.

Judge Beckett, who had been active in Liberal Party politics and had gained a considerable reputation as a civil libertarian lawyer before being appointed to the bench, decided that the public had a right to know about a case involving issues of general concern. But he made an order that limited the media coverage to insure that nothing was reported that would identify the children, parents, foster parents or even some of the professionals who worked with the children. In order to avoid turning the case into a "media circus" and because of the limited space in the court, the judge also ordered that only six news organizations could cover the hearing, and that others be allowed to attend only if some of the original six gave up their places in the court. This ruling, which caused great anguish to editors, actually had the effect of insuring that the case had an unprecedented level of daily coverage—newspapers and electronic media, which normally drop in and out of lengthy trials according to the potential news value of the anticipated testimony, felt obliged in this instance to be there continually, fearing that someone else would claim their seats in the court.

The case began to take on a nightmarish complexity, as it proceeded in a stuffy little courtroom, where the indoor environment was measurably more polluted even than the notorious air of the industrial city outside. The new baby was born, and an application to make her a Crown ward was joined with the original case. This meant two new lawyers coming into the hearing, which was moved to a more spacious, but equally stuffy, courtroom in the Hamilton-Wentworth District Court House. Some of the lawyers originally involved in the hearing had to pull out for personal reasons—one to have a baby with whom she had become pregnant at around the time the trial began. The need for new lawyers to catch up with details of earlier testimony required adjournments, as did various side issues and procedural wrangles that crept into the case. The case became, as Judge Beckett put it, "like a living organism" that grew to almost unmanageable proportions as it dragged its feet through the ponderous legal process.

Public concern began to grow over the monstrous length of the case, the huge expenditure of public funds and the danger that traumatized children and, possibly innocent adults, were suffering because of this protracted legal process. Judge Beckett began to show signs of distress from the public pressure he was under, and his normally patient, good-humored approach sometimes gave way to flashes of temper, in which he used his keen wit to lash out satirically at lawyers engaging in legal wrangles or "interminable cross-examinations."

Just before adjourning the case to await his judgement, Beckett had been provoked into an angry outburst about the "obscene" length of the trial. He railed at lawyers, who, he said, appeared to be wanting to make a career of the trial and seemed prepared to continue interminably a legal process that had been "an act of perverse cruelty to these children."

As was usually the case, a long lunch-break restored the comfortably proportioned judge to a more affable frame of mind. There was an expression of immense relief on his large, sensitive face as he almost skipped out of the courtroom on that January afternoon. At the age of 62, he had just remarried. After a few weeks of hard work on his judgment, he was hoping to be able to take some time off for a honeymoon.

CHAPTER 2
EARLY YEARS

Childhood experiences are often a dominant influence on people's lives. The way people treat their children is frequently modeled on their own upbringing. This natural human characteristic takes on a tragic dimension for a person whose early experiences were of pain and humiliation and whose only model for parenting was one of brutal abuse.

Sharon Wells was such a person. She was victimized by her own parents and other adults during childhood, just as her own children were abused by her and the people she associated with. She was part of what social workers call "the cycle of child abuse," the process by which exploitative behavior is passed on from one generation to the next. As Judge Beckett noted in his final judgment on the case. "An adult who is abused as a child is predisposed to abuse his or her own children since people tend to repeat what they grew up with."

Slum clearance, development and restoration have now transformed the Toronto inner-city neighborhoods where Sharon Wells grew up. One can trace, in the series of addresses where her family lived, the pattern of migration of Canada's urban poor during the last 20 years, as they were driven ever further from the city's center by the wrecker's ball and the needs of a booming real estate market.

It was an exodus that ended in what was to have been

11

the promised land: the efficient high-rise buildings of the outer suburbs. But the milk and honey went only to the developers, as these rapidly deteriorating apartment complexes became isolated enclaves of poverty and crime—the newer and bleaker ghettoes of the dispossessed.

An expensive new town house development now occupies the site of one of the homes where Sharon lived during her abused and deprived childhood. It is now a fashionable district full of art galleries, bookstores, restaurants and boutiques. This development was the subject of a bitter planning controversy in the late 1960s, as citizens' groups fought to preserve a working-class neighborhood. Sharon did not remember the place with nostalgia.

"It was such a bad place to live. We had to move because there was rats and bugs," she said, as she told the court her tragic life history. "They were never really good places. The best place we lived was in North York. But there were still bugs."

Sharon, and thousands like her, escaped the plague of rats by leaving the inner city, and that may have been the only real progress that came from the best intentions of public planners, allied with the perhaps less pure motives of the property developers. Although they did nothing to break the cycle of poverty, they did succeed in sweeping a highly visible social problem off the downtown streets and under a carpet of suburban sprawl.

Low-income housing and welfare rights are no longer such fashionable issues as they were in the late 1960s. The public agenda has moved on to other concerns. Near the top of that agenda is the newly recognized plight of sexually abused children. No one knew or cared when Sharon silently suffered such abuse 20 years ago in the downtown slums.

In Canada, the 1984 report of the federal government Committee On Sexual Offenses Against Children And Youths, which is usually referred to as the Badgley Commission, concluded, "Child sexual abuse is a largely hidden yet pervasive tragedy that has damaged the lives of tens of thousands of Canadian children and youths." This committee did a survey of a representative sample of Canadians and found that about 40 percent of the women interviewed said they had been victims of unwanted sexual acts during childhood. The report described the fear, shame and helplessness experienced by these victims, and noted that three out of four of them kept the assault a closely guarded personal secret. The report commented: "Why did so few of the young victims seek assistance? These persons, or the parents of children who have been assaulted or molested, explain in their own words why most of them did not even tell another family member. Two-thirds were too young when these incidents occurred to know that sexual contacts were wrong. If they did know, then they were too ashamed about what had happened, or they were too afraid of their assailants to tell others. Among the few who later told a parent about these incidents, all were initially disbelieved."

Sharon Wells was one such victim. As she told her pathetic story to the court, shaking and wringing her hands, pausing often as she began to sob or pant hysterically, everyone who listened was conscious of the dreadful irony—she was also describing what her own children had allegedly suffered at her hands.

Sharon was the fourth of six children. Sharon's mother and father split up soon after their youngest son, Mike, was born.

Sharon's first memory of abuse was from when she was about three or four years old. They were living in a three-story brick house with an attic, which led out onto the flat roof. Sharon used to go up to the attic to play. There was a back room in the attic, little more than a cubbyhole. Her father kept a telescope up there. They had a boarder living in the house whom the children called "the redheaded woodpecker" because of his red hair.

Judge Beckett gently told Sharon to take her time and relax, as she tearfully told the court of her encounter with the redheaded woodpecker: "We were playing a game: horsey. My mom used to play it with me on her foot. But I wasn't on his foot. I was laughing because I didn't really understand then. But I do now. I got wet. And we were just playing. He just got mean afterwards, and he put me in the cubbyhole, and said if I tell anyone he would. . . . He threatened me. I didn't know. I didn't know. I didn't understand. But I do now."

It was towards the end of the wardship hearing that Sharon gave this testimony, and she apologized to the judge for her lack of composure: "I'm sorry. I listened to all this through this court. I thought I'd be able to sit here, since I already heard it, and it would be easier to sit here and say it."

She also remembered being abused by her father in the

same house. He stuck his fingers in her, she said. She didn't tell anyone because "he would kill me. You just don't get him angry at you."

One time he inserted a block in her, and her mother took her to the hospital. She didn't tell anyone about how it got there "because you don't make my dad mad. He hit us kids a lot. He would kick my brother, take the boot to him. My brother come home, and said he got beat up at school. My dad whipped him good. He'll kill you, sure as you sit there.

"One time I needed help to tie up my shoes. I asked him to help me. He just said, 'Don't bug me.' He hauled off, and went wham, and I went flying. We had this boarder called Lorne. I used to like to watch him put insoles in his boots. He said, 'Sharon, some day you'll find happiness.' I just looked at him. He said, 'I hope it isn't after you're dead.' I didn't understand what he said. But I do now."

Sharon said her dad put his fingers in her when he got drunk on weekends—not every weekend, but about ten or fifteen times altogether. She said her mom and dad used to fight a lot and one of the reasons her mother eventually left her father was that she caught him molesting her.

Her mother moved with the children to a rat-infested house in the neighborhood, which was slated for redevelopment. From there, they moved to an apartment over a store, in a seedy, run-down district where the housing had deteriorated too far to be worth renovating. This area remains much the same today, except that the corner store is now owned by a chain. The tavern over which Sharon's family lived for a while now seeks to lure the more daring or desperate into its bleak confines with a neon sign advertising "Three Exotic Dancers."

What Sharon remembers most about the apartment over the store is the broken stair, which you couldn't step on, where she once lost her doll. There were two bedrooms, one for the boys and one for the girls, and her mother slept in the living room on a bed. She does not remember how long they lived there, except that they were there for at least one Christmas because the children sold Christmas trees, which the boys had scrounged by telling someone "a sob story."

They lived over the tavern for about another year and Sharon's most vivid memory of this place was a haunting one. Her father was not living with them but he used to visit. One day Sharon's older sister Sally brought her to the window of the apartment and pointed to a stained paper towel on the ground.

"That's Dad's blood," Sally told Sharon, "Dad fell out the window."

Her mother told her that her dad had jumped out of the window. He had been taken to hospital and recovered. He continued to visit them after that, but he did not sexually abuse Sharon any more.

She remembers being physically abused by her mother. She used to try to protect herself from these beatings by laughing instead of crying. This would enrage her mother, but the more the woman hit her, the more Sharon would laugh. Sharon later wondered if this had somehow distorted her emotionally. She said she scared herself sometimes by laughing when she should have been crying. She could understand, however, why her mother would be driven to administer these beatings: "She didn't know any better. Her mother did it to her. Her mother's mother did it."

From the tavern the family moved to a house on a short narrow street, where many of the buildings are now uninhabitable and boarded up. When she was asked to describe this house to the court, Sharon shook her head with an expression of disgust. "There were lots of bugs," she said. "It had a veranda and a backyard covered with cement.

"My mom has a saying: A place can get messy and can get dirty, and her place is always messy not dirty. From my point of view it was always dirty," she told the court.

She said her mother would tell the children to clean the place. On one occasion her sister Sally was washing dishes to get ready to eat supper, when their mother noticed that the table had not been washed. "She made us put food right on the table. She said, 'If you want to eat off a dirty table . . .' I don't like what happened. There was people there, company there."

When Sharon was about ten years old her mother's latest boyfriend moved in to live with them. This perverse and violent man, Anton Laroche, who would later become her stepfather, was to have a devastating effect on the precarious emotional balance of Sharon and her sisters. Anton and Sharon's mother had a child, Lucille, who was born when Sharon was 13 years old. Anton also had a daughter by a previous marriage who was about Sharon's age.

Even before he moved in, when Sharon and her younger sister Lesley would stay at his house with their mother, Anton would join in the games they played with his daughter, and encourage them to touch him sexually.

When Anton moved in with the family, his nephew also came to stay as a lodger. It was he who first persecuted Sharon. She and Lesley used to share the same bed in the basement, and one night when their mother and Anton had gone out, his nephew, whom the girls called uncle, came down to the basement.

As Sharon described her memory of this incident to the court, she said, "When I think about this it makes me so angry inside. I can't believe it. He had his pants down and he was rubbing against me. I kept my eyes closed so he wouldn't think I'm awake, because I'm so scared. A knock came at the door. Mom caught him going upstairs doing up his pants.

"She kicked him out. That was great. I'm proud of her for kicking him out. But he was eating at the table the next day. She threw the sucker out, and to think he was eating at our table the next day. I can't believe that woman," said Sharon, almost shouting in the silent courtroom, as she relived her rage, "I don't feel I've got the worst mother in the world. But I have a hard time believing it."

On another occasion Sharon was in an upstairs room watching a raccoon who was sitting outside on the windowsill. Her mother was having a party downstairs. Anton's nephew came upstairs, grabbed Sharon and pulled down her pants.

"He started rubbing my bum. I was facing the other way. I remember looking at that raccoon, you know, just watching. He started putting fingers in me. He said, 'I do this to my wife. She likes it. You're going to like it.' I thought, 'Hey, that raccoon has some great power. He could stop it.' I said, 'That raccoon is going to eat you,' and the raccoon just left. He kept rubbing my bum.

"That's not the last time. I just can't understand my mom. I didn't tell her about that. Why should I? The guy said nothing could hurt him, and women like being touched there.

"Once he did it to Lesley. I lied there. I didn't do a damn thing to help her. I should have done something. I didn't do anything. And when I turned sixteen, I left. I didn't stay there and help her. I should have done something. I feel I should have done something to help her. I helped me and my sister bolt the door so Anton wouldn't get in. That's all I did. I just lied there. To this day I don't understand why I didn't help her. Why didn't I jump up and beat him?"

But the cruelest abuse came from Anton himself. "He was sick, sick," Sharon told the court. "I don't know how the Lord can make such sick people."

She had some respite after her mother tried to leave Anton following a chaotic period of bitter fighting between them. But eventually Anton moved into their new home, another run-down building in a seedy section of Toronto. Sharon's brothers shared a little room behind the furnace. The walls were painted black and they had decorated the room with objects such as a fearsome skull with a head of hair, which Sharon remembers with horror. Anton used to babysit the children, and when the others went out to play, he would take Sharon to her brothers' room.

"He used to touch me all over and say, 'It's mine. Your tits are mine.' He used to do nasty things. I was so scared. He was just . . . I don't know . . . I guess maybe . . . I don't know. We'd be out playing. He'd call me in to get a cookie or something. He'd put me on the bed. The room was painted black with a skull. He used to tie my hands to the bed. It was around about the time my mom was pregnant that he really did it more."

Sharon choked on her words as she tried to describe to the court the "nasty things" that Anton used to do to her. She said he would stick things into her. Her own lawyer, Arthur Brown, persistently trying to draw details from her, asked her what things. She tried to speak several times, before she hoarsely whispered, "A carrot and . . . other things. I know it hurt. I know I can feel it sometimes. It bothers me a lot.

"My friend, who lived two doors beside us, had an uncle. We used to go to his place, and he used to do things like Anton. Touch us down there and play with us. I just felt like, hey, men do that to you. It's allowed. That's the way they care and love you."

Sharon said this man used to give them money, and sometimes they would go to his house for that reason. She worried that this meant that she was a prostitute.

She said the family moved to government housing—"It looked like a barracks, houses after houses, rows of houses, houses here, houses there, all attached together"—but the abuse continued.

School provided some respite from the home environment. Sharon said she used to stay on at school for sports, plays and other activities. She got on to the cheerleading team. She liked being out of the house. The one school activity she used to avoid was the health classes, which involved sex education: "I used to skip off to the washroom. I didn't like it, because I didn't like the slides and stuff they showed us. I didn't want to know about it. I figured I knew all I wanted to know about it, and I didn't want to know any more."

She told the court, "I just didn't understand. I wanted to understand. I'd not let my kids go through what I went through. No way, when people do things like that to you. You don't understand at that age, who I was, what I was, where I was. I just thought these men are allowed to do this to you. When you finally realize this is wrong, you don't want it. You go to your friends, and their uncle is doing the same thing. I wonder, 'Is it right and is it wrong?' A part of me saying, 'It's right,' a part of me saying, 'It's wrong.' I'm so confused."

"The pain doesn't go away. I'm trying so hard to put it in the back of my mind. You try and live day to day, but you can't forget."

Like many victims of child sexual abuse, Sharon Wells escaped from her home at the earliest opportunity. At 16, she left her school and what little protection her home afforded her. She was sexually experienced but ignorant of any of the joy, or even of the pleasure, that can be found in normal adult relationships. Desperately deprived of love and understanding, she deeply distrusted other people, and had little self-esteem.

Sharon's needs were great, but her expectations were low. Her stunted childhood had prepared her for only one role in life, that of the victim of violent and exploitative men. It did not take her long to find one.

When she was asked in court to describe the natural father of her first child, Sharon said, "Ross was like every man. They start out nice and then they turn."

Sharon first met Ross, when she was 15 years old, while visiting her sister Sally in New Brunswick. The older sister had gone there when she fled their abusive home a few years earlier. It was during this visit that Sharon first learned that Sally had also been sexually abused by their father and then their stepfather. Sally urged Sharon to come to live with her as soon as she turned 16, and promised to send her a ticket as a birthday present.

"I was really glad. I was so happy getting out of there," Sharon said, as she described the optimism with which she embarked on her "fresh start," the first of many attempts to somehow magically cleanse a life that had been polluted at its source.

It was summertime when she went to New Brunswick. She enrolled in school and stayed for a year, but she didn't get a certificate and is not sure what grade she was in, though she thinks it was grade ten. She became friends with Ross, who had a job and would take her out and buy things for her. He used to give her money and buy her lunch. She said they got along well together, until her sister went back to Toronto and Sharon moved into a one-room apartment. She became more dependent on Ross, who started to make greater demands on her. She used to record her personal feelings in a diary, which Ross got hold of one day. Sharon would not say what it was in the diary that enraged her boyfriend, but she said it was after this that he started to get nasty and violent with her.

As Sharon told her story in court, her mood would frequently shift from anger and tearful anguish to a childish, giggly, lighthearted state, which wasn't always appropriate to the harsh experiences she described. At times it seemed that she was enjoying having an audience, and delighting in her role as heroine in her own tragedy. It was almost with nostalgia that she described some of the acts of violence inflicted on her, as if she perceived these acts as an expression of love, and her victimization as an endorsement of her own importance to the man who abused her.

Sharon, who had skipped the sex education classes in school, soon became pregnant. She was still only 16 and she was scared. But she was also happy. She wanted to keep the baby, "because I would have someone who was going to love me, and I was going to love them with all my heart and soul."

She wanted to go home to Toronto. She felt that she needed her mother's help and she believed she could stand up for herself at home now. She didn't think Anton would touch her any more. She said it never occurred to her that her stepfather would have by now found a new victim in his own daughter, Lucille. Lucille was Sharon's halfsister, her mother's daughter, and about ten years younger than Sharon. Sharon said she told Ross that she was going back home to her mom to have her baby. He said, "We'll get married and have the baby, and give the baby a name and that." Ross and Sharon both lived with her family until the baby was born, but they were not allowed to sleep together because it was felt that this might be a bad influence on Lucille. They never did get married.

Sharon said Ross used to hit her during her pregnancy but not hard enough that it would leave marks on her. She said that once when they went to the Canadian National Exhibition together, they got into a big fight and he hit her, and then took her money and left her there. He had a chip on his shoulder, she said, because he was very good-looking and women would be attracted to him. She said she would tell him, "It's not fair to me. You're looking at other women, and I'm carrying your child. You're going to marry me, not them."

Ross got a job in a factory, and, after Janis was born, he and Sharon moved into a small apartment. Sharon's 14-year-old cousin lived nearby and used to visit them to see the baby. It was not the safest of neighborhoods, and Sharon used to ask Ross to walk home with the girl when she stayed late at night. She did not exactly trust Ross with other women, but did not dream she had anything to fear from a 14-year-old girl. When she came home one evening to find Ross and her cousin in bed together, Sharon was astonished and outraged. She felt both of them had betrayed her trust and their relationship with her. When she tried to throw Ross out of the apartment, he beat her up badly. She called the police, who arrived in time to hear him say, "I should have killed you." Sharon said that, on the advice of the police, she charged Ross with assault causing bodily harm, and he was sentenced to two years less a day.

Janis was about six months old when Sharon and Ross split up. After a few months Sharon began a relationship with Gordon Wells, who would later adopt Janis as his daughter. Gordon was a friend of Sharon's older brothers, and she had first met him when she was about 14 years old. She remembered being impressed with his good looks and his skill at drawing. Soon after the breakup with Ross, Sharon went to visit her brother and saw Gordon there, lifting weights. At that time Gordon was going out with Sharon's stepsister, Anton's daughter from a previous marriage, but he and Sharon got together at a party. She said that, when she told him about her relationship with Ross, Gordon said, "If that bastard ever touches you again, I'll kill him. Stick with me and I'll protect you from that guy."

Sharon said Gordon did protect her. "There was a time

when Ross came. But he went away because Gordon said he'd bury him if he came near me. He meant what he said. He was going to protect me. I felt very safe with Gordon. He had muscles and tattoos. He looked very manly. I was 17." Ross remained on the scene, however, until he was sent to jail.

Janis was admitted to the hospital for gastroenteritis when she was nine months old, and it was noted on the hospital record that the baby was dirty when she was brought in by the mother. After Janis was released from the hospital, a public health nurse visited Sharon's apartment. The nurse reported to the Metro Toronto Children's Aid Society that the apartment was "a disaster area," with dirty clothes, garbage and food on the floor. Janis's crib was missing some screws and was not safe. When asked about the baby's diet, Sharon said she fed her steak, pork chops and Kentucky Fried Chicken.

Sharon moved before the Children's Aid Society (CAS) could follow up on this report. She denied suggestions made by a CAS lawyer at the wardship hearing that she was attempting to get away from the social work agency when she moved into an apartment in the building where her father lived. It turned out to be her last contact with her father before he died several years later, and it was a negative one. At her dad's insistence she went out one night with a friend of his, who liked her and wanted to see her again. She later stood him up for Gordon, and this enraged her father, who called her a tramp.

Sharon moved in with Gordon. She said he loved Janis and knew that she and Janis were a package deal. She knew he was her brothers' friend and wouldn't do anything to hurt her. They spent a lot of good times together. He drank a lot, but he wasn't nasty, she said. "We'd run around the house, and joke, and put on records. He wasn't that violent. He would talk violent, but he wasn't violent with me before we married."

There was one incident, however, before they were married, that boded ill for their future relationship. They were sleeping together, Sharon said, and she woke up to find his hands around her throat. She said Gordon told her he was asleep and did not remember what happened, but she was not altogether convinced. She said that, as a result, she was always uneasy about sleeping with Gordon.

The picture of Gordon Wells that subsequently emerged from Sharon's testimony at the wardship hearing, divorce depositions and various other statements made in other court proceedings was of a man obsessed with violence: a man who terrorized his wife with threats, and several times came close to killing her. His behavior, as she described it, was so outrageous that it began to take on some elements of black comedy, elements that Sharon sometimes appeared to find quite amusing in retrospect. Gordon was portrayed as a man who would keep a sawed-off shotgun under his bed, clean his nails with a switchblade and trim the Christmas tree with a machete.

When he testified at the wardship hearing, Gordon confirmed many aspects of Sharon's account of their relationship, though he took issue with some of the specific allegations she had made against him. He said she used to bait him and play upon his temper by saying things about Ross. Gordon said his relationship with Sharon was "the complete pits. I could be around anybody, no problems. But, around Sharon, it was like setting off a short stick of TNT."

One of Gordon's tattoos was a depiction of a cartoon character called Hot Stuff—a baby-faced devil figure with horns and a forked tail, carrying a pitchfork. Much would be made of this devil tattoo during the wardship hearing because of suggestions that a satanic cult was involved in the violent graveyard rituals described by the children. The tattooed caricature was given more sinister connotations when linked with some comments attributed to Gordon, such as "God is dead, and I am the devil," and "When I die, I will go to the devil."

Sharon and Gordon were married a few months after they began living together in a dilapidated house in an older suburban neighborhood. Sharon was pregnant again, and it was winter. The house wasn't heated properly, and, Sharon said, it was always cold. She became depressed and began to question whether she should have the baby. After counseling from her doctor, she decided not to have an abortion.

Not long after they were married, Sharon made her first attempt to separate from Gordon. She left him and went to her mother's house. But her mother urged her to return to her husband. She told Sharon, "You made your bed. Lie in it."

Sharon returned, but she was afraid of the gun that Gordon kept. It was a pump-action shotgun, and, according to Sharon, Gordon's father had sawed off the barrel for him. Sharon's fears were realized when Gordon got drunk one day, had an argument with her and threatened to blow her head off.

She said she was also uneasy about leaving her husband alone with the baby. She had a job for a while and used to return home tired after work. Gordon would tell her to go to bed and that he would watch Janis. Sharon would do as he suggested, but used to get up and "creep up on him, to see what he was doing to Janis." One day she explained to him that she was very scared because she had been sexually molested as a child.

"He said, 'People like that should be shot, hung up by their feet—something to that effect—and killed, should not just be killed but castrated,'" Sharon recounted. "So from that day on I was more at ease when Gordon would watch Janis."

Sharon said Gordon never hit the children, but he once picked Janis up, when she was a baby, and slammed her against the wall with such force that he might have put her right through it. She said she told him never to do that again.

Around that time, Janis was treated three times for head injuries, either in the hospital or by the family doctor, Dr. Harvey Knapp. Dr. Knapp was not alarmed by this, as he maintained that two-year-olds are prone to falling or banging their heads. Any fears he might have had were allayed when it was found that a torsion in the child's foot might be affecting her stability, and a foot brace was prescribed to correct it.

After Linda was born, Gordon legally adopted Janis. Sharon, Gordon and the two children moved into a high-rise apartment building in a newly developed area in the outskirts of Toronto. They planned to start afresh in a nice new place. It was to be a different way of life.

The Children's Aid Society, which had been concerned about Sharon's care of Janis as a result of the public health nurse's report, concluded that the older child's situation had improved as a result of the marriage and the move to the new apartment. The agency closed its file on the family for the time being.

The fresh start, however, turned out to be a disaster. The relationship was rapidly deteriorating, and Sharon partly blamed the new apartment, which she described as a "bad luck place. I started getting moody because we lived on the 20th floor, and there was not a lot I could do. I was just totally bored. I loved my kids and everything, but everything started to get to me."

She and Gordon would get into huge fights over little things. Sharon said she got bothered about things like the way he parted his hair. He was drinking more, and Sharon said she was "super bothered" by all the beer bottles that were left around the apartment. She said that when Gordon had his friends over to visit, he would boast to them about what he did in bed with her.

Sharon said she began to feel great anxiety. She started to realize that she shouldn't have married Gordon. She had never loved him, she said, and only married him because Janis never knew anyone else as a father, and because she didn't want to jump from man to man.

"When Gordon thinks I baited him, maybe I did. I took a lot of anger out on Gordon, which I shouldn't have done, and maybe that's what prompted him to do what he did," she reflected, as she gave her testimony in court. "My personal thing that happened to me as a kid was really getting to me. Sometimes I would pick a fight so that I didn't have to sleep with him. Often Gordon ended up sleeping on the couch."

Linda, the new baby, was sickly from birth. She had been treated in the hospital for a bladder infection. Sharon was having trouble feeding her, and was convinced that this was the fault of the medication prescribed for the child.

Little more than a month after they had moved into the new apartment, Sharon insisted that Gordon leave. She would later explain to social workers that it was because he was too sexually demanding and had forced her to have intercourse against her will. As he continued to be seen around the building, the welfare worker and the social worker attached to the housing project suspected that the separation was just a ruse to allow Sharon to collect welfare. They began to investigate her, and later felt guilty as they feared this investigation might have caused her mental breakdown a month later.

Sharon would later describe this breakdown as "an anxiety attack"—a term she heard frequently in court as doctors analyzed her voluminous medical record. It happened the same day she had taken Janis to the hospital for treatment for a head injury. She said she found herself shaking and crying. She didn't know what was wrong with her. She called Dr. Knapp. He asked her where the children were, and either called her mother or told her to do so.

Sharon said that at the time she called the doctor, Janis was crying for something to eat. "I made Janis a sandwich, and gave Linda her bottle," Sharon recalled. "I crawled to the table because I could not stand up. My legs were totally shaken. I went into the storage room, a cubbyhole, because I was very afraid, afraid of me, afraid I might hurt the kids because of the crying. Then my mom came and told me it was going to be okay."

Dr. Knapp noted in his file, "I feel very sorry for her, but everything is very complex. Out of my league at that time to handle this degree of problem."

Sharon was hospitalized for 35 days, and while she was there she took an overdose of sleeping pills—they were pills that she had had at home and had asked Gordon to bring in for her. She said Gordon was "really nasty" when he came to visit. He called her a mental patient and said she was sick. She took her rings off her fingers and threw them at him.

"I felt nobody gives a damn about me, why should I live. Gordon had brought the pills. At that point in my life I just wanted somebody to give a damn about me. I didn't feel that anybody cared."

CHAPTER 3
THE CAS GETS INVOLVED

Social workers were usually more than a little scared when they were called upon to go into the huge apartment complex where Sharon and her children lived. The stark and forbidding high-rise blocks were devoid of any aesthetic appeal, and the minuscule pieces of green space that the developers had provided were usually strewn with trash. A small token playground, for the hundreds of children living in this "family housing development," was sandwiched between the highway and a parking lot. It afforded a dispiriting view of the back of one of the buildings, where the monotony of concrete and glass was broken only by several large garbage containers and the wire mesh that covered the ground-floor windows.

When Marg Wilson, a social worker with the Metro Toronto Children's Aid Society, drove down the short street that separated the development from its immediate neighborhood, she traveled from the security of a quiet, modestly affluent suburb into an area of poverty, violence and despair. She could read this on the threatening faces of the youths who loitered around the drab entranceway, as she prayed that they would not follow her into the elevator.

This was by no means a new experience, however, for Ms. Wilson, who was a seasoned veteran of social work. She was a tough, shrewd woman, whose casual, slightly offhand

26

manner tended to put people at ease. The image she projected was not that of a prying, middle-class do-gooder, but of a busy, caring person, who could relate to the concerns and problems of her clients.

How much Ms. Wilson, and others like her, were able to do for their clients was determined less by their own personal dedication to the job than by the restrictions imposed by the system in which they worked. Their role in that system was fraught with almost impossible contradictions, which are rooted in society's conflicting goals and priorities as they relate to child abuse and family violence.

The Children's Aid Society that Marg worked for was founded in 1891 by a crusading journalist, as a private organization devoted to the protection of neglected children. Ontario government legislation, introduced two years later, encouraged the establishment of similar organizations across the province, and charged them with the administration of public measures for the prevention of cruelty to children. While these agencies have remained private, they are largely financed and controlled by the Ontario government. This unusual status perhaps reflects an ambiguous attitude on the part of governments toward the delicate issue of state intervention into the traditionally sacrosanct, private realm of family life.

Legislation requires that Children's Aid Societies protect children, where necessary, but at the same time support the integrity and autonomy of the family unit. In 1983 a standing committee of the provincial legislative assembly was told that this sets up "an incredible, inhumane dilemma" for the social worker.

Former Minister of Community and Social Services Frank Drea told the same committee, "A CAS worker who is involved with a high-risk family has to walk a very, very difficult line. On the one hand they are there to prevent or to help. On the other hand at the very same time that they are in the household, they are also collecting evidence by just being there. They are looking around and they are seeing things. This is a very, very difficult line, where they have to be, at the same time, the investigator and the remedy."

Their task is made even more difficult because the government has put increased demands on the social work agencies. New laws require that all suspected cases of child abuse be reported and investigated; the Children's Aid Societies maintain that they have not been granted enough additional funds to do the job properly. Yet, whenever they fail to do all that is required of them, public opinion, now highly sensitive both to child abuse and to human rights, is easily moved to outrage, either over the plight of a child whose abuse has gone undetected, or over a parent who is wrongly accused of abuse.

It was about a month after Sharon's release from the psychiatric ward that Marg Wilson first visited her in Sharon's 20th-story apartment. Ms. Wilson found the young mother depressed and overwhelmed by her situation. Sharon told her she was unable to cope and very disorganized in her housework. Janis was very demanding, and, according to Sharon, was getting lippy, would pull at the baby, mess her room, throw tantrums, dawdle, hit other children and spit out food.

Linda was sick with diarrhea and vomiting. A public health nurse had already been in the home to assist with this problem; a pediatrician, who felt that Sharon had a problem feeding the baby properly, recommended that she be encouraged to be more tolerant and take more time with her. Sharon said she wanted to be a good mother and didn't want to hit the children, but felt like she wasn't able to get up in the morning and get her work done.

Sharon's mother had always warned her not to trust the Children's Aid Society, but she was desperate for any kind of support and immediately established a rapport with the sympathetic and practical Ms. Wilson. The social worker made arrangements for a visiting homemaker, and for Sharon to participate in a parenting project that provided guidance to mothers considered to be in danger of abusing their children.

Ms. Wilson had been called upon to visit Sharon because of concerns reported by a social services worker, who became involved with the family when Sharon applied for welfare. Marg knew about Sharon's hospital admission, but she was not aware of the suicide attempt. She was also unaware, until about a year later, of Sharon's prior involvement with the CAS, because that information was filed under Sharon's maiden name. This kind of communication failure was characteristic of the various professional attempts to help the family, as it is in many such cases. Part of the same pattern was the fact that Sharon's physician, Dr. Knapp, was never aware that the CAS was involved in her case, just as he was also ignorant of several occasions when the children were taken to different hospitals for treatment of injuries. In spite of all the best efforts of the conscientious individuals involved, the family's problems were simply too great for any one of them, and their combined interventions were plagued with breakdowns in coordination and communication.

Another problem was Sharon's attitude when help was offered; although she appeared willing to seek help, she was perhaps not as forthcoming as she appeared to be, and certainly was not consistent in following through with all the arrangements that were made for her. It was clear when she testified in court that Sharon was often torn and confused by conflicting impulses. Her own account of what happened in her life was often misleading and contradicted by other evidence. A part of her seemed to dearly wish to be a good mother and do everything right for her children, but there was always something else to intervene, something that she didn't understand, or wouldn't talk about. The long succession of sicknesses and injuries suffered by her children left an overwhelming impression that they were being mistreated. Yet it was only because Sharon was so conscientious in seeking medical attention for these problems that they ever came to light.

These ambiguities were all present when Sally, Sharon's older sister, reported a suspected sexual assault on three-year-old Janis. There was no way of knowing whether or not, if the child was sexually molested on this occasion, it was an isolated incident or part of the ongoing pattern of abuse that Janis would talk about a few years later. At the hearing, Sharon's lawyer claimed that the fact she reported this incident showed her desire to protect the children. But there is some question about whether the allegation would have been reported if Sally had not taken the initiative. According to Sharon's first account of the incident, told to Harriet Jensen, the director of the parenting project she was attending, her 14-year-old brother Mike was staying at the apartment, and Sharon went along with Janis's request that she be allowed to sleep with her uncle on two successive nights. By the time Sharon testified in court, this part of the story had been revised, and she said, "I'm not sure how he got into bed with her." In any case, she said, the child told her afterwards that her uncle had touched her in the genital area, which appeared to be sore and red. Sharon said she confronted Mike and he denied it.

Sharon discussed the incident with Sally, telling her that

she was worried that her husband would kill Mike if he found out about the incident. She told Sally she was confused and didn't want everybody to know about it. She said she was really torn between her relationship with her daughter and her relationship with her brother. Sally also attended the parenting project and said she would talk to Harriet Jensen. Sharon said her sister told her that she didn't want this to go on in the family for another generation.

Sharon told the court that she received a phone call from Harriet Jensen, who said she had a legal obligation to check out the situation. Ms. Jensen took Sharon and the child to the Hospital for Sick Children, where a doctor found no evidence of damage or sexual abuse. But he told them that this did not prove it didn't happen, since a sexual assault need not leave any physical scars. The doctor advised Sharon to keep her brother and her child apart.

When Sharon received follow-up calls about the incident from the CAS and a social worker at the Hospital for Sick Children, she was angry because "I didn't want the rest of the world to know my business." She told Harriet Jensen, "I don't want anything to do with you, or what you have to offer."

Marg Wilson of the CAS found that Sharon was unwilling to discuss the incident. The social worker reported to her supervisor: "Sharon is backing away from CAS as a result of this incident, but I feel she will come back, if given some breathing space." She recommended that the CAS continue its monitoring and support, as this was a high-risk case. Ms. Wilson arranged for a subsidized day-care place for Janis, whom she described as a disturbed child—she was quite whiney and manipulative, and got on her mother's nerves. She said the child's mother was refraining from disciplining her as she was afraid she might not be able to stop hitting her.

Without any actual evidence that abuse had taken place, there was little that the social worker could do, except hope that Sharon would eventually be willing to see her again. As long as a client was unwilling to co-operate with the CAS, there was nothing the agency could do to help the children, unless it had enough evidence to take legal action.

However, the continuing crises in Sharon's life were such that she needed support. The allegations about her brother Mike had precipitated a big family crisis, when discussion of the issue prompted Sharon's halfsister, Lucille, to disclose that her father Anton had been sexually abusing her for years. This revelation led to a suicide attempt by Sharon's mother.

Sharon returned to the counseling sessions at the parenting project, but told Ms. Jensen that she would not tell her about any more abuse, until she had discussed it with her own doctor. A few days later Janis was taken to the hospital with a severe injury to her abdomen and blood in her urine. A hospital report recorded that Sharon went away, leaving her child unattended on a stretcher. Sharon told her doctor that a beam had fallen on the child. She told Harriet that a counter and a television fell on Janis. She said she had bought the three-year-old child, who wore a brace on her foot, some roller skates, and that while she was skating in the living room, she had banged into a counter with a television set on it, and pulled both of them down on top of her.

When Sharon herself went into the hospital a couple of weeks later, she told Harriet it was to have an ovarian cyst removed. The CAS was never informed of Sharon's stay in the hospital, which was in fact for an abortion. Dr. Knapp had recommended the therapeutic abortion, because Sharon was in a distraught state and unable to cope. He said she had found it very difficult to accept that she was pregnant, and at first claimed it was impossible as she had not had sexual relations with her husband for several months.

She explained to the court that after she and Gordon separated, his best friend Don, who had been best man at their wedding, moved into her apartment because he had had a fight with his girlfriend and didn't have a place to stay. She said it came as a shock to both Gordon and her that she was pregnant. She said Gordon told her, "It's not my kid. I'm not going to raise another kid that's not mine."

Sharon said she was deeply hurt by this response because she thought that Gordon fully accepted his adopted daughter Janis as his own. She said he calmed down later and apologized for his cruel reaction, and they agreed that it would be best for her to have an abortion. She said she subsequently felt extreme guilt, and received psychiatric treatment for depression. It was not clear from Sharon's testimony whether or not Gordon had good reason to doubt that he could have made her pregnant, or if Don had played a role in the matter.

Gordon had moved out and was living with some friends, but he would visit her on weekends, in what Sharon said was an attempt to reconcile their differences. The welfare department took a different view of this and on one occasion withheld Sharon's checks on the grounds that they believed her husband was still living with her. During Gordon's visits, he and Sharon would often get into huge arguments. Gordon would take out his frustrations on the furniture. Sharon said he punched a light once—it went flying into the ceiling and broke. She said one time he picked up a coffee table and threw it at the washing machine. Also, she said he put his fist through doors and walls, and on one occasion hurled his machete into the wall, just missing her head.

When Ms. Wilson next visited Sharon, she found the apartment a mess, with dirty dishes and diapers everywhere. The social worker for the housing project also reported that Sharon's housekeeping was dreadful, and that the place was extremely dirty and infested with cockroaches. A succession of homemakers, sent in by the CAS, made little impact on Sharon's housekeeping abilities. One time when Ms. Wilson arrived for an unannounced visit, she found the children alone in the apartment with dirty clothing scattered around. She found Sharon in a neighbor's apartment. Sharon told her that she was taking diet pills and they made her feel drowsy. She said she felt lethargic, immobilized with depression and over-whelmed with the kids and with housework. Sharon said she was no longer seeing her husband, since he told her that his girlfriend was pregnant. She said that had made her come to her senses.

Doctors at the Hospital for Sick Children continued to be concerned about baby Linda's health. She spent much of her first two years in and out of the hospital, and it was noted that, while she remained below normal weight for her age, she would always gain considerable weight while she was in the hospital. She was therefore diagnosed as suffering from inorganic failure to thrive: a condition of weakness that is usually attributed to inadequate care.

As Linda grew old enough not to depend on her mother to feed her, she began to gain weight, though she remained a frail little child. The pediatrician noted a fine tremor in her hands, which he attributed to stress. Both children continued to suffer from an unusual number of injuries, and Janis was treated for infections. Dr. Knapp said he might have had more cause for concern had he known about the family's history of sexual abuse.

Sharon became preoccupied with a fear that the abortion she had had might have rendered her infertile, and, without disclosing the true reason for these fears, saw Harriet Jensen for some individual counseling sessions. The therapist later testified that Sharon told her, at that time, that she was unable to form satisfactory relationships with adults, and depended on relationships with children to meet her needs for companionship and love. Sharon told Ms. Jensen that she was afraid that when the girls grew up and left home, she would not have the ability to produce more children to replace them.

Sharon claimed that she had invested heavily in being a good mother, didn't leave the children with people she didn't trust, and therefore limited her own social contacts to those where she could include her children. She said she was very critical of adults in her life, and cut them off when they did not fulfill her expectations. She told Harriet, "My dream was to have as many children as I can, to do right by them, to have someone to fall back on when I'm alone."

Ms. Jensen was concerned that the incident with Janis's uncle Mike was not a good prognosis for Sharon's ability either to see the danger of sexual abuse or to stand up for her daughters if they were abused by someone who was close to her. In addition, she was afraid that Sharon had a tendency to seek out the kind of partner who may be attracted to children, or who would turn to children for gratification when frustrated in adult relationships. With all her own problems, Sharon would quickly frustrate such men and leave her children as targets. Ms. Jensen formed the impression, while she was counseling Sharon, that there was a high risk that children in Sharon's care would be sexually abused, because she was not prepared to work through the problems caused by her own childhood abuse. She said the way Sharon would turn to her daughters for nurture, wanting them to meet her adult needs, was a typical setup for a child who gets sexually abused.

As far as Marg Wilson knew, the two children got on well at day-care. That is what their mother told her. The Children's Aid Society social worker was aware that the girls were absent from the day-care on occasion, and got explanations for these absences from Sharon. But she heard nothing from the day-care staff to cause her to have any additional concerns about the children.

The day-care staff did have grave concerns about Janis and Linda, but did not think it necessary to communicate all

of these to the Children's Aid Society. They knew that the social work agency was already involved in the case, and was
presumably watching the children carefully, as it was the CAS
that designated them as being at high risk of abuse. While Ms.
Wilson was told about some problems with the children's attendance, she was not made aware of the extent of this problem. She did not know that the girls were absent half of the
time that they were supposed to be in day-care; their attendance at the day-care was mainly to protect them from potential abuse at home. Most of the children's absences were
unexplained.

"There were not many smiles on their faces. That's
something that sort of stood out," the day-care supervisor recalled. She described Janis and Linda, to the court, as pale,
unkempt, untidy children. She said Linda's clothes were often
too big for her, and the child used to tremble "like a little leaf
in the wind." Janis was observed to be a rather willful child,
who did not play with other children and was often unpleas-
ant and aggressive with them.

The day-care workers were also disturbed by Linda's
persistent odor of dried urine on unwashed clothes. They
asked her mother to provide them with second sets of clothing
for the child, but Sharon kept forgetting to do this in spite of
frequent reminders. When Sharon came to the center, the
staff remarked that she often appeared to be unresponsive and
"spaced out" on some kind of drug or medication.

One day while Linda was in the washroom, a day-care
worker noticed bluish marks on her lower abdomen and
thighs, close to her vagina. Having determined that they were
not bruises but some kind of dye, the supervisor asked Sharon
about the marks and was told that on the previous evening
Janis had taken some marker and painted Linda.

A few weeks later, during "circle time," a period when
the children were encouraged to tell stories and talk about
their own lives, Linda announced that her father had held a
knife to her mother's throat the night before. Sharon was
asked about this incident, and confirmed that it had taken
place, explaining that she was having a very difficult time
with her estranged husband.

In November, 1982, Sharon met Gary Evans at a disco
bar. If one accepts Sharon's account of their first meeting, it
involved what must be one of the most unromantic overtures

ever made. Sharon testified that she told Gary, "I have two kids. I'm separated and if you touch me I'll sock you. I'm a package deal. You have to love my kids and you have to love me."

Sharon's relationship with Gary developed slowly. She had been very attracted to him when she first met him. He was a small, slim, dark-skinned young man with a clean, innocent face and carefully coiffured hair. Sharon liked his looks as soon as she spotted him in the crowded disco, and, when she saw him talking to an acquaintance of hers, she had asked to be introduced to him. Sharon and her girlfriend went there for Ladies' Nights, when women patrons could win prizes and were given their first drink free.

Perhaps inhibited by Sharon's warning that he should keep his distance, Gary did not ask to drive her home until the third or fourth meeting, and then Sharon declined the invitation. But they continued to meet at the bar to dance and have a good time. Sharon was quite enchanted with the courteous way this shy, middle-class young man treated her. They became friends and started going out, with the girls, to the beach or Ontario Place. It was, according to Sharon, nine months before she would allow Gary to enter her apartment. She said, "I wanted to make sure he loved me and my kids. The girls liked him. They never complained or anything. I think Janis was more closer to him. Janis always wanted to hold his hand or stuff."

Sharon felt herself falling more and more in love with Gary. She had never before known such a sensitive person. Sharon would describe him as a very quiet, sweet, beautiful guy, like no one she had ever met before. She would marvel at the way they could discuss things, without arguing or fighting. She said he was a virgin until they started to have sex together.

It was after they started sleeping together that Sharon discovered that Gary was a very religious person. She illustrated this with a story about how Gary got Janis a bicycle, after Gordon had promised her one but failed to follow through. Sharon said Gary found a bike in the garbage, and said all it needed was a wheel. She said he then looked out of the window and saw a wheel, and explained, "That's the way God works. He performs miracles like that."

Gary's family also impressed Sharon, as they never

yelled and screamed at one another, or insulted each other.
They were different from any people she had been involved
with before. She could never understand what Gary's father
said, because of his fast clipped speech, and she knew that
Gary's sisters would have rather seen him with a black girl;
she was amazed that none of them was ever mean to her.

Gary and Sharon were not living together. He would
visit her most weekends and would stay over sometimes during
the week. They took the children on a couple of camping trips.
When they went out together in the evenings, Sharon said they
would either leave the kids with a baby-sitter, with Sharon's
mother, with her sister's boyfriend, or with Gordon.

The question of whether or not Gordon had a good relationship with Gary was a disputed issue at the wardship hearing, as the children's allegations suggested that they were
partners in crime, perhaps members of the same satanic cult.
According to Sharon they did not get on at all. Gordon once
called her "a fucking nigger lover," Sharon told the court. "He
did not like Gary because Gary was black. He calls him 'that
fucking black bastard, that nigger.' He would just blow off the
handle, and say, 'That nigger should be shot.' I don't know if
that was his color, or because he was with me. He always
threatened to kill Gary. Even today he threatens that. The last
time I saw him he threatened that."

Although she was happy when she was with Gary,
Sharon became uneasy about her relationship with the
middle-class university student. She explained it this way:
"There was a time when I thought my life was going too good
for me. I asked Gary to get out of my life. I said, 'You're from a
whole different world than me.' His family is such a sensitive
family. They care about one another. Different from what I
grew up with. The whole atmosphere in his home is different.
I felt like a Cinderella sort of thing. I went to his place, and
then went back to my place. He'd say, 'I'll get you out of this.
You deserve better than this.' I didn't feel I deserved better. I
said, 'That's my life. That's the way I live.'"

She asked him to go away, and they agreed to stop seeing
one another. Sharon said the children cried when they were
told she and Gary were going to separate. Then Gary called
her and told her he loved her and wanted to try to make it
work. He said he really wanted to make something of her. He
said he wanted to see her succeed.

With Gary's encouragement, Sharon was trying to better herself by going to school for upgrading classes. She attended sporadically and dropped out after about six months. She said she derived a lot of strength from children and wanted to pursue a career in early childhood education. She said she had a dream of one day opening her own day-care center.

Meanwhile, Gordon continued to terrorize Sharon with his violent behavior. She charged him with assault after he slammed her against the wall during one of their attempted reconciliations. She later dropped the charges. She also had him charged with dangerous driving, when she claimed he tried to run her over at a shopping plaza after she refused to lend him $10 from her baby bonus money. This charge was also dropped, and Gordon signed a letter agreeing that he would not act violently towards her again.

In a divorce application presented to Family Court, Sharon cited these two incidents, and also claimed that Gordon had told her he was getting guns from the United States and would use them to kill the kids, her and himself. When Sharon was convicted of defrauding a bank of about $650, she claimed that Gordon had driven her and the children to the bank, and threatened to kill her if she didn't commit the crime.

"Gordon could be the nicest guy in the world. Just don't get him angry," Sharon later told the wardship hearing.

Sharon described another incident, when she said Gordon hung her over her 20th-story balcony. He had come over to pick up the children, she said, and they got into a big fight. He was very strong and could lift her with one hand. He had her over his shoulder, and she was punching him, kicking and screaming. Sharon said he told her, "I'm going to kill, you bitch," but she held on to the bars of the balcony and eventually he pulled her back.

Gordon later claimed that on this occasion he had saved Sharon's life; he said she tried to throw herself over the balcony during a violent argument. His version of the story was supported by a note made by Dr. Knapp: "Severe depression. Very suicidal that day. Had a problem with her teacher. Told me she had assaulted her teacher and was going to be charged. Said she had nothing to live for. Almost jumped off a balcony. This was the worst I had ever seen her."

Sharon said she was feeling a lot of pressure in her life at that time. She felt she was being torn in two by Gary and Gordon. She was struggling to keep up with school and to attend a center for handicapped children, where she was doing volunteer work. The distances involved in traveling to and from her remotely located apartment made this even more difficult, she said.

She was hospitalized again after taking an overdose of tranquilizers. When she was released, she was advised to get out-patient psychiatric treatment. She didn't follow up on this because of the distance she would have to travel to get there, she said. They should provide such facilities in the community closer to where the patients live, she told the wardship hearing.

Once again, Ms. Wilson knew about Sharon's stay in the hospital, but was never told about the drug overdose. When Ms. Wilson next went to visit, Sharon told her she was too busy to see her, as she was expecting a visit from her husband and Gary. Ms. Wilson went back a week later and was not allowed to enter the apartment. Sharon answered the door, stepped outside and said she had forgotten Ms. Wilson was coming. Ms. Wilson said that, if Sharon was forgetting appointments and not bringing up issues to discuss with her, it was maybe an indication that she no longer needed the services of the CAS. Believing that the children were okay, and knowing nothing about Sharon's suicide attempts or the fact that psychiatrists were pessimistic about her recovery unless she received further treatment, Marg Wilson closed the case in April, 1984.

During the six months after Ms. Wilson closed the CAS file on the case, each child was involved in allegations of sexual assault. In each case it was one of the parents who made the allegations, and in neither was enough evidence found for authorities to do anything other than to continue to "monitor" the family.

In August, 1984, Sharon took Janis to hospital, complaining that the child had been sexually molested at a babysitter's apartment. According to Sharon, Janis was afraid she would be beaten if she talked. The child said she had a dream that a man with one eye and half a nose was hurting her. Sharon said the child's genital area was red, and she did not believe that it was a dream. She said she had been out with Gary that night and asked him to drive her and the child to the hospital.

At the Sick Children's Hospital it was found that Janis did have some small abrasions. The police investigated, but did not find there was sufficient evidence for any prosecution. Sharon felt the police did not do a good job. They had gone to the baby-sitter's apartment, and returned to say that there was no black man there. They then asked Gary if he had touched Sharon's children. Sharon was indignant about that, as she was convinced that it could not have been Gary. It was later discovered that there was a man living in the building whose face was half eaten away by a cancerous disease, but there was no evidence of any contact between him and the children.

The Children's Aid Society reopened its file, and social workers tried unsuccessfully to contact Sharon for several weeks. She would not return calls, although she did go into the CAS office during this period to pick up a food voucher from a worker unconnected with the investigation.

Meanwhile, Gordon had been receiving phone calls from a woman, who refused to give her name, but said she was a former girlfriend of Gary Evans and had had a child by him. She said Gary had threatened her life, and was now harming Janis and Linda. Gordon told Sharon about these calls, and, when she asked Gary if he had a previous girlfriend and fathered a child, he denied it.

When Gordon had the children for a weekend visit, he noticed that Linda was rubbing herself a lot and was red in the genital area. Gordon refused to return the four-year-old child to her mother and took her to the hospital instead. A young doctor at the Queensway Hospital examined Linda and found she had a yeast infection, but saw no evidence of bruising. Linda told him that Gary had not hurt her. The doctor did not think there was any need to consult a gynecologist, as there was no evidence beyond a vague phone call in the middle of the night. If he had known that there was a history of sexual abuse in the family, or that the Children's Aid Society was involved, he said, he might have referred the child for a more thorough investigation.

Gordon returned Linda to Sharon, with a prescription and the doctor's recommendation that she get some treatment for the yeast infection. Sharon did not follow up on this recommendation. Gordon was angry that neither the CAS nor the police took any action as a result of his complaint.

Ms. Wilson finally got to see Sharon and the children the next day. After hearing the mother's account of the two inci-

dents, she talked to both children. After talking to Janis she
concluded that, while there was no evidence for this incident,
the way the child described the alleged molestation suggested
that she had been abused in the past. She recommended that
Sharon should get Janis into a play-therapy group. Ms. Wilson
asked Linda if she had fun with Mommy and Gary, and Linda
replied, "Gary said not to talk about it." Ms. Wilson asked her
if Gary ever touched her, and Linda giggled and whispered,
"No."

"There could be something going on in this home, but
there is no evidence to support this," Ms. Wilson wrote in a
report, recommending that the family should have continuing
help from the CAS.

A few days later Sharon and the children moved to
Hamilton. Sharon claimed that the main reason for this was
that she did not wish to remain close to the neighbor who she
believed was responsible for Janis being sexually abused. She
also said she wanted to get away from Gordon and be near
Gary, who was attending university in Hamilton.

The fact that both parents reported allegations of sexual
abuse was cited by their lawyers at the hearing as evidence
that Sharon and Gordon would be unlikely to abuse the children themselves. However, the judge eventually found that the
parents did sexually abuse the children, and it is likely from
the girls' accounts that this abuse started before Sharon took
the children to Hamilton. There are two possible explanations
for this apparent inconsistency. One is that other case histories
have shown that some people who think they have a right to
abuse their own children will not tolerate other people abusing them. The other, which seems more likely to apply to
Sharon than to Gordon, is that the allegations were some kind
of muted cry for help from people who recognized that they
were harming their children but could not control themselves.

The social worker at the housing project was shocked by
the state of Sharon's apartment when the family moved out.
She said there were holes in every wall and in all the doors.
The fridge, screen door and toilet were all damaged and the
light shades broken. The walls, which were originally an egg-
shell color, were now a blackish-gray. The floors were sticky
with dirt, and the unit was full of cockroaches.

Sharon said the move to Hamilton was to have been "a
new beginning, a different life." She and Gary leased the

ground floor of a newly renovated house in an older, slightly run-down neighborhood. It had a basement and a small paved backyard. It was the best accommodation she had ever had, and a complete change from the stifling apartment where the children could never go out to play on their own.

She did not tell Gordon where they were living because, she said, she did not want him to come to the house. She said she told the children their dad would come to visit them, but they said, "Mom, he'll come and wreck our place."

Sharon found a school for the children and a low-paying job for herself, but the live-in arrangement with Gary lasted only ten days. Gary had not wanted Sharon to move to Hamilton in the first place. He was looking for a job, but he didn't want to work in Hamilton, as he didn't like the city. He was also studying and said he found it impossible to work in the house because of all the demands that were placed on him by Sharon and the children. Although Sharon and Gary had decided that they were going to live together, get married and have a baby some day, they very quickly concluded that they were not yet ready for it.

However, Gary continued to spend a lot of time at the house in Hamilton, and would look after the children when Sharon was at work. He often took them to school in the mornings or picked them up in the evenings, and would baby-sit for Sharon on weekends. On some occasions Gary failed to take Linda to school, and later explained to Sharon that he hadn't been able to, as he had "things to do." He said it was easier for him to take her with him, and drop her off at his parents' house while he was looking for work in Toronto.

At one time Linda used to say that she didn't like going in Gary's car. Sharon said she thought this was because she peed on the seat, and Gary got mad at her. Sharon also noticed that Janis would be red in her genital area more often than she used to. She asked Gary if he had touched the girls and he said he hadn't. Sharon said she believed him and trusted him completely. She said the girls never complained about any untoward contact.

Linda's kindergarten teacher in Hamilton had been a little concerned that, although the mother spoke a lot about the child's medical problem, she did not seem to have gone to the trouble of locating a family doctor when she moved to Hamilton. The teacher later became worried that the child was undernourished and seemed to suffer from jerky motor control.

Janis's grade one teacher in Hamilton was Rose Eddy, a nervous little woman in her mid-50s. She sat grumbling to herself as she waited to testify at the wardship hearing, and confronted the court with a look of indignation as she answered the lawyers' questions. She said she remembered Janis as a very pale, thin and lethargic child, who was unusually slow in her reactions. She said Janis often used to cling to her teacher during recess, never smiled and had no spontaneity.

"She used to look as if she hadn't been treated well at home. She looked as though she'd cried all night or weekend," Ms. Eddy said. The teacher formed the impression that Janis was "so miserably unhappy" that there had to be more going on in the home than simply the problems associated with poverty or marital discord.

The teacher noticed what she described as "an unusual sensitivity in her lips," and she said Janis's eyes always looked red and swollen. Ms. Eddy sometimes had the children do an art exercise where they would take a straw and blow through it to spray paint on paper. Janis refused to do this, saying her lips hurt. Ms. Eddy noted that the child's lips were red and swollen.

Ms. Eddy said she didn't question the child about her home life, because "there are certain limits as to how far you are going to snoop in a child's life." But she said she did talk to Sharon, who spoke in a slow, slurry way, and "seemed in a little world of her own, tired and unhappy.

"You don't say, 'You're not feeding your child properly,' " Ms. Eddy explained to the court. "You just ask if she is getting enough sleep. Mrs. Wells said she was aware of the problem. She said she would see a doctor about it. She seemed to know the right things to say. She seemed to use the right words. I didn't feel a sincerity there, that she was going to do anything about it. But it was not for me to judge. I wondered whether she was really listening to what I was saying, absorbing the full implication of what I was trying to tell her."

It became apparent to the court why Ms. Eddy looked so uncomfortable about giving her testimony when she began to explain what happened in her class during "rug time," a quiet period after recess, when she encouraged the children to rest on a rug. Ms. Eddy explained reticently, "During these times I had observed some of my children like Janis and Andy Jackson kissing and hugging, french-kissing and touching each other in places, where as adults you would call it sexual play. It went on for a period of time before I realized it was not just kids not knowing what they were doing. Some children are very loving and tend to hug and kiss each other. They were a very loving group of children last year."

Ms. Eddy said it was only after another teacher had noticed Janis and Andy touching one another in the playground, and she had received a complaint from a parent, that she understood that what was going on in her class was "more than just a child's innocent play."

She said a few of the boys and girls were involved in this. She saw Janis once grab at a boy's pants, in his private parts, front and the back. "The boys wanted to put their hands under the girls' dresses. I never got as far as to see what they were doing under there. And the girls naturally responded by putting their hands at the boys' zipper area. I don't think it got as far as the girls getting into the boys' pants. I certainly would have put a stop to that. It went beyond the ordinary children's curiosity," Ms. Eddy said. "Another teacher exclaimed to me in horror, in disbelief, 'Look at what the children are doing in recess!' But it wasn't all this one great big orgy or whatever you call it."

"I said, 'There's lots of room on the rug, move apart.' I told them to close our eyes and keep our hands to ourselves. I really believe that was the end of it—on the rug," said Ms. Eddy.

The Hamilton-Wentworth Children's Aid Society was informed of the Toronto agency's concerns about the children, and a social worker, Lesley Morgan, was assigned to monitor the situation. Ms. Morgan was large-boned and slightly heavyset, but an attractive young woman, with a healthy complexion. She got on well with children and had a pleasant direct approach to everyone. She was generally well-liked, except by those who came into conflict with her and considered her to be stubborn and aggressive. She was idealistic about her work, and devoted much of her spare time to activities involving the peace movement and women's issues.

Ms. Morgan helped Sharon to sort out some problems she had with her financial affairs at Christmastime, and encouraged her to get involved in an incest survivors' group at the Rape Crisis Centre, where Ms. Morgan worked as a volunteer. Sharon, who subsequently became very bitter towards Ms. Morgan, later told the court that she still appreciates what the social worker did for her at that time: "I can't forget what she did. She was there when I needed her."

Sharon told Ms. Morgan that she would call her if she ever felt she was going to harm her kids, and she joined the group after being assured that anything she said there could not be subsequently used against her by the Children's Aid.

The sessions at the Rape Crisis Centre opened up "a can of worms" for Sharon. As she remembered all that had happened to her as a child, she started to take out her hostility on Gary, and, she said, began to get short-tempered with the children. She was also experiencing financial difficulties, and had received a letter from Gordon's lawyer, demanding that his client be given access to the children. Then at the end of January, 1985, Gary left to work at an out-of-town job.

"I was having a tough time. My life was going pretty fast for me," Sharon said. "I was upset from a phone call from the lawyer that Gordon wanted to have access to the kids again, and I didn't want him to find out where I lived. I had a shortage in my pay. I had $36 to feed the kids for two weeks, because they took OHIP off me mistakenly. I had to walk Linda home in wet pants, in wintertime. I didn't think it was fair. I was upset. I was going to the Rape Crisis Centre trying to deal with a lot of things. I was really upset. Gary wasn't in town, and I was all by myself. Everything got to me. I didn't want to hurt my kids, and I just needed a break. I needed time to get on my feet. My life was running so fast compared to what I was used to."

Sharon said she was scared of herself. She had recurrent dreams, one of which was about diving into a garbage pail full of water. She felt she was going crazy. She had begun yelling and screaming at the kids and she was afraid that if she kept them with her she would hit them. She felt she couldn't call on her mother to take the children, and she certainly didn't want to call Gordon, so she arranged with Lesley to have the girls put in foster care for a month.

Lesley Morgan received a call from Sharon in the early hours of the morning of February 7, 1985, four months after the family had moved to Hamilton. The mother told Ms. Morgan she was suffering "a severe anxiety attack." Ms. Morgan found her sitting against a wall on the living room floor, sobbing hysterically. Sharon said she was afraid that, unless Ms. Morgan took the children that night, she would physically hurt them.

could use those actions when needed, for the trials have
been rewarding. Phoebe said she would like her office to
have room for Patricia that night. She wore glasses
herself.

PART TWO
THE ALLEGATIONS

CHAPTER 4
THE FOSTER HOME

Janis and Linda were whisked into another world when they were taken to a foster home in the middle of the night. It was a split-level house in a quiet residential neighborhood. To most people it would seem like a very ordinary suburban household, a clean, quiet, well-regulated home, inhabited by gentle and generous people. But Janis and Linda, who were both less than eight years old, had never experienced the simple security of normal family life.

Catherine McInnis was one of the Children's Aid Societies' most experienced foster mothers. During the previous 15 years, she had provided care to more than 300 children. The CAS had nothing but glowing reports of her work. She was described as having a professional attitude, even though she did the work for altruistic reasons. Social workers often chose her home as a placement for particularly difficult cases, as she was well-known, both for her competence, and for the love and understanding she gave to the children in her care. Many of these children would maintain close ties with her for years after they left her home. She was also scrupulous about keeping notes on all her foster children and reporting any concerns about them that she may have had.

In 1985, and for a few years prior to that, she was a provider of short-term or emergency foster care. This often involved taking in extremely disturbed children without any advance notice. She had also adopted some children, who were now teenagers and young adults. It was because of her years of experience and her gift with difficult children that the CAS persuaded her to open her home to children in need of emergency care. These children would usually only stay for a month or two before either returning home or moving on to a long-term foster home. This meant that, while it was important that the children felt as comfortable as possible in Mrs. McInnis's home, and received the nurturing that they usually desperately needed, she also had to be ready to let them go, and could have no expectations of being able to keep them.

Friends and neighbors saw Catherine McInnis as a model of stability. She and her husband of thirty years lived in a split-level home in a quiet residential neighborhood. They were religious without being fanatics, and the church they attended regularly was of a conservative, nonconformist denomination. At the trial, she would speak little of her husband, who seemed to have minimal involvement with the foster children, but would always refer to him with great respect. She clearly saw him as a model of moral authority and good conscience.

Catherine had an idealized reverence for authority figures in society, particularly the police, and would always make a point of telling children in her care to say "policemen" rather than "cops." Respectability and the appearance of respectability were prime values in Catherine McInnis's life. Nothing could be more distressful for her than the thought that other people might think she was crazy, and she would consider it the ultimate indignity to have two police cars parked in front of her door. She was proud that she had always led an upright life, emphasizing that she had always paid her taxes, and never had so much as a parking ticket—a boast that indicated how she perhaps let her own rhetoric carry her away a little, as she did not drive. She also had a great respect for education, and would often put herself down as being "just a simple housewife."

In spite of the rigidity of Mrs. McInnis's life, a certain eccentricity about her came through clearly in her court testimony and in the diaries where she recorded her observations of the children. Both were replete with little digressions in which she displayed an unexpected wit, an obvious enjoyment of a colorful phrase and a loosely bridled sarcasm. She would draw little pictures in her diary to illustrate things she described, and sometimes during her testimony she would mimic a child's voice as she recounted things that the girls had said to her. An avid gardener, Catherine had an intense love of nature, and would make frequent references to her habit of caring for wild and stray animals—practices that she felt she had almost to apologize for, lest someone would think she was "nuts."

Catherine McInnis projected a wholesome, grandmotherly image. She sat up straight in the witness stand and dressed in a dark serge suit with a white blouse that was fastened at the top by a cameo brooch. She looked like someone who would give advice on moral principles, recipes, folk remedies and household hints, rather than some of the most graphic descriptions of sexual abuse and sadistic violence ever heard in a Canadian courtroom. She did, however, manage to include some proverbial wisdom and household lore during her many asides and digressions, but she didn't flinch from any of the obscene words or sickening descriptions that she was required to relate.

Allegations of child sexual abuse often disturb people in a way that elicits the age-old human response of wanting to shoot the messenger who brings bad news. People find it more comfortable to believe that children are natural liars, or that they have been bewitched, manipulated or brainwashed, rather than accept that the sanctity of the home has been desecrated by acts of perverse cruelty. Therefore, as sexual abuse expert Suzanne Sgroi has noted, those who try to assist sexually abused children "must be prepared to battle against incredulity, hostility, innuendo and outright harassment."[5]

People who knew little of the 18 months of testimony that had been presented to the court would assert confidently that the foster mother had obviously made it all up. Defense lawyers at the trial were sure, at the outset, that they would eventually succeed in breaking her down under long cross-examinations, during which they would probe her for signs of hysteria or religious mania. She was put under such pressure that she did eventually burst into tears on the witness stand, complaining about the intensive questioning and ridicule to which she had been subjected. At the end of the hearing the defense lawyers argued that her testimony was highly emotional, and lacking in credibility, but they were not able, on the basis of the evidence that came before the court, to make that argument as strongly as they might originally have wished.

Catherine McInnis was vulnerable to such criticism, because, unlike some of the other people to whom the children subsequently made disclosures of abuse, she was not a professional and did not respond to the allegations in an objective, unemotional fashion. The children were in her care for 85 days, and it was to her that they first made most of their shocking disclosures. She was constantly exposed to the children's macabre preoccupations, was deeply troubled by them, and came to fear for her own safety and that of the children. Eventually she began to respond in some irrational ways, as she became convinced that everything the children told her was true, and that the police were not taking the allegations seriously.

A psychiatrist, who later examined Mrs. McInnis, described her as obsessional and compulsive, but said she exhibited no sign of the kind of psychiatric disorder that would lead someone to fabricate such bizarre stories. The credibility of her reports was also supported by the fact that the children did make other similar allegations to several different people, and that many of the details of the girls' statements, as reported to Mrs. McInnis, were confirmed in other testimony. While the foster mother knew virtually nothing of the children's background before they came into her care, she reported things that later came out in other evidence, such as Janis's "scary dream" in Toronto, their father holding a knife to their mother's throat, his threats to kill Gary and his so-called picture of the devil.

Other testimony indicated that the foster mother had accurately reported even fairly minor details that had made no sense to her at the time. For example, she said the children told her about their mother giving them "drunk stuff" that made them wobble around, and this was later confirmed by Sharon, who said that she had let the girls drink a little wine at Christmas time and that they had all pretended to be drunk. Apart from those allegations, which the girls' parents denied, and for which no external evidence was found, there was nothing that Mrs. McInnis said the children told her about their past lives that did not correspond with what the court heard from other sources. By the end of the trial, even the lawyers representing the parents ceased to maintain that her accounts were a complete fabrication. Instead, they argued that she may have listened selectively to the children, misinterpreting and distorting what they said.

Mrs. McInnis's solid respectability presented the court with a sharp contrast to the uncomfortable presence of Sharon Wells. Sharon was nearly eight months pregnant by the time Catherine took the witness stand. The father, who was now accused with Sharon of abusing her other children, had already abandoned her. Since the court hearing had begun four months earlier, Sharon had attended every day, dressed almost always in the same large sweater and slacks, looking progressively more unhealthy, distressed and distracted. As the foster mother gave her evidence, Sharon would pout and roll her eyes, make angry gestures with her hands, sigh loudly or mutter to herself. Sometimes she would flounce ostentatiously out of the courtroom, or turn around and try to communicate her disgust to the journalists sitting behind her. Her lawyer, Arthur Brown, tried to calm her down on numerous occasions, and once turned round while the court was in session and baldly told her to "shut up."

Catherine's first impression of Sharon was that she appeared to be "scared out of her wits," when she and the social worker, Lesley Morgan, brought the two children to the McInnis home in the early hours of February 8, 1985. The girls appeared frightened too, and Catherine noticed that Linda's whole body was trembling.

As soon as they had got in the door, Linda said she was hungry and asked for something to eat. She struck Catherine as being a bright, talkative little child, but she seemed, to her, to be as pale as a ghost, and her fair hair was as dry as straw. Catherine saw Janis's thin, sad face as being "the shape of a person sobbing." She noticed that both girls had a whiney way of talking. She said this disappeared within a few weeks of their coming to her home.

Sharon told her that the children were "hyper," and produced a bottle of medication prescribed for Linda, who she said had a chronic bladder and kidney infection, and would wet constantly. She warned Catherine that she would have "little puddles," and that Linda would wake at night and scream in her sleep. Sharon hugged the children, and told them they would be coming home soon, explaining that she had "some problems with Gary that I need to sort out."

As they left that evening, Lesley Morgan noted Sharon's

comment to her that she felt good about leaving the children with Mrs. McInnis, because she seemed to be a very caring, motherly person.

The foster mother began to suspect that there was something seriously wrong with the girls soon after their mother left. She felt that both children smelled bad, and decided that, even though it was late, she had to give them a bath before putting them to bed. Catherine said she noticed a sexual odor on Janis. She told the court: "It was clear to me that someone had ejaculated on her since she was last bathed."

As Catherine bathed them, the children cried and screamed, she said, displaying "unbelievable stark terror." Their vaginas were both inflamed, and they both complained that they had sore bums. Then, when she tucked them in bed, Janis held the sheet up to her neck, and had a wild look in her eyes, as if she was scared to death, Catherine said.

Several weeks later the children would tell Catherine that they had been scared when they first came to her home because they assumed that someone was going to abuse them. Catherine testified that Janis told her "she thought everybody would do all those bad things to her all over again. She thought it would be worse even than at home." It took a long time for the girls to realize that they had nothing to fear from Catherine, her quiet retiring husband and their grown-up daughters, Grace and Mary.

Grace McInnis subsequently testified at the hearing and described how Janis and Linda appeared during their first few days in the home. "They appeared terror-stricken the day after they first arrived," she said. "Janis was always looking over her shoulder, always whispering, always scared of somebody else hearing. If someone else came in the room, she would stop talking. And Linda had this strange stare, a really long stare. It wasn't like any stare I've ever seen from any of the other children in the house."

Grace was a student and did not spend a lot of time at home. Her older sister Mary was there even less. They both saw enough of Janis and Linda to be able to describe their behavior in testimony before the court. They both overheard some of the extraordinary disclosures that the girls made to Catherine and were therefore able to corroborate these in court. But they did not spend much time with Janis and Linda, and it was only with Catherine that the children developed a close, trusting relationship.

Two days after Janis and Linda came to her house, Catherine phoned Ms. Morgan, the social worker, to tell her some of the things she had noticed about the girls. She told the social worker that she had "a funny feeling about these children." Catherine had not known Ms. Morgan before she took Janis and Linda into her home, but they quickly developed a good relationship, based on their shared concern for the children. Ms. Morgan asked Catherine to keep detailed notes on what the children said and inform her if there were any further indications that the girls might have been molested or illtreated.

Keeping notes was something that Catherine always did, as a matter of routine. All her life she had been in the habit of writing little notes to herself. Whenever her foster children said anything that seemed important or interesting, Catherine would jot it down right away on a scrap of paper, a grocery bag or an old envelope, whatever was handy. Later on she would transcribe these jottings into a notebook. Usually all her notes on any one foster child would not fill more than a page or two of her notebook. She didn't dream, when she started a new book for Janis and Linda, that four months later, she would have filled nearly 200 pages with her observations and notes of things they said.

For the first two weeks she had nothing particular to report. She was getting to know the two children, slowly winning their trust. It was obvious they were far from happy. Although they had seemed to be undernourished when they arrived, the children seemed to have little zest for the good meals Catherine provided, and would sometimes refuse to eat meat. Catherine did not press them about finishing their meals as she might have with other children. She sensed that these girls needed a lot of patience, understanding and love.

While Linda was naturally chatty and would go on all day about this and that, she would sometimes become totally disconnected and sit staring intently at nothing for long periods of time. She continued to shake a lot and wet her bed a few times at night, but she stopped wetting during the day as soon as she came to Catherine's house. At first Janis was extremely withdrawn and sullen, but she gradually began to open up to Catherine. She told the foster mother one night about the "terrible dream" she had when she was in Toronto. It was very scary, she said, and after that they moved to Hamilton, where Gary found them "a terrific place, with no bugs and no holes in the walls."

When Sharon came to take them out on the Sunday of the first week that they were in the foster home, Linda cringed and said she didn't want to go with Gary. Both girls said that they didn't like Gary, but Sharon reminded them that they did.

One evening, after the children had been with Catherine for about two weeks, she said Linda informed her, quite out of the blue, "Gary puts his finger where the pee comes out."

Catherine said the child dropped down on the floor and spread her legs. "I lay down like this, and he puts his finger and wiggles it, and.I scream. He does it to Janis too," Linda said, and then lowered her voice, as she added, "You don't tell people you know. He thumps the wall when he has finished."

The next day Linda talked to the foster mother again about Gary sticking his finger in her. She said it would happen on her mother's bed: "Sometimes it hurts. Sometimes it tickles. Gary squeezes the thing he pees with, and then he pees into a towel."

Catherine told Linda she should tell her mother. Linda replied, "My mom knows. She was on the bed."

While Catherine immediately informed Ms. Morgan about this conversation, there was something else that Linda told her the same day that she did not mention. She had thought it was strange, and possibly important enough to make some note of, and jotted the child's words down on a paper bag. But what Linda said was so weird that Catherine found it difficult to deal with, and was afraid she would be ridiculed for taking it seriously.

"Elizabeth got dead. A killer got her. He had a knife. He was a killer," Linda said, as Catherine listened dumbfounded. "Me and Gary, and Mom and Janis and Elizabeth went for a drive. Elizabeth was sleeping. She went in the woods."

As Linda spoke, her usual breathless chattering pace slowed down slightly with apparent fear and bewilderment. Janis was frantically trying to get her to be quiet. Linda continued, "I think maybe she walked. Maybe Mom carried her. She was bad. Mom told us she touched things. Mom went in the trees. Gary and us waited in the car. Mom hurried back from the woods. Gary drived fast. Mom had blood on her finger. Mom was scared after a killer got Elizabeth. Mom said she opened her mouth. I guess her mouth opened when the killer got her."

On the IDA drug store bag, on which Catherine noted Linda's disclosure, she also wrote a note to herself: "Should I tell and be a fool, or be quiet and be a bigger one?"

She decided to put the bag away in a safe place, and not say anything more about it for the time being. It was not until two months later, when she had heard a great deal more from the children, that she became convinced that Linda's story about Elizabeth was not a tall tale or a fantasy, but a child's eye view of a real murder.

CHAPTER 5

CHILDREN INTERVIEWED AND MOTHER CONFRONTED

The Hamilton-Wentworth Children's Aid Society offices are housed in a brick building in a quiet, well-to-do residential district about half a mile from the center of the city. It is a homey-looking place, well-suited for such an agency. Lesley Morgan took the children there on March 1 for an interview with the society's sexual abuse specialist, Tricia Donnelly.

They were introduced to Ms. Donnelly in a playroom, where there were toys, dolls and materials for drawing and painting. The room had a two-way mirror, so that observers behind the mirror could watch the interview. Children felt at ease with Ms. Donnelly. She seemed like a really nice, warm lady, who knew how to talk to kids and liked to play games with them. From an adult's perspective, she appeared a little nervous, reserved and cerebral. She was a very neat, carefully dressed, energetic young woman. She seemed scarcely old enough to be an expert, but had interviewed more than 600 sexually abused children.

The children also met Sergeant David Broom of the Hamilton-Wentworth Regional Police. Ms. Donnelly had asked him to sit in on the interview, as this would help to reduce the number of times the children might have to tell their story, if it turned out this was a case of sexual abuse.

Sgt. Broom was a tall, burly man with a pleasant manner. He sat in a corner of the room, while the specialist interviewed each of the children in turn. The interview was recorded and a transcript of this recording was entered as evidence at the hearing. Linda, whom they saw first, struck them as being a chatty and intelligent child, who showed no fear of being there with these two strange adults. When Ms. Donnelly asked her if she knew Gary, Linda said she did. But she said "Yes" a little more hesitantly when the woman asked if she liked the man. Then she asked the child to tell her about Gary, and Linda said, "No."

"Why?" Ms. Donnelly asked.

"It's bad," Linda replied, and after a poignant pause, she added, "If I tell, Gary's going to spank me."

Ms. Donnelly assured the child that she was safe, and that no one was going to hurt her. She gave the children some dolls to play with. These looked like soft, Raggedy Ann dolls, but they were what are known as Anatomically Correct dolls, which, when undressed, reveal a simplified fascsimile of male and female anatomy. They are widely used in the field of child abuse to assist young children in disclosing sexual assaults. Linda was immediately intrigued by the four dolls—an adult and a child of each sex.

Demonstrating with the dolls, Linda said that Gary "sticks his finger in my pee-hole. It hurts. I don't like it. He does it to Janis too."

Linda gave a few more details, played for a while, and then said, "Mom and Gary suck Janis and me. Sometimes we have to suck each other. Do you want to hear another funny thing?"

"Okay," said Ms. Donnelly.

"I stick my finger in Janis, and she sticks her finger in my pee-hole."

Ms. Donnelly asked, "How did you learn that?"

"Mom taught us how to do it."

"Do what?" asked Ms. Donnelly, anxious to insure that there was no misunderstanding.

"Mom taught us to put our fingers between our own legs," said the child, and then added, putting her mouth to the doll's vagina, "I suck Mommy's pee-hole."

The child continued to talk and play for about an hour, disclosing a few further details similar to those she had already told her foster mother. As Ms. Donnelly was taking her out of the playroom to rejoin Lesley, the child soiled her pants.

Arthur Brown, the mother's lawyer, would later argue that this and other interviews that Tricia Donnelly conducted involved a lot of prompting and prodding of the children. But Judge Beckett said he was very impressed with the way the social worker conducted the interviews and did not accept the lawyer's submission, especially as the lawyer said he was unable to provide specific examples of any leading questions that Ms. Donnelly had asked.

Ms. Donnelly was dealing well with a difficulty that faces anyone interviewing an allegedly abused child. Children seldom find it easy to make such allegations, particularly against their own parents, and therefore require constant reassurance. They are also easily distracted and need to be kept on track by persistent, gentle questioning. The use of visual aids, such as dolls and other toys, while facilitating this process of disclosure, also leaves the interviewer open to charges that she has been encouraging the child to fantasize.

Ms. Donnelly told the court that it is very rare for a child to lie or fantasize about being sexually abused by her own parent, and that in the 600 cases she had seen, she had never encountered such a phenomenon. She said the accompanying physical symptoms of distress served to reinforce her belief that Linda was telling the truth. Police officers and defense lawyers would distort this statement, and other similar assertions by psychiatrists, into the patently absurd proposition that "Children never lie."

The interview with Janis produced fewer disclosures than her younger sister had made, but was very revealing. The child appeared to be very nervous, and would glance anxiously around the room. Ms. Donnelly found her a very easy child to play with. She thought she was intelligent, and drew pictures well and very meticulously. When she asked Janis about her mother and Gary, Janis said, "I'm afraid," but said she couldn't tell why.

Ms. Donnelly said that the dolls might help her tell about her mom and Gary. Janis responded to this suggestion by asking if the dolls' clothes came off. Then she demonstrated the dolls putting fingers in one another and the two adult dolls having intercourse. Ms. Donnelly asked if there was anything else, and the child said she was afraid to talk any more. Ms. Donnelly asked her what would happen if she talked. Janis began sobbing uncontrollably, and said, "I'll die, I'll die."

Sgt. Broom agreed with Ms. Donnelly that there appeared to be little doubt that the children had been sexually assaulted. Ms. Donnelly advised Lesley Morgan not to bring the subject up with the children, but said she suspected that more details of abuse would emerge later. She said that there is a generally recognized pattern in children's disclosure of abuse. They start by talking about some relatively minor instance of molestation. Then, if they meet with an understanding response from the adults to whom they make the disclosure, they begin to make progressively more detailed and more serious allegations. Critics of this theory maintain that this is because the receptive adult is feeding the child's fantasies and encouraging her to fabricate more and more.

When the girls returned to the foster home that day, Janis appeared to be in a state of panic. Catherine overheard her tell her younger sister, "Linda, you talk too much. You tell everything. I'll tell Mom. You don't tell on Mom. You just tell on Gary."

Linda interjected, "Gary did it to us."

"With the finger. Shut up," said Janis.

"Well, Mom does it too," Linda insisted, as Janis continued her attempts at silencing her with warnings that their mom was going to be mad. Linda was shaking uncontrollably. When she noticed that Catherine had slipped into the room during their argument, she crawled on to her lap and cried frantically for a long time, eventually falling into an exhausted sleep on the floor.

It was on the following day, March 2, that the children's mother was questioned about their allegations. Lesley had told her to come to the CAS offices, and Sharon thought they would be making arrangements for her to get the girls back. Instead she was confronted with another social worker and a big policeman.

Sgt. Broom noted that Mrs. Wells reacted to the allegations with dramatic swings in mood. He said she paced up and down, threatening to sue the CAS, then looked up at the ceiling and said, "God, why me?" He also quoted the mother as saying: "I knew it would come to this. To a point where I would get hurt. Okay, it did happen. I swore it would never happen to my kids."

The sergeant noted that Sharon asked him if the children said she put her finger in them. He was curious about this because he had not mentioned that allegation to her. When he asked why her child would say she was afraid she would die, Sharon began screaming hysterically, "I don't know. Keep my kids. I don't care."

While the policeman and the two social workers were stunned by the force of her hysteria, Sharon suddenly bolted from the office and ran out of the agency, screaming. Ms. Morgan, Ms. Donnelly and Sgt. Broom were slow to follow, and, by the time they did, Sharon had disappeared from sight. They spent about 20 minutes looking for her. Sharon later said she had thought about throwing herself under a bus, but then decided to return to the agency. Ms. Morgan found her there, took her back into the interview room and talked with her for a long time, while Ms. Donnelly and Sgt. Broom monitored part of the conversation through the two-way mirror.

Ms. Donnelly later described watching the distraught mother engrossed in a discussion of her own childhood, sitting with her hands crossed over her abdomen, as if she was physically experiencing pain. She said the mother also told Lesley about her violent marriage, and her good relationship with Gary, whom she described as a virgin.

Sharon said she would charge the foster mother with defamation of character. She asked if there was enough evidence for charges against herself. Then she said, "I'll charge everyone. It will cost, but I don't care. I won't get caught. I don't believe it. If my girls have been sexually assaulted, it happened in foster care. I truly believe that.

"I'm not two people. I'm one. I don't have two personalities. Gary sometimes thinks I have," she told Lesley. "I feel like you don't do your job right. I shouldn't have trusted you so much. It's not easy to prove you're innocent.

"Why am I the victim and accused? How can I be both the victim and the accused? They don't teach you to defend yourself against that at the Rape Crisis Centre. I can't fight my kids in court. My kids have accused me of sex-abusing them. I remember the first time they saw me put a Kotex on. Now they fight to see who will pull the paper off. I need to see the kids to tell them the truth."

Sgt. Broom compared notes with Ms. Donnelly, and concluded that, while Sharon's statements were strange and suggestive, there was nothing that she had said that constituted an admission of guilt. He found out from Sharon that Gary was working out of town, but was expected at her home at about seven o'clock that evening. Sharon was allowed to return home, and the sergeant waited outside her house for Gary.

However, when the boyfriend had not shown up by 7:30 P.M., Sgt. Broom decided to go home, since his shift was over. He did not get another officer to wait and interview Gary.

This was the first of many indications that this was not a high priority case for the Hamilton police. The failure to interview the main alleged perpetrator at the earliest opportunity, and before his alleged partner-in-crime had a chance to warn him of the allegations, was the first item on what proved to be a long list of police mistakes or omissions. These later served to discredit the police investigation and made it impossible for any court to ever find out the complete truth behind the children's allegations.

Sgt. Broom returned to Sharon's house the next morning, but she would not let him in until she had cleared papers and other things from the floor, and put them in a garbage bag outside. He did not examine this garbage, as he did not have a search warrant. Once he was allowed inside, it did not seem to him that the cleanup had made much of an impression on the messy apartment. He spoke to Sharon and Gary, but they refused to discuss the allegations with him and both declined to submit to lie detector tests.

Later on the same day Sharon visited the children at the foster home. She assured them that they would be going home soon. She clearly wanted to talk to them alone and, though Catherine was hovering around, would whisper to the girls and accompany them to the bathroom. As Sharon left, Catherine mentioned that she found Linda to be a "bright little thing," and the mother responded with a gesture towards Janis, saying, "She is a little slow. Not retarded. Just slow."

After the visit, Linda said, "We'll soon be going home."

"How can we be sure all that stuff won't happen to us again?" Janis asked her.

Linda replied, "Well, Mom and Gary will stop it. We're used to it now. I hate it when Gary . . ."

"You tell too much, Linda," interrupted Janis. "It's not our business what Mom and Gary do. They'll stop doing it maybe."

Linda said, "I like the treats they give us after they do it."

"What kind of treats?" Catherine asked.

"Lollipops and candy," said Linda.

"Sometimes we get money to go to the store," said Janis. "I like that 'cos I can choose the things that I like."

Later Catherine overheard a conversation between the children as they were getting ready for bed. Janis told Linda, "It's Mom's fault we're in a foster home. But Catherine is nice, eh?"

"Yeah, Jan, nobody hurts us here," replied Linda, who went on to talk about her mother fondling her "regina." She said, "It's so crazy. I don't like it."

"Nobody likes it. But we got to like it, because Mom gets angry if we cry," responded Janis.

Mrs. Wells came by again two days later, frantic to talk to the children. She took them outside and whispered to them urgently.

At bedtime Janis said to Catherine, "You know those things we told you this morning. They were just a dream. I told you it was true, but it was a dream. I'll get a licking for telling that stuff."

Linda responded indignantly, "Really. A dream, eh, Jan. It's true. I don't tell lies, Jan. It's crazy but it's true."

Janis said, "I shouldn't say that stuff. Mom is going to give me a licking. Somebody will tell Mom I told."

The next day Linda again came out with a disturbing disclosure, and Janis again tried to silence her. Linda pointed to a little battery-powered "Glow Bug" night-light, and told Catherine, "Mom has a thing like a little knife with batteries. They stick it in, and sometimes it gets poo on it. They stick it in everyone."

Janis, who was playing on the stairs, said, "Shut up, Lin. She's making up stories, Catherine."

Janis herself later talked about what apparently was a vibrator. She told Catherine: "Mom did all those bad things to us before we even knew Gary. They put that banana thing with batteries way up in my vagina. Sometimes I would scream and they would put a towel in my mouth. Gary didn't live with us then. She put it in my bum too. It moves up and down, and in and out, and it shivers. It has batteries in it, and it hurts.

"I'm so scared of it. It's terrible. Your house is so different. I can't believe how people are in this house. It's so safe. Why did Mom hurt me so much? It hurt to sit down. It hurt to walk. I was so sore and so tired."

"Couldn't you rest when you were finished?" Catherine asked.

"But you're never finished," Janis replied. "Everyone's so nice here. How come you are all so nice?"

The two children completely reversed their previous roles when they went for their second interviews with Tricia Donnelly on March 7, 1985, six days after their first meeting with the child abuse specialist. Janis was forthcoming about disclosing abuse, while Linda was evasive. Ms. Donnelly was not particularly surprised by Linda's lack of co-operation, as it is quite a normal phenomenon for children to become scared by the enormity of the allegations they have made, and the response of their parents. Linda told Ms. Donnelly her mother would spank her if she told about Mom's and Gary's secrets.

Ms. Donnelly later explained to the court about a mechanism known as the accommodation syndrome; this is when sexually abused children usually deal with their own feelings of fear, guilt and helplessness by keeping the abuse secret. According to this theory, the child will accommodate her abuse as a part of her normal experience, and only disclose what has happened to her when she feels safe and secure in a different environment. Because her feelings of fear and guilt have become incorporated into her view of the world, the theory states, she is likely to become frightened after making the disclosure, and will then try to deny or retract it. Child abuse experts often cite this theory in court in order to indicate that delayed disclosures and retractions need not necessarily be seen as discrediting children's stories, as they would in the case of adult victims of sexual assaults.

As soon as Janis saw Ms. Donnelly, she said she wanted to talk because "Mom needs help." When the social worker asked what her mother needed help with, Janis said, "Not to do what she's been doing to me and Linda. We should talk, because we have to get Mom better."

She used the dolls to show Ms. Donnelly all the things that Linda had already described to Catherine. Sometimes she questioned whether she should be saying all this, and Ms.

Donnelly reassured her that it was a good thing to do. The child said it was hard to tell, and that if she told all it would take until the next morning. After a while she very proudly told Ms. Donnelly that she felt better, and that she was now able to talk without having the dolls to help her.

"I'll tell you something that's very, very sad," said Janis. "It is very sad about my mom and Gary, and what they do to us."

The children's second interview with the child abuse specialist reinforced a decision that the Children's Aid Society had made a day or two earlier. On March 6, 1985, Janis and Linda were officially "apprehended" by the CAS. Though nothing was actually done that made the children aware of what was going on, this involved initiating court proceedings to have the girls declared "in need of protection" under the *Child Welfare Act*. The CAS obtained an interim court order allowing them to keep the children in foster care pending further hearings. Janis and Linda were told that they would be staying with Catherine for a while longer.

One night as Linda was getting ready for bed, Catherine heard the child singing a sad, tuneless song to herself, with these rambling, improvised lyrics: "I'm getting ready for bed. Nobody can hurt me here. Mommy loves me, but she sticks her fingers in us. And we're going home some day. But she can't hurt me now. I'm getting ready for bed. Nobody hurts us here. We can't go home now, because the boss said, 'No.' I mean the court said, 'No.' "

CHAPTER 6

PORNOGRAPHY
ALLEGATIONS BEGIN

The children were beginning to look healthier than when they first came into foster care. Linda was still nervous and hyper-active, while Janis was very quiet and often withdrawn. However, Janis appeared to Catherine to have changed significantly from the woebegone little waif who arrived at the foster home six weeks earlier. Catherine observed that she was now beginning to be happy, and had rosy cheeks, while before she had appeared so preoccupied that she seemed to be falling apart at the seams, and so withdrawn that she was "almost like a little robot."

The foster mother had established a warm relationship with the two girls, who felt comfortable about telling her things that they would not disclose to anyone else. Catherine facilitated these disclosures by making an effort to hide her horror and disgust at what she heard, and by not asking questions. As she explained in court, in words that could well be quoted in any manual on child-interviewing techniques, "You know how children are, if they are talking and you ask them something: they just stop talking, or start telling you stories."

Catherine said that from time to time the children would tell her never to tell anyone about what happened in

67

their house, "that it's a secret, not people's affairs, and I must not tell. I must button my lips, and keep it quiet. They just want me to know. I must be quiet so Gary and Mom never find out that they told me. They say Dad would really be mad, if he found out. He would be mad at Mom. He would be mad enough to kill Gary."

The girls did repeat some of what they told Catherine to Ms. Morgan, whom the foster mother frequently invited to the house to discuss the horrible things the children had been saying, or simply to see the terrified state that the girls got into when they made some of their disclosures. Catherine explained to the court that the looks on the children's faces were often so painful that "I used to call the CAS, and say 'I want somebody else to come and see this. I don't want to be the only one to see this kind of thing.'"

There were disturbing indications that the prematurely sexualized Janis was beginning to victimize her younger sister. Catherine had noticed the children on a few occasions rubbing tummies and touching one another in ways that she considered too familiar and altogether inappropriate. Then one night she caught Janis in bed with Linda trying to put her hands between the younger child's legs, while Linda struggled to fend her off. Linda looked relieved when she saw Catherine and complained, "Janis is trying to put her finger in me."

Catherine told Janis not to do things like that again, and warned that, if anyone found out she tried to molest her sister, they would think it was weird and other children wouldn't like her. Linda corrected her on that, and said that it's okay sometimes to put your fingers in your friends. Janis told Catherine that other people still like you if you stick your fingers in them, and mentioned that she had stuck her fingers in some of her friends.

"If I wrote with both hands, I couldn't write it all down," Catherine noted in the diary, which catalogued the children's ever more startling allegations of abuse. Catherine explained to the court that all she had done in her 200 pages of notes was to write down each new thing the children told her, and record conversations that she felt were particularly significant. The children would go over and over the same ground in their discussions, so that all these "gross things" were a constant topic of conversation in her home.

The next ugly revelation came while they were watching television one evening. "I couldn't believe my ears," Mrs.

McInnis told the court, as she described how Linda told her: "At my house, I saw myself on TV, with Mom putting her finger in me. And I saw Janis like that too. I saw Gary putting his finger in Janis, and Gary and Mom and everyone doing those things."

The child shivered and shook, Catherine said, as she described how they would use a tape and a thing like a tape recorder, "and when they put the tape in, you see Mom putting her finger in me and Janis."

The girls were due to visit their father, who had just been informed that the children were in foster care, and he had been granted access to them. Janis and Linda warned each other not to tell their dad about what they had been saying. When they returned from this visit, Linda told Catherine, "Dad has a knife."

"I guess it's to kill people," said Janis.

"He held it to Mom's neck once," said Linda. "He doesn't hurt us. He doesn't hurt kids, you know."

Linda went to bed complaining of such a terrible headache that she felt her head would fall off. Then the following day she said something so awful that, Catherine said, "I was shocked right out of my shoes."

"When we are on TV, we don't wear any clothes. They put the bird in me. A real bird with real wings. You know, wings. They put a Kleenex over its head. It was black. They put it in me and Janis. We cried, and they took it out. It hurt. They threw it away after," Linda said.

Catherine said that as Linda was saying this, she noticed on Janis's face "a look of horror that I don't know any words to describe."

In the evening Catherine overheard the children discussing the bird. She heard Linda say, "When they put it in you, you screamed more than me," to which Janis replied, "I really screamed when it was dead, when I knew it was dead."

"It looked awful hanging down between my legs," said Linda.

"It was a dream, Linda. It was only a dream. I thought it was true, but it was only a dream. I'm telling Mom you talked. It's a secret. It's a dream. I dreamed all of that. I'm telling Mom you talked to Catherine. I'm telling Mom that Catherine knows about the bird. I mean that Catherine knows about the dream."

Catherine said the subject of the bird kept coming up in

the children's conversation, as they were reminded of it by such things as seeing a bird on television, or in a comic book. She told the court, "The look of agony on the children's faces, when they talked about the bird, is written on my brain in indelible ink. The faces reminded me of pictures I've seen of people who went through the holocaust."

Catherine did also have some ordinary times with the girls, when she felt a great relief that they could for a while just play "I Spy" or "Snakes and Ladders," or listen quietly to a story. But this relief was always mixed with apprehension, as the smallest thing would suddenly spark some traumatic memory. Often they would be playing an innocent game or having a quiet chat, and Catherine would find herself ambushed by a monster that would crawl out of these little girls' consciousness.

Linda would suddenly remember details like how Gary once put "his thing" in her mouth, and it went in too far, and she was sick. Such comments would trigger similar memories in Janis, who said on this occasion that she hated it when the "pee" came in her mouth, because it tasted awful.

Catherine's daughter told the court how, on one occasion, "Mom made salad for lunch with an oil and vinegar dressing. Linda said she wasn't going to eat that, because it looked like the stuff she had to eat off Gary's pee thing. Sometimes it got stuck in the hole."

It was spontaneous statements such as this, in which a preschool-age child displayed a precise knowledge of male anatomy and perverse sexual practices, that would later convince psychiatrists and others of the truth of the children's allegations. The psychiatrists found the descriptions more convincing because of the language that the girls used, and the fact that they would display such natural childlike misconceptions as the notion that what comes from a man's "pee thing" must always be "pee."

There was a tense atmosphere in the small courtroom as everyone present struggled with their painful responses to these disclosures—none more so than Judge Beckett, who watched Mrs. McInnis intently during her testimony, with a grim expression, bowing his head often and wiping beads of perspiration from his wide forehead. Although the foster mother was displaying no squeamishness about describing the children's words and the gross abuse they had related to her, she did not attempt to disguise her disgust and indignation.

There were tears in her voice as she recalled the horror of hearing every day in her own home the girls' continual disclosures of violence and depravity.

One could have heard a pin drop in the court, and one could scarcely imagine what it would have been like in Catherine's living room, when the children's allegations that they were forced to eat feces and drink urine were discussed. As Catherine described it, Linda had abruptly introduced the topic one day by saying, "The subject is that we ate poo."

"I thought my ears were deceiving me. But I knew by the look of her that they weren't," said Catherine, as she referred to her notes in order to relate the subsequent conversation.

"You ate what?" Catherine had asked.

"We ate poo," said Linda.

"Not me," Janis interjected.

"Oh yes you did. You ate poo," Linda replied.

"I forgot. Remember when Mom put it outside to get cold, to get ice on it."

"Yes, and she fed it to me, and it was terrible."

"It's worse when it's hot," said Janis.

"You ate it hot, but Mom fed you part of the poo with ice on it. I wiped it off my teeth with a towel. Gary got me a towel. It sticks to the teeth you know," said Linda.

She said Linda told her, "When Mom made the poo ice in the back yard, she asked Gary to go get it and he wouldn't go. Mom said, 'You fucking bitch ass,' and she went out to get the poo cup. Gary hid Jan and me in the closet."

Catherine apparently felt, from what the girls told her, that this little scene was, perhaps, part of the scenario of a pornographic video in which the children were unwittingly participating. She saw that, in this context, Gary's display of concern for the girls could just have been part of the script. She inserted an editorial comment into her notes: "Somebody was taking pictures of these things, so even the things that seemed kind were brutal."

In making this comment, Catherine showed a natural understanding of a point that has been made by experts in the field of child pornography. The use of children in making pornography is a form of molestation, over and above any sexual abuse that is inflicted on the children at the same time. Researchers have noted that victims often show more distress over the fact that they were used for pornography than over the sexual indignities that they were subjected to while the pornography was made. While a victim can tell herself that the abuse she has suffered is over and done with, she knows that the frozen image of that abuse, in a photograph, film or video, might remain in circulation for years to come. Examples have been cited of teenagers committing robberies in order to recover pornographic pictures of themselves that had been taken by abusers years before.

Although Janis and Linda were too young to have that kind of sophisticated understanding, they did draw these things to Catherine's attention frequently enough to give one the impression that they were, in some way, deeply disturbed by this objective consideration of their abuse.

Resuming her account of the children's disclosures, Catherine said Linda went on to say, "If we don't eat it, she rubs it on our face and hair. Gary doesn't like it. He takes us and gives us a bath. It got all over the tub. Mom gives us pee sometimes."

"I had to drink the pee out of a beer bottle," Janis then told Catherine, who asked her how she knew it was pee, to which Janis responded, "You know by the smell. Mom worried about us crying, because there were people living upstairs, and she put a towel in my mouth."

"At home we eat supper, and then it's always this stuff," said Linda. "I try to run away, but the walls stop me. But we get treats afterwards."

In their frequent references to treats they received after suffering abuse, the children were echoing their own mother's account of her childhood experiences, as well as the reports of a large proportion of the victims of child pornography and sex rings. Children, who are used by adults for sex and pornography, are given money, presents or treats, not only as a reward, which might buy their silence and compliance, but also as an instrument of psychological blackmail—they will feel guilty about collaborating with their abusers, and therefore more reluctant to tell anyone.

A few days later Linda asked Catherine, "Why does Mom tell us it's not true? Mom knows it's true. She's not telling the truth." And, as Catherine recounted this to the court, she exclaimed, "I felt I should tell those suffering little things 'I do believe what you say!'"

Catherine said that Janis used to get very scared when

she made these disclosures, and would look behind doors and drapes, and open cupboards to make sure nobody was there: "I thought it was the limit when she opened up the fridge door to see that there was nobody listening who might tell her mother.

"I told them it would never happen here, and it shouldn't happen anywhere. I told them, if it did, they should tell a teacher, the CAS, a Sunday School teacher, the police. I don't know why I told them that, because when I told the police, they wouldn't listen. They didn't believe it," Catherine told the court indignantly.

The note for April 12 read, "The children were having fun today. They played. But, when we went outside they talked about the bird. The story was always the same, almost always word-for-word."

Then, two days later, the foster mother wrote, "It was a quiet day. The girls played school and house. It was unusual that they wouldn't be revealing some dreadful thing that I hadn't heard before." She told the court, "Every day I thought, 'There is nothing more. I have heard the worst.' But there would be more horrors."

Shortly after Janis left for school the next morning, she appeared banging and screaming at the front door. She told Catherine that a car had stopped and someone offered her some candy. Catherine observed that, "If there had been a tiger after her, she couldn't have been more frightened."

For days after this Janis would not go to school alone, and talked constantly about the orange car. Catherine was convinced that Janis knew somebody in the car and that she tried several times to talk about it, but something would stop her. The child told her, "They're going to kill me. I am scared they're going to kill me."

"It was worse than I wanted to absorb somehow," said Catherine as she described more things the children told her about vibrators, bananas stuck in their bum, fruit and a red jelly that they had to lick off their mother's body, and some "red stuff" their mother and Gary put on themselves, that appeared to be different from the red jelly.

"Sometimes Mom puts jelly on her bum, or in her pee-hole, and I get to suck it off," said Linda. "Your Jell-O is good, Catherine, but Mom's jelly looks like pee."

Catherine said she stupidly responded to this by saying,

"I see," to which Linda rejoined, "No, you don't see, Catherine. I see. Gary bought me a little flashlight. It's mine, and I get to look up Mom's pee-hole with it and her bum."

For all her horror and disgust at what the girls were telling her, one got a sense from listening to Catherine McInnis's testimony that she really liked these children, that she admired Linda's irrepressible spirit, and loved Janis for her gentleness. The humanity that Catherine displayed in her concern for the children was one of the few elements that gave some solace to those who had to listen to her testimony.

Catherine cried on the witness stand when she had to relate an incident in which the children displayed cruelty to one another. She described how Linda told her, "Mom holds Janis's legs, and I put the battery thing in Janis's poo-hole, and she cries."

"I put in my notes that I have a strong stomach, but I felt sick. Linda kept laughing as she was telling me this story. I felt I had to say something to her. I said, 'You have no right to hurt Janis. It's a dreadful thing to hurt another person, more dreadful to hurt your sister.' Linda said, 'Well, I like watching what they do to Janis.' I said, 'It's not fun, Linda. It's cruel and mean.' Linda said, 'When they've finished, I wipe it off and Mom puts it in the cupboard. I have poo on my hands, and I have to wash them. Then we got a treat. We always get treats.'

"I called the CAS and asked to speak to Lesley. She wasn't there, and that was a good thing. I had reached the end of my rope. I couldn't listen to any more of it, and I was going to ask them to move the children. Then I thought better of it. Just a flash in the pan. I wasn't angry with the children."

Catherine McInnis was finding the situation increasingly hard to accept, and, in their own way, so were the children. Janis and Linda were becoming more urgent in their desire to tell all that happened to them and to have something done about it. Their stay in Catherine's comfortable, normal home had made them realize how much abnormality there was in their previous environment. And Catherine had been telling them that the police and other authorities are meant to stop people treating children so badly. The social workers had explained to them that perhaps their mother was sick, and that by talking about what happened, they could help make their mother better; they could help her to stop harming them, so that they might be able to go back home.

But Linda conceived a more radical solution to their problems. "I wish Dad was a killer, because I want him to kill Gary," she said one day. "He has a knife; I want him to cut Gary's neck. I hate Gary. I want Dad to kill him. Gary puts his fingers in me. I don't want him at my house. I want him out of there."

In relating this conversation, Catherine observed that Linda "had a terrible look on her face. It wasn't just idle chatter. She meant business."

Janis, who had previously been the more reluctant of the two children to talk about what had happened in her home, suddenly launched into a detailed description of what appeared to be pornographic moviemaking sessions. She talked about licking the red jelly and peanut butter off Gary for the TV. She said, "I hate licking Gary's pee thing and all that. I cry, and everybody laughs. I can't remember where the place is. We go there at night. We go to bed, and then get up and go in a car to that place. They laugh. They say 'Channel something TV.' Sometimes we're bare. Sometimes we have some clothes on. They laugh. They have a camera. Mom and Gary and us do these awful things. I cry, and Linda screams, and they take our pictures. And then, after, later at home or at that place, we see all the things we did on TV.

"There is a couch there, and some women and men taking pictures," the child continued. "The next day, it's the same thing. We are hurt again. We both get the fingers and the battery thing. They hurt us, but then they give us lots of treats, and we hold hands and we sing songs. We hold hands, and sing songs, and dance round and round, one leg up and one down. Pictures are taken of everything. Then we go to sleep. Lots of times they wake us at night, and we go to this place for pictures, and we can be on TV. A man talks like in the movies."

Catherine listened to this monologue in silence, and noted down Janis's words soon afterwards, while they were still fresh in her mind. She believed that here, as elsewhere in her notes, she recorded what the children were saying as accurately as possible. She tried to recall all the details, as she felt these might be helpful in investigating Janis's allegations. She explained to the court, "She talked about so much. I couldn't remember it all. But I marked down what I could remember accurately and exactly."

Janis said, "Then we hold hands, and we sing again,

twirling and spinning. And then they get the battery thing out. Catherine, it's awful."

"Janis was so eager to talk," Catherine told the court. "But I felt ill, and I couldn't listen another minute. It had to be pretty bad because I'm strong. I went for fresh air. When I came back, she didn't want to say any more. She said, 'Don't tell anyone. It's a secret. It's an ugly secret.'"

Catherine said the child then told her, "You are sweet. You have pretty hands." The foster mother told the court, "I thought, that's strange because I have working hands. I take care of my kids, not my hands."

The next morning Janis told Catherine, "I know where that place is, I think. There is an '11' on the building. I think it's white with some colors."

As Janis described the building and the square sign outside it, Catherine thought she must be referring to a CHCH-TV Channel 11 studio in Hamilton, which did have a white sign with a number 11 on it, and a flower-shaped colored logo.

Catherine said the children described "naked bodies and people doing every mortal perverted thing I ever heard tell of, and a lot I didn't." She said she wrote in her diary, "Could there be corruption in high places?" But she hastened to add that this was just her own observation.

She recorded in her notes, "Janis said that the people took all their clothes off. But one man was more modest, because he left his socks on. They were all laughing."

The children drew pictures of the room at Channel 11, describing little mats on the floor, a couch, a camera on a stand with crooked legs, lights hanging on wires. Janis said that, when they were taken there at night, they would go in and turn to the right.

Sgt. David Bowen, the senior investigating officer on the case, later testified, "I was shown Catherine McInnis's notes with the drawings of crosswires over a lamp and mats. I was satisfied those diagrams seemed to reflect portions of the [Channel 11] building. I didn't understand what they meant, until I went in the building. There were spotlights with very thin wires, and a large number of mats shoved up against each other. I accepted that these diagrams showed the inside of the building."

A television company executive later confirmed that if you enter the [Channel 11] building by a side door, you have to turn to the right in order to get to the studio.

Janis told Lesley that her mother had burned down a house at the Channel 11 place. Police reports subsequently obtained by the CAS indicated that there had been a fire, a case of suspected arson, at a building next door to the studio, which was used to store costumes and property. Sgt. Bowen said he was never made aware of Janis's allegation about the fire.

The police began to conduct a surveillance operation at the studio, but soon abandoned it, when they believed that they had discovered that some subsequent allegations made by the children were untrue. Police received conflicting information about the level of security in place at the studio; it was only used occasionally by the television station for certain special productions. A 1984 signout list of people who had access to the studio had been destroyed in January 1985, and Sgt. Bowen was told by commissionaires who guarded the building, that the security was not very sound. But management representatives at the television station responded defensively to the suggestion that anyone could have used the studio for making pornographic movies. They convinced the police that the security was tight enough that no one could possibly have gained unauthorized entry, and would have had to have great technical skill to operate the equipment.

Subsequent court testimony indicated that some of the equipment could have been operated easily by someone with some basic technical knowledge. It was not necessarily very difficult to beat the security system to gain unauthorized entry into the building. The television company later instituted new security measures as a result of the allegations.

Sgt. Bowen obtained photographs of some, but not all, of the television station employees who had access to the studio. He showed these to Janis, who was frightened and would not look at the pictures. Catherine asked him to go through the pictures with the child again more slowly, but he declined to do this. The Hamilton police also showed pictures of Janis and Linda to a Toronto police task force on pornography, and were told that these children had not appeared in any pornographic material seized by police in the Toronto area. The investigating officers gave no indication that they were aware that this was not a very significant finding, since professionally produced pornography is often sent abroad for processing, and sold in markets as far removed as possible from where it was originally produced.

Authorities in the United States have estimated that the child pornography business is worth from $2 billion to $3 billion a year, and involves more than one million children. The Canadian government's *Report on Sexual Offenses Against Children and Youths* concluded that there was no reliable evidence on the extent of the pornography trade in Canada. It found that detection mechanisms were beset with "crippling problems," but found that on the basis of evidence available, there appeared to be no commercial production of pornography within the country. However, the report warned that law enforcement agencies would soon face a situation of different proportions, with the increasing availability of videotape equipment facilitating the cheap and easy reproduction of child pornography.

The sophisticated nature of the child pornography trade can be seen from a description of how such material is circulated. A 1984 study of child pornography and sex rings stated: "The mail is a major facilitator for the circulation of child pornography. A laundering process is often used: buyers send their responses to another country; the mail received by the overseas forwarding agent is opened, and cash or checks are placed in a foreign bank account; the order is remailed under a different cover back to the United States. This procedure insures that the subscriber does not know where the operation originates, and law enforcement has difficulty tracing the operation."

The same study noted, "Few law enforcement agencies have investigators trained as child pornography investigators, and few of these agencies believe child pornography exists in their own cities or towns."[6]

Sgt. Bowen concluded, on the basis of what he and his partner had learned, that it was "completely impossible" that the pornographic sessions described by the children had taken place at the Channel 11 studio.

Catherine contacted Staff Sergeant John Gruhl. He was a friend, who said he looked upon Mrs. McInnis "as a pretty special person, because of all the children she has taken into the house and done what looked like miracles within the short time she had them."

She asked the staff sergeant to drive her and Janis past the Channel 11 studio. He agreed to do this and drove them by the studio three times, noting that on each occasion the child fell silent as they drove by. Catherine observed that the child "turned as red as blood, and I noticed something I'd never seen before, because she never perspires, a drop of sweat on her lips. She turned her head and glanced, and turned her head. At that time she didn't say anything about anything."

When they got home, Janis told Catherine, "I saw the place with the '11' and the flower." Catherine asked her why she had not told Sgt. Gruhl, and Janis replied, "I thought he might take me in there. I thought he might drag me in there. Most people are bad. I thought he might be bad. I was scared."

CHAPTER 7
THE "FLORID" ALLEGATIONS

The children spent a weekend with their father at the beginning of May. After this visit Catherine McInnis began reporting a series of lurid and bizarre allegations of murder and ritual violence. A psychiatrist who subsequently examined the children described these as the "florid allegations"—a term that Judge Beckett later adopted in his final judgment.

It was plain to see, both from her notes and courtroom testimony, that the foster mother was shocked and frightened by these allegations. She had struggled with her own initial disbelief in what seemed to be preposterous stories, and then she became convinced that the children were telling the truth. She now had to struggle with the devastating emotional impact of hearing the girls' daily horror stories of sadistic violence. She also put her own credibility on the line by reporting these stories to skeptical people, whose first response would likely be to question her sanity. Under this stress her notetaking and reporting became more erratic, and her judgment less sound.

During the first two months that the girls had been in the foster home they had made a few references to children being killed, and talked about a strange character, whom they called "the Blob." While Catherine had found the details about Elizabeth being killed disturbing enough to jot down on a paper bag, though not in her notebook, she had generally not paid much attention to such references. "I played them down in my mind," she said, surmising that "someone had told them stories."

The conversation that led Catherine to begin to take these strange stories seriously took place after she returned from attending a friend's funeral. She told the girls she was at a funeral, and Janis asked her who had been killed. She explained to the child that her friend had died, but had not been killed. She described what a funeral is and talked about going to a graveyard.

Janis picked up on the reference to a graveyard, and said, "That's where Gary and Mom buries the people he and Mom kill. He buries them in the woods. He kills them in the woods, and buries them in a graveyard. Mom kills the boys and Gary kills the girls."

"I said, 'That's sad. Were you sad?'" Catherine testified, quoting Janis's unexpected response to this question: "Sometimes, and sometimes not. Some of them were mean to me too. Sometimes I cried, or else I didn't care."

With a trembling voice, which frequently broke into tears or tones of outraged indignation, the foster mother launched into a detailed description of the girls' allegations about child murders and "sexual orgies with the dead and the living at the graveyard and in the woods.

"They break their hands before. They break them back like that," she said Janis told her, holding her right hand with her left and forcing it backwards with a violent gesture. "They rip their faces too. They rip the faces up. They rip the mouth all up.

"Sometimes the man from 11 is there. He takes pictures of how they do terrible things to the kids. Even when they are dead. They stick lots of big things in them, and they put them in the trunk of the car, and take them to the graveyard. There are stones there. They dig a hole and put them in."

The foster mother described how Janis held up ten fingers and said, "They killed that many that way."

In a somewhat disjointed series of notes, Catherine recorded how the child went on to tell her that some of the kids seemed to know they were going to be killed and were crying when they were in the woods, while others didn't know and were sleeping on the way to the graveyard. Sometimes they are choked, and at other times a knife is stuck in their neck, Janis said. From the child's description, this seemed to have taken place in late summer or autumn, as she spoke of leaves falling from the trees. She said everything was photographed. Catherine noted that when Janis told this, she had a look "of stark, unbelievable horror."

Janis referred to a place in Toronto, much like Channel 11, a place where pictures were taken and things done to children and other people. Janis named children who she thought had been killed. She told Catherine about seeing a dismembered hand on the ground. Sometimes, Janis said, she would have to take a child into the woods, pretending that they were going to play, and then her mother or Gary would kill the child. Catherine said Janis described people who had something stuck in their mouths, or a towel tied around their mouths. She said they would be tied up and would have things stuck in their pee-holes.

"I heard about this every day until they left and how they did terrible and awful things to them, and everything would be photographed," Catherine testified.

Catherine recorded in her notes: "Other children besides Linda and Janis were involved at Channel 11 place. Great baths, lots of people in tubs, lots of soap, lots of water splashing. Janis said both she and Linda were there when Elizabeth was killed. Janis said, 'Some were killed in Hamilton. Some are drived here, or go to Channel 11.' When they were in Toronto, it was a long drive to the woods and the graveyard. It seems by what she said, a number are buried in the same area."

Catherine said Janis snuggled up to her, her face a deep crimson, and told her, "I don't know if I feel well or not. I get so scared when I think about it."

In a conversation recorded in Catherine McInnis's notes, Linda asked Janis one morning to tell Catherine about her dream about a graveyard and a killer.

"I dreamed I was in the graveyard. Mom was sticking her fingers in me," said Janis.

"What graveyard? A real one?" Catherine asked.

"Yes, near the woods. A real graveyard where you bury people. It was terrible. I'm scared."

"Did you see the hand, Jan, did you see the cutoff hand?" Linda prompted.

"Oh, Linda!" Janis exclaimed.

"That's where Elizabeth is, our friend Elizabeth," said Linda. "She got dead by a killer."

Janis said, "Gary said he'd kill me if I told. They'll kill me if I tell. They said that."

"When you tell, the killer gets you," Linda confirmed. "Janis, did you see the hand at the graveyard? Did you see the woods in your dream? That's the killing place."

"Yeah, they tie them up and punch leaves in them, in the belly. They stick knives in them. They cut them. They stick big sticks in them. We have to do things too. I take them in the woods. The man from 11 is there, and so is the lady. Sometimes Mom goes back in Gary's car. Gary has a big shovel. Sometimes they cut the neck, ugh. They stick fingers in us too. They take pictures in the woods and the graveyard," said Janis.

She pointed towards her genital area and said, "They stick knives there too. They cut something off."

"What?" asked Catherine.

Janis and Linda did not answer. Janis told Catherine, "Well, they tear the face sometimes, and Mom likes to break their hands all up. Gary too."

"Elizabeth's mother knew. She went phew. She breathed in when she finded out that Elizabeth was killed," said Linda.

"The man from 11 helps Gary dig the graves. They use a flashlight," Janis said.

When Janis came home from school that evening, both children began to talk again about the same gruesome things. Janis said that parts are sometimes cut off dead children and stuck in her vagina. She tried to describe the graveyard, which, she said, had a crooked path and some kind of grating from which smoke or steam came out. Sometimes it seemed they could smell something off the smoke. She drew a picture of the grate. She told Catherine that you can see the word "Love" on the stones. She would spell it LVOE. She talked about a house in the woods, and two other houses nearby, one of which she thought was red brick with a blue roof. Catherine, who was trying to note down every detail that might lead investigators to the graveyard, also recorded that Janis mentioned the colors yellow and brown as she described the houses.

The notes record that Janis said the brown man and Gary dug graves, while someone else stayed in the car in case they had to get away in a hurry. If a car came or anybody came near, they had to grab their knives and run. There was a reference to a building with a hole in the floor. The children said that the brown man and Gary had cameras, and would use a flashlight, holding an umbrella to shield the light. They described stones shining in the moonlight. They said the graveyard was in the country, and spoke of "the dead place" as being up a little road near the graveyard, with a gate at the end. They said, "It's a home where little kids get killed. Not mothers, not fathers, just kids."

"They spoke of the Blob," Catherine read from her notes to the court. "The Blob is Gary's friend. He is huge, like a giant. The Blob comes from somewhere, when he hears screams. He almost got Janis and Linda before they came to Hamilton. Gary drove hard. Gary's friend wanted to kill them. If they tell, they will be killed. Afterwards the Blob and Gary and Mom were friends again. Linda laughed and sang, 'The Blob does not know where we live in Hamilton now. He doesn't know nothing now.'"

She said the girls told her something was stuffed in the mouths of the victims to stop them screaming, but sometimes you would hear a little mumble. Catherine said, "The children always had to take knives and stick them in whoever was being killed. If they didn't, they would be killed themselves. Both mentioned this numerous times."

Janis drew pictures of the graveyard and the two houses. These simplistic child's drawings showing stick people without some of their limbs were filed as exhibits with the court—eloquent testimony to the severe disturbance of these young children, who had not yet learned to read and write. Catherine testified that while doing one of these simple sketches, Janis told her: "There's ten kids, but I can't make ten kids crying."

Janis told the foster mother that there was a long way, and a shortcut from the parking lot to the graveyard, and if you went the long way, there were lots of holes. She said, "The long way is the sad way."

Catherine said the girls wanted to give her a full description of the houses near the graveyard, where children were killed, so she could "get lots of big men, and the police, and go there and knock them down."

Mrs. McInnis said she reported the girls' allegations to

the police that day, and on many other occasions: "They believed that there was probably a little bit of diddling around, but the main things they did not believe." She said Sgt. Bowen once told her, "These poor children are fantasizing. It's beyond believing."

She said she told the sergeant, "It may be beyond believing, but it happened to these children."

The response of the police was a source of extreme frustration to Catherine. The two officers who were supposedly investigating the case never came to her house to talk to her, or to interview the children, and had not looked at her notes. They had apparently not followed up on the sexual abuse allegations, and indicated on several occasions that they did not believe the stories about pornography and murder.

Catherine had told Sgt. Bowen several times about a child called Andy, who the girls said used to live across the street from them and who was involved in the sessions at the television studio. They took no steps to locate this child. Eventually Catherine did her own little investigation by getting her daughter to drive Janis and herself down the street where the children used to live, and asking the child to point out Andy's house to her.

She described the police response to this: "I had called the police. I said, 'There's something terrible that has gone on with these children.' Sgt. Bowen said at one time that the children were fantasizing. I said, 'I'll take Janis myself, and find out where these people live.' Later I went into the police station and showed him my notes and the number of the house. I said to Sgt. Bowen, 'These children aren't lying,' and again he said that they were fantasizing."

The police officers cited the low incidence of missing children in Canada as one reason to be skeptical of the children's stories. This explanation gave Catherine little comfort, especially when she came across an article in the *Hamilton Spectator* under the headline, "Child Molesters Prove Well Organized Group." This story referred to "an undeclared war on children," stating that child molesters have their own newsletters, and that 50,000 of the 1.5 million missing children in the United States are believed to have been abducted by strangers.

Catherine described a furious argument she had with Lesley Morgan about the lack of police investigation of the case. She said she asked Ms. Morgan if anything was being done about "any of this mess," and the social worker told her, "You'll have to wait. The police will look after it when they're ready. You have to respect the police."

"I said, 'I can't respect people getting paid to do a job and doing nothing.' I told Lesley it was her turn to go to the police station and stand up and be counted. I told her I was going to take all those old notes I made and rip them up. Lesley said, 'If you tear up those notes, the police will put you in jail.' I said, 'They won't come when they are told someone has been murdered. I've spent months without any time for myself or my family.'"

In her diary Catherine wrote: "No more notes ever, in this world or the next one."

Ms. Morgan went to visit the foster mother and persuaded her not to give up. They went for a drive, and when they returned Catherine repaired the notebook from which she had earlier torn out some pages in her rage and frustration.

The disbelief shown by the police was a major disillusionment for Catherine, who had always maintained an idealistic image of the police force. She felt that society was failing her, and that one of her strongest principles had been taken from her.

"When she broke down in tears saying she didn't know what she would do if anything happened to her own children, she apologized for losing control. She is a person who likes to be in control of things," said Dr. Gail Beck, a psychiatrist who subsequently did an assessment of Mrs. McInnis. "When police did not believe the children were telling the truth, she was feeling very frustrated, not knowing what to do. She was preoccupied with the idea that children were being slaughtered and police don't care."

It required great courage for Catherine to continue to listen to the children's stories as they began to describe revolting scenes of cannibalism. Catherine noted that the children talked about eating flesh at the Blob's house, and sometimes eating flesh at the graveyard. As she described the allegations in the notes, "At the Blob's house, or their house, the flesh would be cooked. He cut the flesh off the children, after they are dead and he cooked it. They always shared it around, and people would get the pieces they liked. He would cut off the head and cook it. Gary took pictures. At the graveyard they would cut off the pee thing, and the two things that hang down, and it would be torn apart, and cut apart, and all shared around. Everybody had some of it."

"It was no wonder that when they first came to my home, the girls would leave food on their plates, refuse roast beef, pork and chicken, and ask for bread," said Catherine.

One of the aspects of the children's disclosures that later helped persuade the psychiatrists that they were telling the truth was the way that everyday things seemed to remind the girls of painful memories and bring these to the surface. This tended to show that Janis and Linda were spontaneously recalling buried experiences rather than fabricating or reciting material that had been implanted in them.

For Catherine it meant that her home was a mine field in which innocent familiar objects would suddenly trigger nightmarish descriptions of disgusting practices. A painting or a little ornament could inspire discussions describing horrendous sexual abuse. Flashlights reminded the girls of the vibrators that were used to torment them; candles made them recall satanic rituals; and boxes conjured up images of coffins. Worst of all for Catherine, who loved gardening and the outdoors, was the way that these girls' terrible experiences had perverted their view of nature itself, so that planting seeds would remind them of burying bodies, and animals had become associated with bestiality and degradation.

Catherine described to the court a conversation with the children that took place early in May, when she had gone into the garden to plant beets and had taken some crumbs to feed to the birds. She said some starlings and crows came flapping around, and Janis told her, "Those birds are not as big as the chickens that Mom and Gary take to the graveyard."

When Catherine asked the child if she was talking about real chickens, she said Janis replied, "Yes. Mom sticks her finger in the chicken, and Gary and the Blob and the Channel 11 man, they put their pee things in the chicken. And then they pull the eyes out of the chickens, and pull the neck off, and the head off. And then they have it bleed into this dish, and we share around the blood. And they make that thing, that star, that sign with the circle around it on something with the blood. They pulled all the feathers off the chicken. That's fucking chicken, Catherine."

The foster mother tried to correct the child by telling her she must mean, "plucking chicken."

She said Linda replied, "No, no, no, Catherine, you are stupid. That's fucking chicken. That's what it is."

Linda told her that they had to eat the chicken, and all the stuff inside, and drink the blood: "It's awful. I branged up and branged up but we have to eat it 'cos if we don't they'll kill us."

This was not the only story that Catherine found so personally repugnant that she did not write it out in her notebook. During her court testimony she also explained a note that referred to the possibility that bodies were buried in existing graves. The note had simply stated, "Are bodies being placed in someone's coffin? Are bodies being placed in recent graves? Are they digging in recent graves and tossing in bodies?"

This was in fact a cryptic reference to another conversation with the children, one that was also prompted by an everyday event. Catherine told the court, "I don't want anyone to think I'm cat crazy because I'm not. I can't stand to think of little animals freezing and starving. I put a shelter out for stray cats. Linda saw this and said that she had been in a box away down in the ground. She said, 'I was in a box away down in the ground in the graveyard. I was in the box, and, after we do what we have to do, we can put our hands up, and somebody would help us get out. I was down in that box. It was open. It was slippy in there. There was something wet in there, and my feet went right through it. There was bone in there, and there was hair in there. I was so scared I just shrieked and shrieked. The stink in there was like shit.'"

On another occasion Catherine was planting pansies in her backyard. She said she was shoveling holes to plant flowers in, when Linda started talking about graves and dead children. She referred to an elevator that slants and goes up and down. This made Catherine wonder if the graveyard was near a quarry. Then Linda told her, "When they bury kids, they lie. The Blob mixes a big soup in a big pot with a wooden spoon. It's a lie. It's lye. They say it's lye. The Blob makes a soup to give the dead kids a drink. After he makes the soup, he pours it on the dead kids. Then he takes some white stuff in a bag. It's like sugar. No, it's like salt. He shakes it over the dead kids. Then they throw in the ground and the dirt and they bury them, and they make a little pile of stones."

Catherine described how the constant exposure to these stories threatened her own sanity and peace of mind. She said, "If once in a while I didn't take a 15-minute reprieve away from the children, I'd find myself talking to my cookbook."

As the children's stories got progressively worse, Catherine had obviously become more and more disturbed, and this was evident from the notes she recorded in her book. At the beginning she had simply recorded the children's statements; now she was starting to insert cryptic comments and editorial remarks. At first she tended not to ask the girls many questions and let them tell their stories in their own words. But Catherine began to believe that she had a responsibility to glean all the details she could from the girls so that their allegations could be investigated. When she ceased being a relatively detached reporter, her notes became more difficult to interpret.

Certain things that the children said disturbed her so much that she did not record them at all except through her own coded reference. The reference to the children being lowered into graves was an example of this. The most serious omissions from the notes related to the children's father. On May 11 the children told Catherine that their father was also involved in the killings, and she wrote in her notebook, "I won't hear. I won't remember. And someone helps too."

"I didn't know what on earth to do, who I could go to," she said. "I was getting all this information, finding out that somebody else is killing people. How on earth am I going to bring anybody else into this, when nobody believes."

She was apparently very afraid of Gordon Wells, whom she had met when he came to pick up the children for the weekend visit. The children had described him as a violent and dangerous man. Catherine realized that the police were not taking her reports of the children's allegations seriously, and she was afraid of risking both their added disbelief and Gordon's anger by reporting the girls' statements about their father. Each time the girls talked about their father, Catherine recorded the conversations with notes like, "Surprises, surprises, surprises," "Secrets," or "The news gets worse."

She told the court that she used bad judgment in not recording the girls' allegations about their father, especially as the CAS was allowing the children to visit him on weekends. She explained that the children had been most insistent that they didn't want their father to know they had implicated him. She said, "I couldn't see embarrassing myself by adding more names, telling them someone else was involved. I didn't tell Lesley because I knew she would go to the police, and I couldn't stand the embarrassment of having them think I was crazy."

Dr. Beck, who later examined Mrs. McInnis, did not conclude that she was crazy or had any form of psychiatric disturbance other than an understandable reaction to the stress to which she was being exposed.

The children would later say that their father had killed three people. However, when they first implicated him in murder, it was as an accomplice in the bizarre climax to the story of the Blob and the Channel 11 man, who the children said were killed and mutilated in the basement of their Hamilton home, and then buried in the backyard. The children's story makes sense as the script of a sick, home-made movie, but it apparently did not occur to any of the adults, who were aware of the children's allegations at the time, to view them in that light.

The police lacked the imagination to grasp the concept that, if two very young children had been forced to participate in violent pornography without understanding what was going on, it would not be inconsistent for them to give lurid and detailed reports of violent acts. In this context it would hardly be surprising if the acts that the children described as real events were beyond belief from an adult perspective. The police could not have considered this possibility—or they would not have called off their investigation of the alleged pornography, when they quickly concluded that the murders did not take place.

Linda told Catherine that the Channel 11 man lived in a penthouse apartment in the housing project where they used to live in Toronto. She thought that he was a superintendent there, and said he had a son called Billy. She said Billy was one of the children who was killed: "They hurt him bad. They took pictures of Billy begging not to be killed." The children said the Channel 11 man's wife, or girlfriend, was Elizabeth, the mother of little Elizabeth, who was also killed.

Catherine said the children described how the Blob, the Channel 11 man and big Elizabeth all "got dead at our house." She said that Janis told her that they all had to stick knives in the Channel 11 man and that Gary "got him good in the neck, and his head was half off." The child then told Catherine that Gary "cut off his pee thing and put it in the garbage, the eyes too."

The children told Catherine that they were also forced to help in the killing of the Blob, and that their father helped too because "Dad is fast with the knife."

Catherine said Linda told her, "It was asgusting, Catherine, it was asgusting, when those people were killed. We had to help take those knives and plunge them into the people. It was asgusting. Of course I was scared. We had to do it, or Mom would kill us."

They said three people were buried in the backyard, and somebody was thrown in the water, fastened to something. They said they watched through a window as Gary ran water from a hose on the paving stones in the backyard all night long so that there wouldn't be any clay on the stones. The court was shown one of Janis's drawings, depicting two figures with a rectangular shape beside them. Catherine said Janis told her, "That's where the Blob is buried, and that's the Channel 11 man."

The police found this story so unbelievable that they did not consider it necessary to search for evidence, though they did hop over the fence at 2 A.M. one morning and examine the paving stones in the small backyard. They concluded that the earth beneath the stones had not been disturbed.

Lesley Morgan, who also heard the same story from the children, was asked in court if she believed that the Channel 11 man and the Blob were still interred in the backyard. She said that the children had told her that they thought the bodies were moved somewhere else afterwards. "The evidence is probably long gone," she said, referring to a police occurrence report in which Sgt. Broom noted that he told the social worker on May 28, 1985, "It is apparent that if there was any evidence that could assist in this investigation, it has long since been disposed of."

Ms. Morgan, a very earnest young woman, who was completely convinced of the children's sincerity, told the court, "Something went on and the children should not return [home], whether or not we can prove there were murders." She said that, if they were to go home, "they will continue to be abused by the same people who were abusing them, except for the Channel 11 man and the Blob."

On the day after they told the stories of the murders in the basement, the children had a visit with their mother at the Children's Aid Society. Ms. Morgan noted that the girls were almost out of control after that visit, and Catherine recalled them acting strangely when they returned. She said they wouldn't sit down, and later wept profusely. She said Linda told her, "I was scared Mom will take us out to the graveyard and kill us. I'm scared. My stomach feels stuck. It feels twisted. Just hold me. I'm scared."

Ms. Morgan returned to talk to the children that day, and made a tape of their conversations. On the tape the girls talk about their fear that their mother would kill them at the graveyard with a knife. The court heard Linda say on tape, "I was very, very scared, very, very, very, very, very, very, very scared."

Catherine said the children told her that, when they went to the graveyard, they used to drive by Canada's Wonderland, an amusement park just north of Toronto. She said they spoke about witches, the devil and God, and referred to people wearing masks and costumes. They told her that the Blob sometimes dressed up as a clown. He would always take a book to the graveyard and someone would read from it. They said their father would call out the number "666," a number they often referred to, and always seemed to associate with fear.

As the children continued to talk about the graveyard sessions, it seemed clear to Catherine that some kind of satanic ritual was involved. They said their father's friend would go to the graveyard with a mask and that she would be dressed up. Janis said her mask was torn and she had to paint something on her face. They told Catherine that their father had a sign, and a picture of the devil that he kept behind another picture. They said he wore a mask and a scary costume at the graveyard and would look like the devil. Then they said everyone would spin and twirl around and sing queer songs.

They also told Catherine that their father moves his knife very fast; that he once twisted his boot on someone he had killed, and that he ran over someone in Toronto and killed him. Catherine testified that the girls told her they had to pretend their father didn't come to see them in Hamilton, but he would come.

The children often used to draw a five-cornered star

with a circle round it. They also drew an eye symbol and a heart, but would never tell Catherine what these meant. She said they would tell her, "It's a secret."

Catherine said Janis's artwork was often colored with a black crayon. When she was questioned in cross-examination about the children's coloring, she said, "Their favorite color was black. They put red in there for blood to brighten it up sometimes.

"Day after day the children drew the same things, talked about the same things, and that was all they talked about. That was their world," Catherine said.

"It was so sad to see a small girl's artwork tell such a gruesome story. Every night it was something similar. Janis wouldn't bring home some lovely little thing with butterflies and bees and pretty things," Catherine said.

Once, while she was drawing at home, Janis asked Catherine, "How do you draw a picture when they don't have any legs and feet, and the pee thing and head are cut off? How do you draw a dead person when you take them out to be buried in a bowl?"

She produced more of the girls' drawings for the court, together with notes she had made of the children's explanations of them. One of Janis's drawings was a stick figure of a girl with a glum face; she said this was little Elizabeth; she was crying because she didn't want to die. Other stick figures had hands or heads missing; there were heads without bodies and faces that were missing an eye. Catherine said Janis explained that one drawing was a picture of her [Janis] standing by a grave with her throat cut, and blood all over the ground, saying, "I have to say, 'I love you, Mom,' or else I end up here."

A picture that attracted a lot of interest from Arthur Brown, the mother's lawyer, showed a house and something standing beside it, which was labeled a knife, but looked as if it could have been a tree. It appeared that someone had crossed out the word tree, and then substituted knife. A psychiatrist later suggested that it might have represented both to a child. Catherine's explanation that the knife was larger than the house was, "It is possible that the knife stood out in her mind much more than the house did. She knew more about knives than she did about homes."

Another strange exhibit was a duplicated arithmetic question sheet that Janis had brought home from school.

There was a series of sums on the paper with boxes provided for the answers. Linda had drawn a little human figure in each box. Catherine said she found this sheet and subsequently explained, "I just drew the kids in the graves."

After several days on the witness stand, Catherine McInnis was asked by John Harper, the Children's Aid Society lawyer, if there were any further allegations made by the children that she had not told the court. She said there were some things that she hadn't mentioned, "just revolting things: about things to do with, say, the dog. One morning, early, before I started doing my housework, I was out on the patio with Linda having a cup of tea. We saw a woman walking a dog. Linda said, 'That's different from the dog my mom had in Toronto.' I said, 'I didn't know you had a dog.' Linda said, 'It was a long time ago. My mom had a dog and she stuck her finger in the dog.' I said, 'He would show his teeth.' She said, 'Catherine, you don't know anything. She didn't put her finger in the dog's mouth. She put it in the dog's bum. Gary and another man put their pee thing in the dog's poo-hole. The dog's dead now.' I said, 'Even a dog is lucky sometimes.'

"Janis said things like this to me too. I didn't put it in my notes, because I tried to tell the police things that were less revolting. It's easier to nail water to the wall than to tell something to the police. To save myself from embarrassment and having somebody think I was crazy, I didn't say too much about the really revolting things. I hoped and prayed they would do something about what they already knew."

She described another allegation where the children were forced to eat bananas that had been used in grotesque sexual acts. She said, "I found it so revolting, I couldn't write it down. Their mother made them do it, and, if they didn't, they would feel the cold blade of the knife pressing into their necks. Even when they brang up and brang up and coughed and spat, they would do it, because if they didn't, *they* would be cut up, and handed around for people to take home on a plate."

Catherine said that sometimes, when Janis was remembering such horrors, her body would shudder, her head would go up a little and her eyes would roll back, half open under thick, swollen lids. She would come out of this state when Catherine wiped her face and wet her lips with a cold cloth. Catherine would cuddle the child and then she would be okay, she said. "These were times when she'd be past tears."

In spite of all the personal difficulty that Mrs. McInnis experienced in listening to the children's disclosures, she was still able to give them the love, care and sympathy that they desperately needed. In this way she was helping to revise the blighted view of human nature that the girls had learned from their harrowing experiences.

CHAPTER 8

SATANIC CULTS

May 16, 1985, was a day of revelation for Catherine McInnis. The revelation came from her television set in the form of a documentary report about the victimization of children by satanic cults. This was the first time that she felt she was not the only person to have heard the kind of horror stories that her foster children had told her. She learned that other people all over North America would be receptive to what these children were saying and sympathetic to her own plight. With this reassurance, however, came the horror of learning that, while there were other similar victims and other similar crimes, what she had been hearing in her living room was possibly part of an evil and powerful conspiracy.

Until then Catherine had never taken any interest in the occult and knew virtually nothing of satanism. From listening to the children she was aware that some kind of ritual had been involved in the gruesome graveyard scenes that they described. From her readings of the Bible she knew that "666" was the number that would identify Satan; this was the mark of the beast according to the Book of Revelation. She noted with concern that the children would write that number in their coloring books, and was also worried by the references to witches and devils, dances, masks and costumes.

Drawing on a wealth of evidence and quoting reputable

sources, the program described how links have been found all over North America between satanism and "perverse, hideous acts that defy belief. Suicides, murders and the ritualistic slaughter of children and animals. Yet so far police have been helpless."

The documentary cited records of more than 15,000 animal mutilations and the discovery of ritual sites where satanic paraphernalia were found; these included pictures of the devil, the inverted five-pointed satanic pentagram, the upside-down cross, the evil eye and references to "666."

After discussing a recent revival of interest in satanism in popular culture, referring to films such as *Rosemary's Baby* and *The Exorcist*, and the preponderance of satanic symbolism in heavy metal rock music, the program went on to explain that devil worshippers generally fall into three categories. The first was the "self-styled satanists," who are usually teenagers who dabble in satanism with the aid of such popular books as Anton LaVey's *Satanic Bible*. The second category was "religious satanists," who are members of LaVey's Church of Satan, or similar organizations that claim to eschew any illegal activity. The third group was "satanic cults," which, the program stated, appear to be "highly secretive groups, committing criminal acts, including murder."

With comments from police investigators, a psychiatrist, alleged victims and relatives of victims, the television report examined some of the characteristics of the kind of abuse that the cults allegedly inflict on children, who have a central role in their rituals. Sexual abuse, pornography and forcing children to eat feces and drink urine were described as key elements in the cults' systematic assault on children's morale and moral values, encouraging them to accept evil and degradation as natural. Child murders were described and it was said that children were forced to stick knives in the victims, and also forced to help kidnap victims by pretending to play with other children in order to lure them away. There were descriptions of cannibalism, and it was said that this and drinking human blood were integral parts of the rituals.

Police officers interviewed on the program said there was ample evidence that such groups exist and engage in these shocking practices. But they are so secretive and well-organized that they have so far defied any police attempts to gather concrete evidence of these activities. One former police chief said, "When you get into one of these groups, there's only a couple of ways you can get out. One is death. The other is mental institutions. Or third, you can't get out."

Enlightened, comforted and alarmed by all this, Catherine immediately phoned the local police. She testified that she talked to "one of the police officers working on the case, or not working on the case, and told him, 'Maybe the children got places mixed up, but I believe them, or I would not repeat what they said.'"

While the Hamilton police were apparently no more impressed with the information contained in the television program than they were with anything else that Mrs. McInnis had reported to them, background knowledge of satanic ritual abuse gleaned from this and many other sources did have a significant influence on social workers and psychiatrists who subsequently dealt with the children. It made them less inclined to dismiss the children's allegations as aberrant fantasies or weird distortions of some sordid but more mundane reality. What the children were saying fell squarely within the framework of the rapidly expanding knowledge of this new, disturbing phenomenon of ritual abuse. While such allegations may be extremely difficult to believe, and are even harder to accept, professionals working in the field of child abuse were beginning to find it impossible not to take them seriously. They were hearing about similar cases all over the continent, and many were encountering them in their own work.

In 1986 Catherine Gould, a clinical psychologist, published a list of symptoms of satanic ritual abuse that she observed in her work with abused preschool-age children in the Los Angeles area. This list of 29 symptoms included several that were relevant to Janis's and Linda's allegations and behavior. Dr. Gould notes that such children have a preoccupation with feces and urine, will talk about feces or urine on the face or in the mouth, will refer to it being smeared in the bathroom and frequently discuss these things at mealtimes. She said a consequent fear of the bathroom may make it difficult to toilet train such children. The list includes aggressive play, in which a child appears to enjoy hurting other children, a fear of ghosts and monsters and a fear of bad people taking the child away, breaking into the house or burning it down, or killing the child.

The symptoms also included references to mutilation, in which the child acts out severing, sawing off, twisting or pulling off body parts. Dr. Gould said these children will talk about animals being hurt or killed. They may also be preoccupied with death, sometimes asking if dead people are eaten, or if their death will occur at the age of six. The psychologist noted: "Questions are distinguishable from normal curiosity about death by their bizarre quality." She also referred to bizarre songs or chants, or ones that follow the "you-better-not-tell theme," numbers or letters always written backwards in the devil's alphabet, discussions about films or photographs being taken. She said children will also talk about scary costumes, and refer to television characters as real people, "because perpetrators take on names like Fred Flintstone so a child's disclosures will be dismissed as television-inspired fantasies."

Roland Summit, a California psychiatrist whose theories on how children disclose sexual abuse are world-renowned in the field and were referred to during the wardship hearing, has studied more than 40 cases that involve these ritual elements. He has noted that "another hallmark of whatever this is, or wherever it comes from, is the insertion of instruments such as sticks into bodies, and the use of narcotics and sedatives, usually used as a liquid, a pink liquid."

Dr. Summit, like several other child abuse experts who have become concerned by these reports, has been careful to avoid coming to any categorical conclusions—although many children in different places have said the same things, this does not prove the existence of satanic cults that are engaged in this kind of abuse. He has cautioned that as long as there is no concrete evidence of the existence of such groups, and no one has come forward to say that they belonged to cults that committed such atrocities, one must keep an open mind and accept that there may be other explanations.

Although Dr. Summit has expressed an inclination to believe that there is truth in the numerous "dismally consistent" allegations, he has also warned that it may do a disservice to children to slavishly believe that everything they say is true. His concern has been that children's sincerity should be respected, that their disclosures should be heard without prejudice and that they should get the protection and therapy they need. Too often this does not happen, he said, because "these cases throw people into irrational kinds of prejudice. Some people believe it is true, and the world is going to be taken over by satanists. Others say 'It's too spooky, and it can't happen in this country.' They are likely to abandon the children, dismiss the case, and throw it out."

Many therapists in Canada and the United States have also reported detailed accounts of satanic rituals from a different source—adult survivors of child sexual abuse, who, during therapy sessions, remember details of past ritual abuse. Therapists who report such accounts are usually not child psychiatrists, and are therefore not necessarily familiar with the kinds of allegations that children have been making. However, the adults' accounts of abuse inflicted on them a generation ago often contain details of ritual, symbolism and abusive acts that are identical to those reported by children today.

One such survivor, a woman from Victoria, British Columbia, described in a 1980 book, *Michelle Remembers*, how she was subjected to abuse involving a dead bird, and forced to eat what she believed was human flesh during satanic ceremonies. She also remembered being put into a grave, and witnessing the sacrifice of children and the dismemberment of dead bodies. Lawrence Pazder, the psychiatrist who treated her and coauthored the book, has said that he has since worked with eight similar cases.

Victims of child abuse often deal with their traumatic memories by trying to shut them away in a separate compartment in their minds. In some extreme cases this attempt to seal off painful emotions and responses can lead to the development of a split personality. Psychiatrists who treat patients with multiple personality disorders frequently find that the illness is associated with a history of child abuse. A Chicago psychiatrist who noticed a high preponderance of reports of ritual abuse in the history of such patients conducted a survey in 1986 of 250 therapists working in this field, and discovered that about 25 percent of them had patients who said they were exposed to satanic rituals during childhood.

In Hamilton, Ontario, while the wardship hearing was in progress, at least four adults were involved in therapy sessions at which they discussed their memories of satanic ritual abuse. A former police matron in Kamloops, British Columbia, now working as a sexual assault counselor and involved with her tenth ritual abuse case, followed the Hamilton case with great interest and stated, "It is my belief that as more and more therapists acquire the skills to hear children and adults who have been sexually and physically abused, the more they will hear about the happenings of the cult-related assaults,

which have a different set of problems for patients and therapists. I am grateful for the case in Hamilton getting out in the
open, so that others, who have been assaulted as children in
this manner, can get the courage to tell and not fear that they
will be killed for doing so."

The many therapists and a handful of police investigators who have become convinced of the existence of secret and
sadistic satanic cults tend to see this as a phenomenon that has
existed in society since the Middle Ages. History is also in-
voked by those who maintain that the belief in satanic ritual
abuse is a manifestation of a mass hysteria that was spread by
gullible people obsessed with children's fantasies. They say
that the recent spate of court cases dealing with children's allegations of ritual abuse resemble the witch-hunts of the 16th
and 17th centuries in Europe and New England.

No matter what point of view one takes, the historical
comparisons reveal striking similarities between the current
concerns and the preoccupations of the past. According to historian Jeffrey Russell[7], the ritual murder of children, often accompanied by cannibalism, was one of the most common
charges leveled against witches. Just as children were most often seen as the victims of witchcraft, they were also the source
of many of the accusations against witches. A case in Salem,
Massachusetts, in 1692 was a famous example of this: two
small girls, who began exhibiting nervous symptoms after ex-
perimenting with divination, were subjected to intense questioning by doctors and other adults, and eventually made
accusations against three women.

While many of the so-called confessions of witches were
extracted under torture, and merely conformed to a formula
predetermined by the inquisitors, there was evidence of some
serious judicial attempts to discover the truth about witchcraft. One such hearing was a late-17th-century inquiry at the
French court regarding allegations that Black Masses were being performed in aristocratic circles. Evidence was heard at
this inquiry about the sexual abuse of children and the brutal
murder of newborn babies, whose entrails were used in rituals
that also involved cutting a bird's throat and collecting its
blood in a goblet.[8]

To some people all this is evidence of the survival
through the centuries of child-murdering satanic cults; to
others it all represents archetypal human fantasies. Historian
Norman Cohn maintains that scholars who consider that

witchcraft allegations are indicative of the existence of some such cult are "grossly underestimating the capacities of the human imagination."[9]

Sigmund Freud, before he discovered or invented the concept of such subconscious urges, recognized what he considered clear evidence of child sexual abuse that had been suffered by his female patients. He was also struck by the similarity between what these women told him and the accounts of the witchcraft confessions of the 16th century. He wrote in a January, 1897, letter to a colleague, "But why did the devil who took possession of the poor things invariably abuse them sexually and in a loathsome manner? Why are their confessions under torture so like the communications made by my patients in psychological treatment?"[10]

In the last few years, there has been a rash of cases all over North America in which adults have been prosecuted or children removed from their homes as a result of allegations from children. These allegations often include bizarre descriptions of murder, mutilation, bestiality, cannibalism and satanic ritual. In at least 40 places in the U.S., authorities have been grappling with children's allegations of ritual abuse. In California and Minnesota, in particular, a spate of highly controversial cases has sharply polarized public opinion.

In Manhattan Beach, California, in 1984, friends of the seven people accused in the notorious McMartin Preschool case took out newspaper advertisements that compared this case with the Salem witch trials; in this case there were accusations against the preschool operators and staff involving the alleged molestation of hundreds of children. The same comparison has been made in connection with a spate of cases in Bakersfield, California, and in Jordan, Minnesota, where 24 people were accused. Bizarre stories of rituals, murder, cannibalism, bestiality, pornography, eating feces and drinking urine, as well as extreme sexual abuse, were recurring themes in these cases, as they were in the other cases in different parts of the United States, and in the Hamilton case. One theory adopted by defense lawyers in most of these cases, and also advanced in Hamilton, is that child abuse professionals all over the continent are in the grip of a kind of mass hysteria that inspires them to coach children into making allegations—allegations that become more and more fantastic under the pressures of intensive questioning.

Ralph Underwager, a psychologist who has testified as

an expert witness on behalf of defendants in many such cases in the United States, was sought as a witness by defense lawyers in the Hamilton case. However, he was not available until after the defense case was closed, and Judge Beckett refused to delay the trial in order to wait for his evidence. Dr. Underwager said in an interview that he has been involved in 28 cases where there was a similar progression in the development of allegations over time: "a pattern beginning with an initial statement from young children that somebody touched them, progressing to allegations of fondling, to penetration, to oral-genital contact, to monsters and strange bizarre behaviors, sometimes drug use, ritual behavior and murder of animals. It gets put together in allegations that children were murdered in cultic behavior."

This kind of material is present in the fantasy world of children, Underwager said, and comes out when gullible adults, predisposed to belief in a satanic conspiracy theory, delve into the children's fantasies, producing more and more allegations that they reinforce with their belief: "So you get police officers digging in backyards for bodies, looking for pornography, cultic objects. They have never been found. No empirical data for any of this material has ever been discovered." Mentioning the similarities between the cases in Jordan, Minnesota, and Salem, Massachusetts, Underwager said, "What we are trying to fight is stupidity on such a massive scale." He maintains that "adults who are true believers victimize children by subjecting them to pressure."

What this view fails to explain, however, is why the allegations that children are making in these circumstances are so strikingly similar in so many different and unrelated cases. In Salem the children had indeed been exposed to some voodoo practices by a Haitian nurse, who was the first person they accused, and the 17th-century religious and cultural climate was such that everyone was quite ready to accept that they had been involved in devil worship. But satanism is not a phenomenon that one would expect social workers and psychiatrists to readily give credence to in the late 20th century. It is also hard to understand why they would coach children to make allegations that would heap massive skepticism on their allegations of sexual abuse. Dr. Underwager and others who advance this theory make reference to the richness of children's fantasy world, but have so far failed to provide any detailed explanation of how young children can conjure up, from their imaginations, graphic and detailed accounts of ritual violence, accompanied by sexually explicit descriptions of abuse.

An alternative explanation that is advanced by some people who vigorously support the prosecution of cases like those in California and Minnesota is very disturbing. This theory is that groups of people in society either practice ritual child abuse or use the trappings of ritual to terrorize children, while forcing them to participate in pornography or group sex. This theory has been endorsed by police investigators in many parts of North America. Apart from the allegations of many hundreds of children and adult survivors of sexual abuse, the evidence is slim for any link between child abuse and satanic cult activities. The history and literature of satanic worship does, however, point to a tradition of child sacrifice, and a preoccupation with corrupting and degrading the innocence that children represent.

In recent years there has been considerable evidence of a burgeoning of interest in satanic worship in North America. It has been inspired perhaps by the decline in traditional belief and the need felt by many people for magic solutions to personal problems in an increasingly alienating and materialistic society. There has been a steady growth of such legal and ostensibly harmless groups as The Church of Satan, which boasted more than 10,000 members by the late 1970s. This is the largest of several satanic organizations in North America, and has chapters in Toronto and British Columbia. It was founded in San Francisco by Anton LaVey, a former lion trainer who played the part of the devil in the film *Rosemary's Baby*, one of a number of films that fostered popular interest in satanism during the past 20 years.

While The Church of Satan claims to have no involvement in any illegal activity, another satanic group, The Process, the Church of the Final Judgement, has enjoyed a less savory reputation. This cult made Toronto one of its headquarters in the mid-1970s, and its members occupied a house in the same inner-city neighborhood where Sharon, her brothers and sisters and Gordon Wells grew up. The Process achieved brief notoriety in Canada in 1971 when a Toronto newspaper revealed that this satanist group had been awarded a federal government Local Initiatives Program grant for a social service project in the city. It has since been disbanded, though former members in Toronto have recently been meeting again under the name New Cycle, and there is also believed to be a group of cult members living in Hamilton.

On a religious level The Process was an attempt to reconcile Christianity with satanism; it worshiped four deities, including Christ and Satan. It had an apocalyptic vision of the Last Judgement, and saw motorcycle gangs as an instrument that would bring about this plan of ultimate annihilation. A recent history of the cult, written by a sociologist who was a friend of its leaders, describes it as only indulging in violence at a rhetorical or philosophical level. This study conceded that the cult tended to recruit and appeal to very alienated and disturbed young people, and often had problems with its more sociopathic fringe members.[11] One person who said he was influenced by The Process was Charles Manson, who shared with this cult a preoccupation with the Book of Revelation and the satanic number 666, which was scrawled on the wall at the scene of the murder of Sharon Tate in California in 1969.

Satanic beliefs and practices have nothing in common with traditional pagan witchcraft, which has also seen a revival in the last 30 years, and is now being espoused by many feminists and radicals as a new ecological religion. *The Encyclopedia of American Religions* makes the point that there is distinction to be made between the public groups that adopt a satanist theology and "what are frequently termed the 'sickies.' There are disconnected groups of occultists who employ satan worship to cover a variety of sexual, sadomasochistic, clandestine, psychopathic and illegal activities. From these groups come grave robberies, sexual assaults and bloodletting (both animal and human). These groups are characterized by lack of theology, disconnectedness and short life, and informality of meetings. Usually they are discovered only in the incident which destroys them."[12]

Heavy metal rock music and videos by bands such as Ozzy Osbourne, Motley Crüe, Venom and Slayer celebrate violence and frequently use satanist symbolism. They have helped spur the current high level of interest among teenagers in this aspect of the occult. Richard Ramirez, a 25-year-old serial killer known as the Night Stalker and a self-styled satanist, was heavily influenced by an album called *Highway to Hell*, by AC/DC, a band whose name is seen by its satanist followers as meaning Antichrist/Devil Child. In July, 1984, a Long Island teenager was fatally stabbed 17 times in what his murderers admitted was a satanic cult ritual, and one of the killers, also a teenager, subsequently hung himself in jail.

Paperback copies of LaVey's *Satanic Bible* and *Satanic Rituals* have been found on the shelves of many recent teen suicides. In April, 1987, there were media reports of two such cases, one in Sackville, Nova Scotia, and one in Kitchener, Ontario. The father of the boy in the Kitchener case was quoted as saying that he was told that there are satanist followers in almost every school in the Kitchener area. Charles McLeod, of the Cult Project in Montreal, said in an interview that such a claim is quite realistic and would probably be true of any urban center in Canada. "LaVey's book has probably done far more harm than he has," said McLeod.

A teenager who killed three people in Toronto in 1985 was preoccupied with satanism, and, in the same year, police in Chatham, Ontario, reported concern about the presence of satanist material at the home of a young man suspected of murder in that city. In 1985 in Valleyfield, Quebec, satanic literature was found at the home of a man who killed, dismembered and burned a pregnant woman. A Halifax prostitute was killed in 1986 with a knife on which the number 666 was displayed. Many similar cases have been documented in the United States. Throughout Canada and the U.S. there have been persistent reports in recent years of animal mutilations and vandalism, especially at graves and mausoleums, that have been interpreted as being connected with satanic rituals. In 1986 the small country town of Delhi, Ontario, was put into a panic by some teenagers' disclosures that they had participated in satanic rituals allegedly involving animal sacrifices in a barn. A local priest counseled the youths, who had been frightened by their own experiments in the occult, and the barn was subsequently burned down by an arsonist.

Early in 1987 police in Verdun, Quebec, investigated reports of a satanic gang that, according to McLeod, "supposedly uses a lot of satanist insignia (tattoos, etc.), uses ten-year-old girls in Black Masses and recruits them into child prostitution." McLeod said local people who had publicly protested the activities of this gang were subsequently harassed by someone who painted the number 666 on their houses. The police investigation was inconclusive. McLeod said he was also concerned about a Montreal-based organization called Continental Association of Satan's Hope (CASH), which mails out material promising that satanic magic can bring financial success.

Santeria, a Cuban cult derived from voodoo, has also been associated with the use of children in violent rituals. There have been reports in the Toronto area of rituals involving chickens, which are said to resemble the practices of this cult. A gruesome discovery made at Chicago's O'Hare airport in October, 1984, was drawn to the attention of people investigating the Hamilton case. Police at the airport became suspicious of a package that had arrived on a freight flight from Miami. The package was opened and contained what was apparently a dead fetus, a human skull, wooden sticks, some dead birds and two Halloween masks. Miami police were consulted about this discovery and a specialist from Miami told the Chicago police that these were things usually used in Santeria rituals.

There have been some successful prosecutions in the United States of child sexual abuse cases involving ritual elements. In Malden, Massachusetts, there were allegations of sex in "magic" secret rooms—adults dressed as clowns, still and video photography (of which no evidence was found), and stories of ritual slayings of small animals. A jury, however, convicted a day-care center operator, largely on the evidence of sexual abuse, after hearing the testimony of nine children. Jurors subsequently said in interviews with John Novak, of the *Malden Evening News*, that they believed the kids were telling the truth, and that they couldn't have been describing oral sex out of thin air. In Miles, Michigan, the proprietor of a preschool was convicted of abuse involving satanic activity.

The most notable of the successful prosecutions was in Miami, Florida, where the owners of a baby-sitting service in an exclusive suburban neighborhood were accused of multiple counts of child molestation. As in the Hamilton case, there had been allegations of pornography, but a van load of material was spirited away just before a search warrant was executed, and no evidence of pornography was found. Children alleged that they had been drugged and then forced to drink urine and eat feces. They also said they had been sexually abused. Allegations involving costumes and incantations were downplayed at the trial, which resulted in a sentence of six consecutive life imprisonment terms against the male proprietor, and a light sentence for his young wife, who testified against him. It is interesting to note that psychiatrist Lee Coleman, who testified for the defense in this trial, still maintains that there was no evidence against the accused. This is in spite of the fact that the court was overwhelmingly convinced by the testimony of the proprietor's wife, evidence of allegations made by anguished and fearful children and the fact that the proprietor's eight-year-old son suffered from gonorrhea of the throat.[13]

Dr. Coleman, one of the leading lights of the campaign against such prosecutions, challenges the interviewing techniques employed by child sexual abuse specialists. He claims that these techniques are leading and manipulative. This raises a crucial issue—one that the courts are continually forced to grapple with. Roland Summit, who advocates passionately on behalf of sexually abused children, and is often called as a prosecution witness in such cases, maintains that it is necessary to reassure the children that it is good to tell the truth and that they have nothing to fear from doing so. The kind of positive reinforcement that he considers necessary to gain the confidence of a child is seen by Dr. Coleman as a kind of emotional blackmail.

This debate often focuses on two issues, both of which were referred to frequently in the Hamilton case. The first is the myth that children never lie about sexual abuse. Dr. Coleman maintains that this is Dr. Summit's position, and takes every opportunity to ridicule it. Summit has stated that very few children, perhaps two or three in a thousand, have ever been found to exaggerate or to invent claims of sexual molestation. He says he is not advocating slavish belief in children's allegations, but rather that their statements be taken seriously and not automatically dismissed as fantasy as has often happened in the past.

The second of these issues is Summit's child sexual abuse accommodation syndrome, a theory that accounts for the pressures on children not to disclose abuse suffered from a family member, and often to retract their truthful disclosures because of feelings of fear or helplessness. Coleman sees this as a "Catch 22": when children disclose, they are telling the truth and when they later say that it was not true, they are lying. Summit's observations about the difficulty that children have in disclosing abuse explain the gradual process by which a child will begin with a relatively simple and minor revelation, and gradually work up to talking about the more extreme and

traumatic forms of abuse that they have suffered. This progression, which is present in nearly all sexual abuse cases, is
often cited by defense lawyers as further evidence that allegations have been drawn out of children by manipulative interviewers.

All these issues came into play in Minnesota and California. The extravagance of many of the children's allegations,
the almost fanatical zeal with which the prosecutions were
undertaken, the almost total absence of corroborating evidence, and a polarized and hysterical public reaction to the
cases, all contributed to making the cases spectacular disasters
that wreaked havoc on the lives of everyone involved in them.
In the McMartin case hundreds of children became embroiled
in an investigation that became completely unhinged as children started to make more and more bizarre claims—they
talked about being taken to exotic locations, caverns, tunnels
and, in one case, a house where there were lions in the basement. The children's allegations, which had previously concentrated on sexual abuse at the preschool, had also included
ingestion of feces and urine and the murder of babies.

The investigation appeared to have been hopelessly
compromised from the very beginning because police had sent
out a letter to all parents with children at the school asking
them if their children had complained of abuse. A judge had
found enough evidence, however, to commit five people for
trial after a lengthy preliminary hearing. However, the case
had also become the subject of a political controversy. A newly
elected Los Angeles district attorney withdrew most of the
charges, blaming social workers and their suggestive questioning of children for the collapse of the case.

A similar sequence of events unfolded in Bakersfield,
California, where children and parents have continued to
make allegations about satanic sacrifices after a series of court
cases in which four defendants were convicted and sentenced
to a combined 1,000 years in jail. Another related case was
dismissed, and charges were dropped against several other defendants. The judge who dismissed the second case, involving
130 molestation counts, took this step after learning that the
children, who had alleged satanist human sacrifices as well as
sexual abuse, had not been allowed to be examined by defense
doctors. This issue surfaced in the Hamilton case when defense lawyers were denied access to the children for psychiatric examination, and their motion for a further independent

assessment of the girls was denied. In Bakersfield a 1986 grand jury expressed concern about what they considered obvious mishandling of the children, who were denied interaction with members of their family and had excessive exposure to law enforcement investigators.

In Sacramento, California, allegations of sadistic child pornography were heard when two groups of children testified that they watched other children being killed and multilated while cameras were moving. One of these children said he was forced to participate in the murders. But a judge dismissed charges at a preliminary hearing, ruling that a grandmother had, through persistent questioning, led two girls to believe they had been molested. The judge described the grandmother as "totally obsessed with matters sexual." Connections were inevitably made in the media between this finding and attacks made by defense lawyers and witnesses in one of the Bakersfield cases against another grandmother, who had been one of the people who instigated police investigations. This woman had previously been labeled as obsessive about molestation, and was placed in a locked psychiatric ward after threatening to kill her husband. A defense psychiatrist maintained that she "seems to have presented her own time bomb of psychological explosions in response to every real or imagined revelation by the minors."

In Jordan, Minnesota, sexual abuse charges against 22 people were dropped after an investigation failed to find evidence of ritual murder and pornography. The case, which had begun with sexual abuse charges against one man who had a prior criminal record for sexual assault, had expanded to place 15 families under a cloud of suspicion, and remove 25 children from their homes. Children's allegations included sexual games in concert with adults and other children, killing of animals, eating of feces and the murder of children. Investigators had been horrified by the realistic detail of the children's stories; they were considered so striking that police officers concluded that the descriptions of murders must be authentic.

Once again no evidence was found. Some children retracted or changed their stories, and conflicts arose between different agencies that became involved in the case. A report by Minnesota's attorney general concluded that, because of inadequacies in the way the cases were investigated and prosecuted, "it is impossible to determine whether such abuse actually occurred, and if it did, who may have done these acts." The report stated that children were questioned too often, by too many people, with insufficient reporting and exchange of information on the part of investigators. It noted that suspects were seldom interviewed, or their backgrounds investigated prior to charges being laid, and concluded, "The haste with which charges were brought often precluded a search for corroborating physical evidence. Surveillance techniques were not utilized. Search warrants were rarely obtained."

While no one accused the Hamilton police of proceeding too hastily with their investigation, they were criticized, like their counterparts in Minnesota, for a lack of surveillance, a failure to obtain search warrants in order to interview people at the earliest opportunity and failure to check into the background of alleged perpetrators. Defense lawyers attempted unsuccessfully to suggest that the way the children were interviewed in the Hamilton case was leading and suggestive and the methods used were similar to those used in the American cases.

The failure of many of the ritual abuse cases in the United States not only tended to discredit investigators and child abuse specialists who believe children's accounts of such abuse, but also caused massive disruptions in the lives of the children, whom the authorities had set out to protect. In the light of these experiences, Roland Summit, who has followed these cases more closely than any other expert in the child abuse field, has become wary of the criminal justice system as an avenue for pursuing such potentially explosive allegations. He advised child care workers attending a conference on sexual abuse in Toronto in March, 1987, that it may be better not to reveal allegations of ritual abuse until very thorough investigation and surveillance has been undertaken. He added that such bizarre, though convincing, allegations leave child care workers like the protagonist in a science fiction novel who wants to put the town under guard because of an alien threat: "We may think there's an urgent need for the children to be protected, but we can't promise to provide it."

The Hamilton wardship hearing perhaps provides an answer to Dr. Summit's fears, by showing that it is possible to respond to bizarre stories of ritual abuse in a way that can protect the children while subjecting their allegations to public scrutiny. The allegations made by Janis and Linda were strikingly similar in many ways to those made by other children thousands of miles away. The response of authorities to their story was similar in many respects, but the court case that resulted from all this was fundamentally different. It centered around what solution would be in the best interests of the children, and it provided a forum for a detailed examination of all the facts of the case, without either suppressing the more bizarre aspects of the children's story or chasing off after them into some tangent, where the basic issues of child abuse and neglect could get lost. The 18-month-long hearing was widely criticized for its length and exorbitant cost. It did not provide all the answers to the questions it posed, but it could serve as a model for a cool and levelheaded approach to a volatile issue.

The Hamilton case had the advantage of being a family court hearing, where the emphasis was directed less towards proving or disproving the strange allegations than to deciding what custody and access arrangements would be in the best interests of the children. The *Ontario Child Welfare Act* and the rules of the Unified Family Court, where a district court judge presided over a variety of family and juvenile cases, also allowed for plenty of latitude in dealing with such material as hearsay evidence of children's statements, videotapes of interviews and therapy sessions and expert opinions. With a presiding judge who was clearly personally distressed by the trauma that the children appeared to be suffering and deeply committed to the pursuit of truth in the matter, the hearing soon turned into perhaps the most careful and comprehensive examination of a case of ritual abuse ever undertaken.

CHAPTER 9

THE "PLAN" AND
ITS AFTERMATH

It was just after Victoria Day, Firecracker Day as the children called it, that life in the McInnis home was disrupted with an explosion of fear.

The children had spent the holiday weekend with their father. Catherine McInnis admitted when she testified in court that she had used very poor judgment in allowing the children to go off on this visit; she had not informed the Children's Aid Society of all that the children had told her about their father. She had explained her reasons for withholding this information, but could not justify continuing to do so when she knew they were going to be spending three days with a man whom she believed to be a murderer and a satanist.

Gordon Wells had promised to bring his daughters back to the foster home at about 6 P.M. on the Monday evening, and Catherine had begun to worry about them when they had still not appeared by nine o'clock. Their father, however, did phone soon after nine to say that he would have them home in about an hour. Both Catherine and her daughter testified that they felt there was something a little disturbing about his behavior when he arrived with the girls at about 10 P.M. They said he came into the kitchen with a package of sparklers and a bag of cereal he had brought for the children, and then paced nervously about, peering through the door into the living room. Catherine offered him some tea, which he declined, saying he had a toothache. She said she then looked casually out of the door, which he left open, and, as soon as she did this, the man left hurriedly.

After their father left, the girls mentioned something about a plan, and then began crying. Catherine said the children said strange things to her that night like, "I love you. I love you. I wish I had a thousand dollars. I don't know what I'd buy you. I love you. You're so good."

Catherine said the girls made similar comments the next morning, and talked to one another about a plan while they were waiting for a visit from Lesley Morgan, the social worker. The foster mother observed that they seemed reluctant to talk to Lesley and acted strangely while she was there. They told Ms. Morgan that they were soon going to live with their father in Toronto. Catherine noted that, while they had previously expressed hatred when they spoke of Gary, their mother's boyfriend, that morning they kept saying things like, "I like Gary. Gary is a nice boy."

When Ms. Morgan left, the children started screaming and crying and holding on to Catherine. She said they asked loudly, "Why does Mom think you're so bad? Why does she hate you? Nobody was ever so good to us. This is such a safe place. Your kids are so nice. Why does Mom hate you?"

Then, to the foster mother's great surprise and consternation, they told her that Gary and their mother and father had all come to Catherine's house a week or ten days before, while Catherine's daughter Mary was having a party. They had come and listened at the windows, the girls said, and Sharon had actually slipped into the house. Catherine said she recalled getting up one morning, at about that time, and thinking it rather strange that the double windows and the screen were wide open.

Catherine testified about the girls' description of this incident, and was unable to resist injecting a little sarcasm into her account: "She came in the bedroom, and she had a big knife. She held it at Linda's neck—something that, by now, Linda should have been used to. She said, 'You have a big mouth. You tell Catherine everything. You tell one more word, and I will stick this through your neck.' She stuck pins in a Cabbage Patch doll, and said 'That is what I'm going to do to

Catherine with the knife.' She took the box that the Cabbage Patch doll came in, and, with a pencil, poked out the eyes and made holes in it. 'That's what I'm going to do to Catherine with the knife. You don't tell anybody about what I do. It's none of your business.'"

The court was shown a green box with a picture of a doll printed on it. The box was punctured by a series of holes on the face and body of the printed doll. Catherine testified that the girls produced this box from their bedroom, and told her again how their mother had threatened, "I'll poke her all over with the knife, where she'll never talk again." Catherine said Linda demonstrated by poking two holes in the leg of the printed outline of the doll.

Catherine testified that as Linda did this she said, "We will have to help kill you. We always have to stick knives in people they kill. We'll just stick a knife in your foot. I don't know why Mom says you're so bad. She said she is going to cut out your mouth, dig out your eyes. I couldn't dig out your eyes, Catherine, but we will have to stick knives in you."

The foster mother said the children then told her about the plan that they had heard their mother, Gary and their father making over the weekend. Their mother was not supposed to be present when they were on an access visit with their father, but they assured Catherine that she had been there, and had made soft chocolate cookies. They told Catherine that the three adults had talked about killing Catherine and her whole family. The girls said the plan was that, when their dad brought them back to Catherine's house after the weekend, Gary and their mother would be hiding in the car. Catherine said the girls told her that everyone in the house was to be killed "and then they'll cut you all up and they'll set fire to the house."

Catherine said that the children warned everyone in the house not to go outside, because they were afraid their father would run them over with his car. The foster mother's own children testified that they had never seen the girls so terrified. Impressed by this show of fear, and knowing much of what the girls had said already, the whole family believed that they were indeed under an imminent threat.

When Catherine was later cross-examined by Arthur Brown, Sharon's lawyer, she explained that some details of what happened that day had escaped her memory: "A plan to carve, and cook, and hand you and your family out to cannibals, doesn't do a lot for your memory. I shook for days. I couldn't write what I wanted to put down."

Mr. Brown ridiculed this fear, noting that there were six people in the house, which was located in a well-populated suburban neighborhood. He said the foster mother should have realized that what the girls described to her was "a completely fantastic childlike scheme."

"I did not see it as a childlike scheme," said Catherine. "Nor did those terrified, shaking children. They were well aware what their mother and father and Gary could do. Six people wouldn't be any match against three people very good with knives."

When Mr. Brown questioned her skeptically about the story of Sharon appearing in the children's bedroom, Catherine responded with heavy sarcasm. Mr. Brown asked how Catherine thought the children's mother might have gained entry to the house, and the foster mother replied: "I think she came in the window. Unless she slithered under the door."

After hearing the girls' story about the plan, Catherine called the Children's Aid Society. Ms. Morgan was not there, and, not wanting to have to tell anyone else about what was happening, Catherine decided to wait until Ms. Morgan was able to come to the house in the evening. She said she didn't call the police because she didn't think they would believe her. When Ms. Morgan arrived, Catherine and the children were so relieved that they ran up the driveway to meet her. When she had been told about the plan, Lesley phoned her supervisor, who then called the police. Eventually a police officer, Sergeant Bruce Elwood, came to the house. Catherine said, "I remember I was so thrilled to think somebody came, and I had a chance to tell someone."

Sgt. Elwood, who was the first police officer to actually interview the children, had not been involved in the case before. He was an experienced officer of the old school, clean-cut, conservative and mild-mannered. He told the court that he responded to the call he received from the Children's Aid Society, but "I found all that I was being told very hard to believe. I was very skeptical of what was being said—children being killed, cannibalism—I found it very hard to believe."

He asked to talk to the children separately, and testified that Linda told him she overheard her mother and father talking about killing the McInnis family. He said, "She kept referring to it as 'the plan.' At one point she saw my notebook, and said, 'My daddy has a notebook like that, and he put the plan into it.' She was talking of friends of hers that had been killed, that were gone.

"I felt I should stay there until I had a better grasp of the situation. They had towels over the sheer [drapes]. Mrs. McInnis said she was not going to bed. It looked like a household where everyone was going to stay up all night. I felt, under the circumstances, I should stay."

He interviewed Janis and he said, "After much coaxing suddenly she seemed to relax, and she began speaking of a graveyard where ten kids were buried, about her father having a mask and a picture of the devil. I was shown a picture that Janis had drawn of a graveyard. She said, 'You pulled into a parking area. You have to go over the bridge through a wooded area. Kids are buried in a circle.' I asked her who the kids were. She said she could write down one of the names. She wrote 'Billy.' "

Janis wrote on an envelope, which she gave to Sgt. Elwood, "Dad kild Karen." The policeman asked her to draw him a sad picture and a happy picture. She drew a picture of a man with one of his hands between the legs of a smaller person. She told him that it showed her dad putting his fingers in her. She had drawn smiles on the faces but then changed them into glum faces, saying, "It's not a happy picture. It's a sad picture."

Sgt. Elwood stayed for several hours talking to the children and Mrs. McInnis. He told the court, "After speaking with the children, I cannot explain or understand how both tell such details of bizarre happenings. I find it very difficult to understand how a young child could be so consistent with the same stories. What impressed me more than anything was how normal childhood conversations would lapse into other subjects without prompting. I find it hard to understand how these children were not telling the truth."

He phoned Sgt. Bowen at about 11:30 that evening and strongly suggested that he should come to the house. He said that Bowen stated that there was nothing he could do that Elwood had not already done, and refused to come. Bowen then phoned Lesley Morgan and told her that he didn't believe anything the children were saying.

Sgt. Elwood phoned Sgt. Gruhl. He said that the McInnises were very level-headed people, who were not known to be alarmist. Sgt. Elwood was not able to stay any longer. Before he left the house, however, he requested that Sgt. Gruhl order the officers on the beat to do some additional patrols of the area that night. He later wrote a strongly worded report in which he recommended further police investigation, and that the children's father and mother and Gary Evans all be advised that the police had been informed of the allegations.

Sgt. Bowen responded sarcastically in his report: "Suddenly now the children report that their father is involved in the mass killing of babies. They prove they are telling the truth by urinating in fear as they tell the story. We do not believe what they say, because of the stories they have told us that are untrue."

He later explained to the court that the untrue stories he was referring to related to the murder of children, and to the man with a son called Billy, who was supposed to be the superintendent of the apartment building where the girls used to live. The police had checked at the building and discovered that the superintendent was not dead, and did not have a son named Billy. They also ran a computer check on missing persons; there were no missing children who had names similar to those mentioned by the girls, and who the girls had claimed were dead. He said he was also skeptical about the alleged plot because "from what we knew about the relationship between Gary Evans and Gordon Wells, we didn't for a minute suspect they would join forces to do anything."

Sgt. Bowen agreed that if he had gone to the McInnis home the night "the plan" was reported, he might have obtained some first-hand information from the children—but he said that he had other priorities that night. He said he and his partner did drive by the McInnis home several times during the night, and saw nothing suspicious. He said he had been busy investigating an assault on a witness in a murder case.

Judge Beckett questioned Sgt. David Broom closely, asking why the girls' father was not interviewed immediately when these new allegations surfaced. "I am curious to know," he said, "why you took from May 23 to July 5 to interview an accused person in a sexual abuse case."

The sergeant replied, "We were required to work on other duties. Maybe the frustration of investigation was dwelling on us at this point."

The judge pursued the issue: "You had a brand-new

lead: allegations of sexual abuse, wearing a mask, a picture of the devil. All those allegations are extremely serious, if true. They were made to Sgt. Elwood, an experienced officer whose opinion you would rely upon."

Sgt. Broom responded, "Our superiors told us to stop the investigation for a while."

Catherine told the court: "When Sgt. Elwood left, we just cuddled together in the kitchen like scared rabbits. I had the same feeling as if we were in some remote area like New Guinea, where you don't have protection of any kind."

The next day the Children's Aid Society decided to move the whole family to the Holiday Inn for a few days to insure their protection. Before they left, there was a phone call from Gordon Wells. Catherine said she told him, "Your wife and her boyfriend were in my house last week." She said the girls' father replied, "Oh, my wife would never do that." She let Linda talk to her father but had to cut her off when the child started to say, "We're going away on a trip."

The McInnis family stayed in the hotel until they could make arrangements for new security measures at their home. When they returned, however, it would be without the foster children.

At the hotel the girls continued to talk about the murder and cannibalism and the plot to kill the McInnis family. One day in the restaurant Linda had a steak-on-a-bun meal. Catherine and Grace both described how the child took a bit of the meat and then said, "I can't eat her. I can't eat this because she's sad, her face is so sad. She didn't want to die. She is crying. She didn't want to just be meat. They killed her. They'll kill us too. When they feel like it, they'll kill everyone."

On the children's menu at the restaurant there was a cartoon with a picture of someone holding a shovel. Catherine said the children told her, "That's the shovel they take to the graveyard."

Catherine heard from neighbors that a suspicious car had been seen around her house after they left. The police were asked to check this out, but did not find anything that caused them to be concerned.

While they were at the hotel, Catherine came to a painful decision. Her whole family had been badly shaken by the threat on their lives. She was afraid that as long as the children remained in her home they were all in danger, and she felt that the worry would prevent her giving the children the care and attention that they needed. After consulting with her husband and daughters and CAS representatives, Catherine decided that she had to ask that the children be moved to another foster home. She sat down with Linda and Janis and told them, "You know we love you, and we really like you. But because of the danger, and because of the plan you told us about, you have to be moved so that you can be safe somewhere."

Catherine sadly explained to the court how "Janis kept saying, 'I thought you would never tell anyone the things we told you.' I said, 'I have to tell, to make the world safer so that all of those things won't happen to little children.' She seemed to block out the real reason. She was angry at me. She said, 'you just don't want us.'"

Janis and Linda were moved to a new foster home on May 24, 1985. Catherine never saw them or talked to them again. The girls never subsequently spoke ill of their first foster mother, although they continued to harbor a deep resentment over what they considered a rejection and a betrayal from the only person they had ever trusted.

After they were moved to their new foster home, the children continued to make disturbing disclosures. Their new foster parents, Helen and Stanley Kovaks, were down-to-earth country people, who started off being extremely skeptical of the girls' stories and usually tried to discourage them from talking about such things. For a long time they were afraid to take Linda to visit their friends and acquaintances, fearing that the child would blurt out, "My mom put her finger in me."

The Kovakses wanted to believe that their simple way of life and the caring environment they provided for the girls would soon dispel what they thought were morbid fantasies. But they soon found that, in spite of their disbelief, they were having to wrestle with the suspicion that the children were telling the truth. They were concerned by Linda's lack of modesty, the way she would often lie on the floor and spread her legs widely. One day they were disturbed to discover Janis lying on top of Linda, kissing her younger sister on the mouth and neck.

The foster parents were mystified by the way the younger child associated her father with the devil. She told them, "When he dies, he will go to the devil." They were alarmed one day when Linda watched Mr. Kovaks use a knife to cut a melon and remarked, "That's smaller than the knife my dad used to kill little Elizabeth. She's buried in a never-ending graveyard." On another occasion the foster parents were out with the children and they drove by a graveyard. Janis started talking about skeletons, and asked Mrs. Kovaks if she had ever seen bones on shelves.

The incident that convinced Stan Kovaks that the girls might be telling the truth also involved a knife. It was a big curved knife that he used for cutting bush. Janis saw it lying around one day and said, "You wouldn't kill us with that, Uncle Stan?" Mr. Kovaks later testified that he saw sincerity and real terror in the child's face that day. "I knew then they had really gone through something," he told the court. "I figure now a lot of it has happened. It's awful hard to believe."

Stanley Kovaks said Janis had a way of staring that looked as if "someone has scared her half to death, or she's thinking of something that happened." He said Linda did the same thing sometimes: "Her face will screw up. She opens her mouth. Her tongue hangs out, and, if she's eating, she'll have food fall out of her mouth."

Just before she was due to testify at the wardship hearing, several months after the court case began, Mrs. Kovaks sat down with the girls individually and asked them to tell her what they could remember about what had happened to them before. Linda told her that her dad had killed two people and her mom had killed seven people. She spoke about the abuse with the bird, and the killing of Elizabeth. She said that her mom killed children in the basement of their house in Hamilton, laid them on the floor and would then clean up the blood with a cloth. There was a space under the basement steps where Linda said she used to keep her bike so it wouldn't get blood on it. She repeated the allegations of pornography at Channel 11 and talked about the Blob, saying that "he's dead now," and that Daddy killed him.

Janis also talked about the bird and the other sexual abuse allegations. She said her father had killed five girls and her mother had killed five boys. She said, "They took their heads off." She talked about the killing of Elizabeth and murders in the apartment in Toronto, where she said her mother would clean up the mess with paper towels and then throw them in the garbage. Like her sister, Janis spoke about the Blob and the Channel 11 allegations. She drew a picture of the graveyard, and talked about going there with bodies in the back of Gary's car.

"I thought it was hard to believe. But, when a little child tells you the same thing over and over, I believe she has experienced some of it or seen it," Mrs. Kovaks said.

Mrs. McInnis's ordeal was not over when she reluctantly concluded that Janis and Linda should be moved out of her home. A cruel trick of fate embroiled her in a similar case that led the court to conduct a further probe into her sanity and credibility. For several months after she parted with Janis and Linda, Mrs. McInnis had not felt able to take any new foster children. However, when a CAS social worker appealed to her in November, 1985, to take in some very difficult children who were in a state of great distress, she agreed to do so.

The two children, Lorne and Mary, were slightly older than Janis and Linda, but both under ten years old. They had apparently suffered a lifetime of abuse in a transient family that was involved with motorcycle gangs. They had come to the attention of the Children's Aid Society as the family moved from one community to another. Their father, who had served a prison term for assault with a deadly weapon, once threatened the CAS with his biker connections. The Hamilton-Wentworth CAS sent the children to Catherine McInnis because she was particularly adept at dealing with problem children. No one at the agency could possibly have foreseen that these children would begin to relate, to the foster mother, stories of sexual abuse, murder, cannibalism, sodomy and bestiality that were similar to the allegations made by Janis and Linda.

The startling revelation that the same foster mother was reporting similar bizarre statements from a second pair of children seemed, at first, to present the easy solution that defense lawyers and many observers were hoping for—that the foster mother was obviously crazy. Although the allegations of Lorne and Mary were to be the subject of a separate Crown wardship hearing, some of the evidence in their case was presented to Judge Beckett during the Wells hearing in order to shed light on Mrs. McInnis's credibility.

This trial within a trial showed that the second pair of children made similar statements, sometimes with more detail, to several people besides Mrs. McInnis. Judge Beckett said that after hearing this evidence he was "satisfied Mrs. McInnis was truthful in her evidence concerning this other case." The court did not probe further into the new allegations, to answer the question of whether or not this was another disturbing case of satanic ritual abuse. If it were, it would clearly give credence to Janis's and Linda's stories, and would corroborate, to an alarming degree, the suggestion that there is some kind of satanic cult practicing murder and violent ritual in southern Ontario. However, evidence from an unrelated case was only admissible insofar as it shed light on the credibility of a witness.

There was also another quite feasible explanation for Lorne's and Mary's stories—that these disturbed children had somehow found out about Mrs. McInnis's involvement in the case of Janis and Linda, which was at that time already being publicized by the media, and had engaged in a very sick joke. After Mrs. McInnis had testified about the new foster children's stories, Judge Beckett asked if it had ever occurred to her that she had been set up. She replied that she had wondered about this, but came to believe the children's stories of satanic ritual. "In my wildest imagination I would have never thought that in a lifetime I would have been connected with it again," she said. The judge later told defense lawyers that the issue was Mrs. McInnis's credibility, not her gullibility.

While the allegations that gave rise to these speculations were, in many respects, similar to those of Janis and Linda, there were many crucial differences. The children themselves were very different. For all the dreadful experiences they had to relate, Janis and Linda had maintained a quality of innocence. They seemed to be basically sweet little children, deeply traumatized, but sensitive and sincere. Mrs. McInnis said she also came to like Lorne and Mary, but they were definitely street-wise kids.

Lorne and Mary talked about other children being killed, tortured and cut up with a saw. They spoke about eating raw chicken and drinking its blood, going to a graveyard, wearing masks and costumes, dancing, singing, killing people and sharing out flesh to eat and take home in bowls. They talked about a man with a camera, and described going across the U.S. border from Windsor, Ontario, where they used to live, to find victims. They said the man with the camera liked to kill and eat people, and was called "Camera Man." The children said they had to help lure children into being kidnapped by playing games with them. They also described bestiality and went into graphic details about "sex and slaughter sessions," which, Mrs. McInnis said, contained "brutality beyond description." She said the children told her things "that would curl the paint off the walls."

Catherine observed that, unlike Janis and Linda, these new children "never cried and never showed emotion. They would laugh a rather nervous laugh when they spoke about people begging for their lives, and how scared the children are when they see the saw."

These children did not seem to have anything like the same reticence as Janis and Linda when disclosing the alleged atrocities. Some of the things that Lorne and Mary said appeared glib and childish; however, they contained some grotesque elements that had never surfaced in the Wells children's allegations. Some of the more believable details in Lorne's and Mary's stories were related in a subsequent interview with a police officer. This helped the court to reach the conclusion that, whether or not the children were telling the truth, they had indeed told Mrs. McInnis what she said they had told her. Defense lawyers who tried to challenge the foster mother's evidence on this did not later question her credibility in their final submissions to the judge.

Catherine McInnis described to the court the turmoil that these new children's allegations put her in. She said she told her husband one night, "I'm in an awful mess. I don't know what to do. I'm certainly not going to tell everybody this happened to me again." She said her husband told her, "You have to do what's right." She said she consulted Ms. Morgan and explained to her that she was afraid, because "I felt people thought I was crazy for the first time." She asked that Lorne and Mary be removed as soon as possible so they could make their disclosures to somebody else. She asked Ms. Morgan to be discreet about her involvement, because "I didn't want anybody to know that I had children telling me anything as bizarre as this again. I was afraid what people would think."

Lorne's and Mary's allegations were more detailed and specific than those of Janis and Linda in their references to satanism and ritual. In describing what happened at the graveyard, Mary said, "We twirl and dance. Big people swing each other. We sing, 'The devil is good.' We sing how nice Satan is, that he's so good and smart."

They talked about people dressing up as devils and witches, and spoke of the Prince of Power. They described burning candles, and putting needles in a doll before burying it. They said they were made to drink a mixture of blood, wine and urine; this is a known satanist ritual that parodies the Christian Eucharist. The children told the foster mother that a teenage girl involved in these rituals said, "God is a dumbbell, stupid and I hate his guts." They described another person singing, "Jesus humps everyone, poisons everyone." One of the children once told Catherine, "I hate Jesus 'cause I know he's bad. Jesus is ugly."

While it was hard to believe all that these children said, it seemed quite likely that they had been exposed to some quite bizarre practices. In a statement that ominously echoed comments made by Janis and Linda, Mary quoted a man, who, from her descriptions, appeared to be the leader of the group of people engaging in these rituals: "Mike says nobody will ever catch them. They know what they are doing."

Mike may well have been right. It was certainly not the job of Judge Beckett's court to try to catch them. Once the judge had decided that Mrs. McInnis's credibility had not been impugned in any way, the parallel story of Lorne and Mary would no longer play a part in the case of Janis and Linda. However, when Mr. Wells later mentioned that his wife had once taken Janis and Linda to visit an uncle in Windsor, the scene of the other children's alleged abuse, several people involved in the case began to speculate, albeit with flimsy evidence, that there may be some link between these two similar accounts of savage rituals.

PART THREE
THE INVESTIGATIONS

CHAPTER 10
POLICE INVOLVEMENT

The investigation of child sexual abuse involves many sensitive and complex problems, and requires the involvement of specialists in several different fields. It can be seen as a social problem, a crime, a disease, or all three at once. Depending on how the situation is perceived, the goal of an investigation might be protecting the children, preserving the family, punishing the offender or getting medical treatment for the perpetrator and the victim. Usually these goals coalesce, but sometimes they come into conflict. This is why it is generally recognized that good communication and teamwork between social agencies, doctors, police and prosecutors is essential in sexual abuse cases.

Rather than co-operating with one another in investigating the allegations of Janis and Linda, the Hamilton-Wentworth Regional Police and the Children's Aid Society pursued separate goals, reached completely different conclusions and ended up openly hostile to one another. Part of the reason for this lay in the different assumptions and predispositions the investigators each took to the case. Behind such assumptions one can see a difference in training, methods and philosophy. One cause for conflict was that the police only felt responsible for investigating the matter if it could lead to criminal charges, while the CAS had the goal of protecting the children. The social workers and psychiatrists listened to the children's story, analyzed its credibility and assessed it in relation to the girls' history and that of other family members. The police officers looked for physical evidence. They did not find the type of evidence they were looking for, and therefore concluded that the children were not telling the truth. The child care professionals concluded that the children were telling the truth, and were frustrated that the police did not take the children's allegations seriously.

The police and the CAS began their investigations of the Wells case with the best of intentions. A protocol had recently been agreed to in Hamilton-Wentworth that was supposed to insure co-operation and a free exchange of information in such cases. In accordance with that protocol, police were present when the children were first interviewed by the agency's child abuse specialist, and social workers were there when the mother was confronted with the girls' allegations. Information was passed back and forth about the further disclosures that were made in the foster home, and the police responded to these when they were called upon to do so.

At the beginning of the case after attending the specialist's interviews with the children, Sgt. Broom believed that the girls had been sexually abused. But when the mother denied the allegations, Sgt. Broom was in a position where the only evidence to support his belief was the statements of two young girls whose testimony would probably not be accepted in a criminal court, given the rules of evidence that applied at that time. Some questions were raised at the hearing as to whether better police work, even at this early stage in the investigation, might have resulted in evidence being uncovered. Sgt. Broom missed his best opportunity to confront Gary Evans about the children's statements on the day Sharon Wells was first confronted at the CAS.

On March 8, 1985, about nine days after they were first informed of the children's allegations of abuse, police executed a search warrant at Sharon's home. Sgt. Broom went with Sgt. David Bowen, his partner, who had been away the previous week. Bowen was slightly older than Broom, and the senior officer on their two-man team. Although they worked well together, the difference in style and character between the two men was as great as the contrast between Broom's thick dark hair and Bowen's partially bald head. While Broom was reserved and reticent, Bowen was aggressive and opinionated. The older man was perhaps sharper and better educated, but he was not always a good listener and was prone to sarcasm.

According to Sgt. Bowen's testimony at the hearing, the search, which was conducted while Sharon and Gary were absent from the house, produced no evidence. Lesley Morgan, the social worker, testified that police told her they removed some towels, which they thought might be stained with semen, during the raid, but neither of the officers mentioned this in their evidence or referred to it in their written reports.

In his testimony before the court, Sgt. Bowen agreed with lawyers' suggestions that the best course of action on hearing the allegations would have been to move quickly to search the house, so there was no time to dispose of evidence. But he said that Broom did not know that the girls had mentioned being abused with a vibrator until after the March 7 interview, and it was only after that disclosure that a search was deemed necessary. He also agreed that it is normally desirable, where there are two alleged perpetrators, to interview them separately and early on in the investigation.

On March 11 the police closed their investigation of the case, stating in a report that "it is quite evident that both of these children have been sexually assaulted, yet because of their age their evidence in court would be unsworn. Since neither of the suspects have admitted to this offense and there is no corroboration to prove what these children are saying is true, there is not enough evidence at this time to lay any charges."

When the children began making their more serious allegations of pornography and ritual violence, the CAS urged the police to reopen their investigation. Although they did so, it is clear from the statements made to the foster mother and social worker and in police reports that Sgt. Bowen, the senior officer on the investigating team, quickly concluded that the children's stories were "beyond belief." He reached this conclusion without talking to the children, whom his partner had found believable when they made their earlier disclosures.

Judge Beckett stated in his final judgement, "The reluctance of the police who investigated the case to believe more than sexual abuse allegations was understandable—they reflected the natural abhorrence of any normal person at the very thought that children in our community could possibly be involved in such matters."

If natural abhorrence to the alleged crime was the basis for closing a case, few police investigations would ever be undertaken. The police clearly had a duty to investigate any allegation, however bizarre, so Sgt. Bowen and Sgt. Broom did reopen the case. They opened it and closed it five times between March 11 and July 26, on each occasion following up on additional information provided by the CAS and each time failing to find evidence that they considered significant.

As police officers became more incredulous of the children's strange stories, social workers and psychiatrists became more convinced that the children were telling the truth, and began complaining about inadequacies in the police investigation. These complaints were explored during the hearing. The police explained that they had begun a massive surveillance operation when the allegations of pornography were first made but abandoned it when the children's stories got more bizarre and further investigation showed that some of the information provided by the girls was false. The CAS representatives responded that the police officers had not taken the trouble to find out the exact contents of the children's statements. It was not a case of the girls giving wrong information, but the police misunderstanding what they had said.

The exchange of information between the police and the CAS degenerated to the point where the Children's Aid Society had to obtain a court order to obtain police reports on the case, and, when police wanted access to the agency's files, they were told they would have to get a search warrant. The conflict between the two groups was so pronounced that, during the Crown wardship hearing, the CAS lawyer, John Harper, attempted to have the investigating police officers declared as hostile witnesses. He also tried to have senior police representatives cited for contempt of court in connection with an alleged attempt to persuade a court official to disclose what he might have overheard lawyers saying about the case. When Lesley Morgan reported a break-and-entry at her home soon after the police testified in the case, CAS representatives accused the Hamilton-Wentworth police of conducting the break-in to search for compromising material about her or the foster mother. An Ontario Provincial Police investigation of this allegation concluded that it was without foundation, and a private investigator working for the CAS was charged with public mischief.

This grotesque breakdown in communication and, co-operation was epitomized by a somewhat comic episode in July, 1985, when police took the children and Lesley Morgan on a trip to Toronto in a quixotic search for evidence of ritual burials. The excursion ended with an exaggerated version of the intense frustration well known to parents who have to take young children for long car rides in hot weather. The children refused to help look for the graveyard where they said the rituals took place, because they were not allowed to go on the rides at Canada's Wonderland. Although the police promised them ice cream cones, and, according to Sgt. Bowen, Ms. Morgan pleaded on her hands and knees with Janis, the girls maintained this hard bargaining position. When the police threatened that they would not be allowed to go home until they found the graveyard, Linda began to identify several unlikely places as the scene of the bloody rituals. A psychiatrist who saw a transcript of a tape recording made by police that day later told the court: "For the last third of this interview I don't think anybody in the car was in their right mind."

Sgt. Bowen and Sgt. Broom taped conversations in the car that day without informing Lesley Morgan. This infuriated the social worker and her superiors at the Children's Aid Society, particularly as the police officers did not tape record a conversation with the children's father on the same day. It seemed to underline CAS workers' suspicions that the police were more intent on trying to catch the children in a lie, or the social worker in some attempt to manipulate the children, than they were in challenging the people the girls had accused.

Sgt. Bowen said the conversations were taped because he doubted the accuracy of Ms. Morgan's perceptions. He said he and his partner forgot to tell her they were making a tape. When he was asked in court if the social worker was under suspicion, he said she was not, but added "she came under suspicion for something else, which has nothing to do with this case." He did not explain to the court that the "crime" of which the police subsequently suspected Ms. Morgan was painting shadows on a city sidewalk to commemorate the anniversary of the bombing of Hiroshima, and that the reason that they suspected her of this offense was that she openly acknowledged that she had done it.

Sgt. Broom was more diplomatic in his explanation to Judge Beckett, who was obviously disturbed by the notion that police should secretly record conversations with a professional person with whom they were supposed to be collaborating, but not bother to do so when they talked to a suspect. "It was a long day. There was no intent to deceive. It was only meant to assist as an investigative tool. I don't know why it was not on with Gordon Wells," Sgt. Broom said.

It was, as Sgt. Broom said, a long day. On the way to Toronto the children began complaining of the heat in the back of the car, and the police officers explained to Ms. Morgan, who sat in the back with the girls, that the air-conditioning was not working. When told that they would be going to stop by their father's house before they went looking for the graveyard, Janis said, "I don't want to go to my dad's home." A little while later she complained, "I'm sick and tired. I don't want to go anywhere." Her sister echoed her sentiments by responding to a question, "I'm not telling you. I'm sick and tired." The irrepressible Linda did start talking to the policemen eventually, and Janis told her to "shut up." Janis was told that her help was needed to find the graveyard, and she replied, "I ain't gonna show anybody nothing, and I don't have to."

The first stop in Toronto was in the center of the city, where the police were looking for an occult store that had a bad reputation, according to an Ontario Provincial Police officer who specialized in cult investigations. They parked in front of where the store should have been, but found that it was no longer in existence. While the two policemen were out of the car looking up and down the street, Janis looked up towards the empty storefront and said, "Oh, 666." Ms. Morgan could not see the number written anywhere, and asked Janis if she had seen it, but the child changed the subject.

The next stop in an excursion that was becoming quite a frightening ordeal for the children was the housing project where they used to live in Toronto. There the police questioned the children about the character to whom Sgt. Bowen referred to as "the infamous Blob." This was a rather confused conversation, because the police officers were under the impression that the Blob and the Channel 11 man were the same person, and that the children had said that the Blob used to be the superintendent in their building. The police had established to their satisfaction that nobody answering the description of the Blob or the Channel 11 man had been superintendent of the building. They were not aware that several different people had acted as assistant superintendents at the project while the children lived there. They were also convinced, as a result of their earlier investigations, that children who Janis and Linda had said were dead were in fact alive, and were in the children's classes at school. But it emerged from the interrogation of the children that day that the police officers did not have a clear grasp of many of the details of the children's allegations.

They drove to the house where the girls' father, Gordon Wells, was living. When the girls saw their father, they ran up to him and hugged him, saying, "We love you, Daddy." The police officers later mentioned to Ms. Morgan that they were surprised at this reaction, but the social worker indicated that it is common for abused children to continue to express love towards an abusing parent.

This was the girls' first contact with their father since the Victoria Day weekend. His access rights had been abruptly withdrawn after the girls' story about the plan to kill the foster parents. Ms. Morgan had talked to him on the phone a few days later. He had denied the allegations and told the social worker, "I'll sue the shit out of you." He was very angry and went on to exclaim, "Gary and her in that goddamn house. Sharon has those kid so screwed up. The kids are mentally unbalanced. They are treating them like a bag of dirt. Of course they're going to have imaginations."

The police had never seen Gordon until they arrived with Ms. Morgan and the children on July 5. He told the police officers that he would not allow them into his house without a search warrant. They attempted to obtain one later in the day, but were unsuccessful. They spoke to Gordon outside the house and asked him about the devil picture. He produced a drawing, which he said he had done ten or fifteen years before, of a sinister face with long dark hair and a black beard. He said that Sharon's sister, whom he described as a Jesus freak, thought it was a picture of the devil. The police officers did not see it that way, but Ms. Morgan said it reminded her of pictures of Satan that she had seen in books. Sgt. Bowen later noted in a report: "Like everything else in this case, horror is in the eye of the beholder."

The police officer noticed that the man had a tattoo on his arm of "a chubby little devil." He told them he was not a satanist and denied the alleged plot to kill the McInnis family on the Victoria Day weekend. Sgt. Bowen later described Gordon Wells as "a bit of a rounder, somewhat violent and short tempered." Although the man did not have a criminal record, Sgt. Bowen said, "I would argue he fits my definition of a criminal: the way he talks, his attitude, his associates, the way he talked about Sharon, very vehement about how much he hated her. He insists he's not a kiddy diddler, and that he was very upset about what happened to his children. He talked in language that you often hear from people from perhaps his social background that he looks down strongly on kiddy diddlers. I don't believe for a minute that he is a satanist. I find no evidence to support this. I believed that he didn't plan to kill the McInnises with his ex-wife and Gary Evans."

Gordon Wells did not seem very smart, Sgt. Bowen observed. When he was asked in court how he came to that conclusion, he said, "By his talking. Smart people don't talk to police."

Sgt. Bowen's view of what happened during the rest of the day was quite different from what the social worker reported. The tape recording, which the police had made because they did not trust the social worker's perceptions, proved to be a considerable embarrassment to them, as it clearly showed that their version of the conversations with the children was incorrect.

Sgt. Bowen said the children emphatically denied the allegations "often and throughout the day," even though Lesley Morgan "produced many and various inducements to get them to talk." He told the court, "Janis specifically said there were no dead children and I believed her. I asked her if the stories of the dead children were true. She asked, 'What happens if it's not true?' I said, 'Nothing.' She said, 'It's all a big story.'"

He told the court that Lesley Morgan subsequently pleaded with the child to tell the truth, falling on her hands and knees and shaking her, saying, "It's very important for other children." Ms. Morgan denied this scene, Sgt. Broom did not see it and Sgt. Bowen did not record it either in his reports or his notes.

Sgt. Bowen also told the court, "When Janis wanted to go to Canada's Wonderland, I wouldn't promise her anything, quite properly so. It was my impression Morgan was saying they could see Wonderland later on." When challenged on this, he was not able to find the relevant quote in the transcript of the tape. Asked to give another example of the social worker's inducement to get the children to talk, he referred to a line in the transcript where Ms. Morgan was quoted as saying, "We're not going home until . . . [inaudible]." He said she had gone on to say something about finding the graveyard.

"We believe, when taking statements from accused or witnesses, you have to let them tell their stories. The CAS, in dealing with children, accept that you manipulate and oppress them until they tell you what you want to hear," said Sgt. Bowen.

The tape recording, which John Harper played to the court during his cross-examination of Sgt. Bowen, showed that the children were upset about not being allowed to go to Canada's Wonderland, and very reluctant to talk about the graveyard. Janis said, "I know, but I don't want to tell you, because I don't want to go there." The older child did begin to talk about the murder allegations: "I know why they killed the Blob, because he's too mean." She started to talk about the graveyard, but Sgt. Bowen interrupted her with a challenging question based on his confusion of the Blob and the Channel 11 man.

Sgt. Bowen had to agree when Mr. Harper suggested, "You didn't let them tell their story?

"You were obviously giving them the wrong facts," said Harper, quoting a passage from the transcript where the sergeant said to Janis, "'You told Catherine that the Blob was the superintendent,' and the child replied, 'No I did not. I didn't tell her that.'"

Referring to another section of the transcript where Janis talked about seeing "the dead kids," Harper said to Bowen, quoting from the transcript, "You directly challenged Janis. 'Did you make up the story about the dead kids?' Janis said, 'No.' Linda suggests that, 'Maybe Mom did.' Janis said, 'No.' When Janis said, 'We went to Channel 11. Mom and Gary and Andy's mom stuck fingers in us,' you challenged them again. Janis said, 'She did. It did happen at Channel 11.' I suggest to you that in spite of persistent and many challenges, and wrong facts put to the children, the children were telling you what they had told others up to this point."

Sgt. Bowen was again forced to agree, and was then further embarrassed by the next quotations from the transcript, which showed him telling the children, "Just show me where the cemetery is, and we'll go straight home," and then saying,

"I'll help get you guys up to Wonderland some other time. You can come some other day, and they'll bring you."

"I suggest it wasn't Lesley Morgan who suggested that the children would get to Canada's Wonderland. It was you," said Harper.

Sgt. Bowen replied, "I was trying to leave it as vague as possible, but I understand. I agree I was the first to give in."

"I'm suggesting to you that you purposefully misled this court the other day," the lawyer went on, "indicating many and various inducements, citing Canada's Wonderland when the evidence clearly shows it was you. After the children stood up to many of your challenges, I suggest, Sergeant, on this long hot day, you finally got your denial."

The denial came after a meandering excursion through the countryside with Linda, who scarcely knew left from right, gallantly but quite arbitrarily directing the two policemen on a wild-goose chase in search of the graveyard to which the children had said they were driven at night more than six months before. Janis steadfastly refused to give directions, but did start to draw a picture of the graveyard for the police. She drew the house where she said the Blob lived, but scribbled it out when Sgt. Bowen aggressively told her that she had previously said that the Blob lived in an apartment in Toronto, and asked her, "Are you lying now, or were you lying before?"

In a report the following day, Sgt. Bowen wrote: "We have reached that stage when we've got a denial and they don't believe it. We can't prove or disprove it." He said the children's stories "are probably based on some fact, then exaggerated beyond all truth. But the CAS believe what they said, and have the psychiatrists swearing that children never lie."

One of the psychiatrists who later assessed the credibility of the children's statements said after reviewing the transcript of the police tape recording, "They were asking kids questions there is no way kids of that age could answer, dangling the bribe of a trip to Canada's Wonderland and ice cream cones, then becoming frustrated, and alternating between putting the kids down and putting pressure on them."

CHAPTER 11

INVESTIGATION RESUMED

Hamilton-Wentworth Crown Attorney Dean Paquette was concerned. His review of Sgt. Broom's and Sgt. Bowen's investigation indicated that there were many unanswered questions. "Further investigation is warranted," he said in a letter to the police that listed 40 specific items that he wanted them to check into. He described the allegations as "bizarre and difficult to believe," and went on to state, "The fact that something such as this could take place in this jurisdiction is hard to accept for anyone. All steps should be taken to determine whether or not what the children allege is true, and if true can it be presented in a criminal court of law. To successfully investigate this matter will require innovative police investigation by individuals committed to the task. . . . It is hoped that through full exchange of information between the Children's Aid Society and the Hamilton-Wentworth Regional Police the truthfulness of these allegations can be determined."

Hugh Atwood, the lawyer representing the Ontario Official Guardian at the wardship hearing, referred to this letter in his final submissions when he argued that the court should not consider Sgt. Bowen and Sgt. Broom to be credible witnesses: "The fact that the Crown Attorney for Hamilton-Wentworth had to send a letter to the police outlining the

responsibilities in the investigation speaks volumes to Sgt. Bowen's and Sgt. Broom's lack of effort on this case."

In fact, the first item on the list of matters for further
investigation exposed what would appear to be a glaring hole
in the police work. On August 9, 1985, five months after the
police heard convincing allegations from the children that
they had been grossly sexually abused by Gary Evans, they
were asked to find out where Evans lived and worked and
whether he had a criminal record. The police had previously
received confusing information from Sharon about where her
boyfriend was working, because he was working at two different jobs, one of which required him to travel. She had been
vague about where he lived, claiming she did not know his
parents' address although she had visited their home, which
was also Gary's official residence, many times.

When police officers had tried to talk to Gary at
Sharon's home, he told them they were putting his life in jeop-
ardy and that they should investigate the matter further, but
refused to say any more to them. As the police officers made no
attempt to probe Gary's strange statement, one can only speculate about what kind of involvement this man had that
caused him to feel his life was threatened and what it was that
he thought they should investigate further. Sgt. Broom told the
court that he was mildly surprised that Gary had refused to
talk to the police. "I found that unusual, considering the se-
verity of the situation. But in 17 years of dealing with people
I've found a lot of odd people on the street."

In response to Paquette's letter, the police officers stated
that Gary Evans had no criminal record and gave Paquette the
other information requested, noting that Gary's family was
very protective. The Crown attorney had also requested that
the police do some research on voodoo and examine any possible connection that Evans might have with this Caribbean
sect. The police reported that the literature on voodoo contains references to the sacrifice of children and animals, but
no references to eating feces, drinking urine or performing sexual acts. They said that Evans left the Caribbean region in
early childhood, and that his family was Christian. A warrant
to search his room at his family home near Toronto was obtained, and in order to execute it the police said they had to
fight their way into the house amidst much screaming and ob-
struction. They said they found no evidence of pornographic,
voodoo or satanist material. They did find several hours of vi-

deotape recordings of Christian religious services or lectures, Sgt. Bowen said.

The Crown attorney's list included checks of medical records, further investigations of opinions of doctors and psychiatrists, investigations of people who may have been named in the children's stories and research on the backgrounds of the children's parents and their relationship. The police were asked to question Gordon Wells about whether he had been threatening his ex-wife. They reported that Wells denied any threats, but admitted that he was "ready to kill her" when he found out she was moving to Hamilton.

Gordon Wells admitted to police when they interviewed him on August 13 that he kept a machete in the back of his car. He also told the police that he did not see the children for several months after they moved to Hamilton. This conflicted with information Lesley Morgan had about visits the girls' mother made to Toronto, but, as a result of the breakdown in communication between the police and the CAS, the social worker and the police never exchanged notes on such details. The girls' father also mentioned to the police officers that his ex-wife had a videocassette recorder while she was living in Toronto. No VCR had been found when her Hamilton home was searched in March, 1985. Judge Beckett asked Sgt. Broom at the hearing if he had ever questioned Sharon Wells about the VCR, and the sergeant replied, "I'm not sure we ever covered that."

Paquette asked the police to obtain pictures of all the employees of the television station, in order that they could be shown to the children by "someone with whom they are comfortable and not the police." CHCH television would not comply with this request. Lesley Morgan would later testify that she formed the impression that the television station was more anxious about avoiding being implicated in a scandal than about helping a full investigation of the children's allegations.

The Crown attorney also asked the police to obtain a list of cemeteries around the northern section of Toronto, and to visit these in order to compare them with the diagram made by the foster mother when she listened to the children's stories. Sgt. Bowen and Sgt. Broom subsequently did a quick check on every cemetery they could identify in the area, and found nothing that matched the children's description. They explained in court that they had rushed from one cemetery to another, only stopping for a few moments at each one. They did not include private cemeteries in their search, though there are several in the area.

The police did some research on satanic ritual. Sgt. Broom told the court, "Other people came to us saying there is such a thing. I must believe there is some type of satanic cult that is available on the streets today." Harper had suggested he contact a San Francisco policewoman who specializes in occult investigations, and a sheriff in Toledo, Ohio, where police were attempting to unearth bodies that were supposedly interred by a satanic cult. But, Sgt. Broom said, "that proved to be erroneous."

Sgt. Broom was correct that the Spencer Township, Ohio, investigation into alleged satanic ritual murders of children did not succeed in unearthing bodies, but posts were found that could have been used for binding people, together with a headless doll with a small pentagram ornament nailed to a board, an eight-inch dagger with blood on it and a crucifix mounted upside down. This finding is typical of the kind of tantalizing, but ultimately inconclusive, evidence that has been encountered in attempts to corroborate allegations of satanic ritual crimes.

Ritual crimes pose a peculiar dilemma for law enforcement officers. Dale Griffis, the former police chief from Tiffin, Ohio, says that satanic allegations "put a lot of law enforcement people in limbo. They get nailed either way." If police appear to fail to take allegations seriously, they can be severely criticized, as the Hamilton police have been, but they can also very easily be made to look foolish if they go on a fruitless search for bodies in unlikely places. A sheriff who was convinced that children in Bakersfield, California, were telling the truth was subjected to considerable public ridicule when his attempts to dig for bodies were unsuccessful.

"We are all trying to figure out how to deal with this new element," Larry Dunn, a sheriff's deputy from Port Angeles, Washington, who specializes in training police officers in child sexual abuse investigations, said in an interview. He said the bizarreness of the cases makes them more difficult, as do the fear and control exercised on children to prevent them from talking and the skill that the cult groups seem to have at covering their tracks. He explained that the lack of evidence is often misleading, since children's perceptions can easily be distorted by drugs or by illusions created by adults.

He said these cases require more investigation, because "you are dealing with a lot of information that doesn't bear out. It doesn't mean that what the kids are telling you is not true. We're feeling our way right now. It's so different and we just don't have the training."

"We're swimming. A lot of agencies are treading water. We're trying to assess what we're dealing with. I feel that if these groups exist they're way ahead of the game," said Dan Clarke, a police detective from San Bernardino, California. Detective Clarke is one of a small but steadily increasing number of law enforcement police officers across North America who have looked at the alarmingly consistent hallmarks of ritual abuse and concluded that there is a clear possibility that there might be an organized network of satanic cults engaging in torturing and molesting children. He says he is persuaded by "the number of reports coming in, the number of victims, the consistency, that somewhere out there is such a group of people doing that sort of thing." Yet, he admits, it is so hard to believe: "We can accept a person being involved in mass homicide. But, for some reason or other, this is hard to accept.

"It seems to be based on behavior modification of children, a brainwashing type of abuse that takes away anything the children identify with or have faith in," Detective Clarke said in an interview. "There are small indications that it might be an organized movement. We're trying to determine if it's valid. I don't think there is a Crimes Against Children Unit that hasn't run into it." His speculations about the motives for such a group "sound pretty bizarre," the detective admits. "There are people who do it to appease a deity of some sort. Some are really religious. There are other people who are just seeking power and sexual gratification. Behind the whole thing there may be a motive of people trying to change the thinking of youth for a future generation."

All this is completely beyond the experience of traditional criminal investigators, who expect perpetrators to be motivated by greed or passion, and are certainly not used to dealing with crimes where the physical evidence is scarce, the witnesses are confused and frightened children, and the prime resources are psychiatrists and experts in the occult. In the past, when ritual elements have been found in a child abuse case, that aspect of the crime has generally been ignored and suppressed as police concentrated on a prosecution for sexual abuse. The criminal cases in the United States that have concentrated on the more bizarre ritual aspects of children's allegations have usually floundered in a sea of controversy, while the more successful prosecutions of this type of case have tended to downplay the ritual aspects, and often have completely excluded such elements from the evidence presented to the court.

When police officers do believe these strange allegations of ritual abuse, they often find themselves in conflict with their peers, their superiors and prosecutors, and vulnerable to ridicule and attack from defense lawyers, the media and members of the public. Child sexual abuse expert Roland Summit said in an interview, "We have a poor history of dealing with the cases. Once the issue of murder comes up and there are no bodies, it is used to ridicule the investigation and intimidate the kids."

The conflicting views that such allegations inspire among law enforcement officers were illustrated in an ambiguous but disturbing report that came over the Canadian Press wire just a few weeks before Judge Beckett delivered his final judgment in the Hamilton wardship hearing. The report from Edmonton, Alberta, stated:

> Devil worshippers may have been involved in several unsolved child abduction cases in Alberta, says an RCMP constable who has studied satanic cults for the past four years.
>
> "Children have a strong significance in satanic rituals and there are suggestions they may be used," Constable Jim Brown wrote in a report on the subject.
>
> He said satanists are believed to have been involved in an attempted child kidnapping in Red Deer in the summer of 1985 on one of 13 annual satanic "holy days."
>
> Spokesmen for Edmonton police and for the RCMP's Alberta headquarters in Edmonton discounted the possibility of a cult connection with well-known missing children cases.
>
> There is no evidence to substantiate that a satanic cult was connected with the January 1983 disappearance of six-year-old Tania Murrell, said city police spokesman Lori Nagy.
>
> RCMP Sgt. Wayne Gesy said Tania Murrell is one of five children the police have wanted to find for years.

"I'm not aware of any specific investigation towards any cult," he said.

Brown wrote that satanic cults are likely responsible not only for some child abductions but for a string of other crimes in the Calgary and Red Deer areas since 1982. The other cases include assaults, extortions, animal mutilations, grave robberies and "ritualistic sacrifice of hitchhikers," he said.

His report said satanists are rarely prosecuted in Canada because they go to great lengths to avoid detection.

"You can't get much evidence because satanic cults are so clandestine and cover themselves up well."

Rena Kirkham of Childfind Alberta, a group which tries to locate missing children, said she knows there is a suspected connection between abductions and satanic cults.

"It's definitely possible," she said in an interview. "If you look at the dates some of the children went missing there's a pattern."

Of the five most mysterious disappearances investigated by Childfind, she said, two took place on the day of satanic festivals and two occurred during the same week as satanic festivals.

Brown, who started probing satanism while investigating animal mutilations in the Red Deer area, said the biggest obstacle in nabbing devil worshippers is that most police officers "think it is all hocus-pocus."

Red Deer RCMP Insp. Larry Pearson said he supports Brown's investigations. "There are lots of things that happen and I don't think they could all be coincidences," he said. "I think the satanists are real. I know they're out there."

The Ontario Provincial Police (OPP) had one intelligence officer who specializes in following up on reports of occult involvement in criminal activity. He does not consider himself an expert in the field, and referred a reporter who was seeking background information on satanic cults to Dale Griffis. Griffis visited Toronto to give a lecture to a university group in the fall of 1986, and said that police in Ontario are increasingly concerned about cult involvement in crime.

Sgt. Bowen contacted the OPP occult specialist in July, 1985, and later testified, "He told me there is no concrete proof of a satanic cult operating in Ontario, although there are a lot of suspicions. He told me that there should be reports of naked people at any satanic rites and the sound of ringing bells. There are no such reports from the children." Sgt. Bowen noted in a police report, "He mentioned some incidents during satanic rites such as killing of a child that should occur and the children are obviously not relating them. It is quite clear no satanic cult is operating here."

The police continued to follow up all the leads that the Crown attorney had asked them to pursue in order to conclude an investigation that Harper said was largely a matter of "going through the motions." Sgt. Bowen and Sgt. Broom talked to many people who claimed to have information on satanists in the Hamilton area. One of these people had what had seemed to be a promising lead about Gary, but that turned out to be a case of mistaken identity. Most of these informants were not very credible. One man talked to the police about his belief that black witchcraft had been involved in a child murder in Hamilton in the early 1980s. This informant, who called himself The Ambassador, also tried to interest local television reporters in his story, but did little to enhance his credibility with them when he phoned to cancel an appointment because he had been unavoidably detained in the psychiatric hospital. A man who called himself Mickey Mouse was also anxious to help anyone who would listen to him. One reporter felt he had a hot lead when an informant promised to direct him to the site of a cult meeting, but was unable to follow up on this as the informant had multiple personalities, and the reporter was never again able to reach the right personality over the phone.

The police replied to the Crown attorney's letter on September 12, 1985: "For a number of reasons we have reached the conclusion that the children are mixing up reality and fiction. This case highlights some of the inherent conflicts between the social welfare philosophy and legal requirements necessary for a criminal conviction. The children's revelations result from leading questions made in the presence of each other. In a treatment atmosphere this may be appropriate, but not in a legal forum. We are drawn to the irresistible conclusion that the children have been assaulted, probably by Sharon and Gary Evans. The only evidence to support this is the vague ramblings of the two girls. They obviously cannot testify. Even if they did so, in a formal court setting in the presence of the abusers, they most likely would deny it happened. In the absence of any other evidence, we find that there is no evidence to support criminal charges."

CHAPTER 12

PSYCHOLOGICAL ASSESSMENTS

It was not enough for the social workers to say they believed the children. They had to show that it was a belief based on professional judgment rather than simple credulity. Then they had to present the evidence on which this judgment was based—the children's allegations—in a way that would convince a court that the children were telling the truth.

A team of two psychiatrists and a social worker from the Hospital for Sick Children played a crucial role in this process. They conducted an analysis of the children's statements that they believed was the most comprehensive of its kind ever undertaken. They concluded that the children were indeed telling the truth. Although Judge Beckett finally decided not to rely on the psychiatrists' conclusions, their report did lay out very clearly the basis upon which a reasonable person might decide that the children should be believed.

This conclusion was reinforced by assessments of the adults involved in the case carried out on behalf of the Children's Aid Society in the summer of 1985 by psychiatrists from Hamilton's Chedoke-McMaster Hospital. Social workers also gathered information on the family's background, attempting to contact day-care staff, teachers and other professionals who had dealt with the children.

Soon after the children were placed in their first foster home, the Children's Aid Society sent them to Dr. Alice Oliviera, a well-respected child psychiatrist, for therapy. After 26 play therapy sessions with the children, Dr. Oliviera concluded that Janis and Linda were describing their own experiences when they talked about sexual abuse, being forced to eat excrement and drink urine and witnessing events that they interpreted as murders. Dr. Oliviera said she did not think it possible that Janis and Linda were fantasizing in making these statements because they were peculiarly unimaginative children.

This opinion was underscored by the findings of a psychologist who conducted a series of personality tests with the children in the summer of 1985. Mani van der Spuy reported that he was struck by their lack of imagination. Janis particularly responded in a very uncreative way to a test in which she was asked to make up a story on the basis of pictures shown to her. Her stories were mostly extraordinarily detailed descriptions of what she saw in the pictures.

Dr. van der Spuy said he formed the impression from Janis's response to the tests that "there is a lot of darkness and sadness in her situation. She feels quite immobilized. She feels everything she has may be taken or destroyed by forces beyond her control." He said Linda's performance in the tests indicated a fragile hold on reality, and a poverty in relationships, feelings and thinking. "I almost get the idea that she experiences life, not in terms of cause and effect, but as a mine field, with here and there an explosion."

Dr. van der Spuy concluded, "I do not believe what they have reported about the past could be taken as fantasy. Their inner fantasy is too poorly developed to have fabricated those reports. Children who are inclined to confabulate may have somewhat pathological fantasies, but have a rich fantasy life."

While the emotional scars left by child sexual abuse are easily discernible on its victims, there is often no physical evidence, or, if there is, it is ambiguous and hard to detect. This seemed to be the case with Janis and Linda. The symptoms of psychological distress were clear for anyone to see, and the accounts of abuse so graphic, detailed and consistent that it was hard to come to any other conclusion but that they had been grossly abused. But a medical examination uncovered no conclusive evidence of physical damage. This lack of definitive medical proof of injury was another factor that made the police reluctant to lay criminal charges in the case.

To the lay person it sounds inconceivable that the kind of sexual assaults that the children described, involving numerous occurrences of abuse with vibrators and other foreign objects, could leave them physically unmarked and intact. Sgt. Broom told the court he believed that sexual abuse occurred because "[although] being a family man I know that children sometimes will lie, what they were saying appeared fairly graphic. They had to have some firsthand knowledge. But I find it difficult to believe the dildo wouldn't leave lasting telltale marks. I also found it difficult that there was no medical evidence of the blackbird's head being inserted."

But this lay understanding of the issue is incorrect, according to medical evidence heard by the court. The commonly held belief that doctors can determine whether or not a child has been sexually abused is a myth that, like the mistaken notion that such abuse is usually inflicted by strangers rather than friends or family members, stands in the way of understanding the nature of child sexual abuse. Unfortunately the fact that it is possible to inflict all kinds of sexual abuse on children without leaving any physical evidence is well known to many pedophiles, which can give them the edge over people who are seeking to protect children.

Angus MacMillan, an expert pediatrician from the Chedoke-McMaster Hospital, explained this to the court. When a child is being molested, he said, she is not necessarily aware of what part of her genitalia is being touched. Any touching in that area can cause intense pain and trauma. Fingers or objects may be inserted into the vaginal opening without penetrating beyond the hymen, and would cause great pain if they touched the hymen. Dr. MacMillan also explained that the hymen is an elastic membrane that is normally perforated with small holes of up to 4 millimeters in diameter. He said research has indicated that it is possible to insert an object with a diameter of up to 20 millimeters through one of these holes without tearing the membrane, thus leaving no physical evidence.

The most important aspect of any examination to determine if children have been sexually abused is, therefore, what the children themselves have to say, Dr. MacMillan explained.

Here he endorsed the CAS child abuse specialist's comments by telling the court, "We know that children rarely, if ever, lie about things of this nature. The *Journal of Child Abuse* will accept an article if you can show in detail how children lied about sexual abuse."

However, in the case of Janis and Linda there were also physical indications that they may have been abused, Dr. MacMillan said. He had first examined the children before they went into foster care, because of difficulties they were having at school as a result of Linda's hyperactivity and Janis's emotional problems. At that time he was not looking for any signs of sexual abuse, but rather was concerned that Linda's medical record indicated that she had suffered from a vaginal yeast infection five months earlier. At her age such an infection was, he said, an extreme rarity, and would lead one to consider the possibility of a foreign body being introduced to the vaginal area.

Dr. MacMillan found no physical evidence of recent abuse when he examined Linda at the request of the Children's Aid Society soon after the children had made their allegations of abuse. But his examination of Janis at that time revealed that the child had a particularly wide vaginal orifice. The holes that perforate the hymen are normally no wider than 4 millimeters, but Janis's were 7 millimeters in diameter. It would be possible to insert an index finger, he said, while leaving the hymen intact. This suggested that the orifice had in fact been expanded by perforation by a finger or some other object, he said, but the evidence was not conclusive.

In reviewing the medical history of the two children, Dr. MacMillan noted several injuries and illnesses that he said were warning signs of child abuse. He said he had never seen a child with a history of as many head injuries as Janis, who was treated five times in one year for bruises or cuts on the head. Dr. MacMillan said he also would be very concerned about the fact that Linda was treated for trauma on three occasions in three different hospitals between the ages of 20 months and two years.

Arthur Brown, the mother's lawyer, who usually questioned experts at length, started to quiz the doctor about the allegations concerning the bird. The foster mother had mentioned that she had the impression from the children's descriptions that the bird they were referring to was a grackle. Mr. Brown asked Dr. MacMillan if he was at all familiar with a bird known as a grackle, suggesting that it was quite a large bird and unlikely to be inserted into the girls without causing injury. After asking the lawyer if he was referring to the Common Grackle or some other species, the doctor displayed a fund of ornithological knowledge, and explained with the help of drawings how the grackle, which has a relatively small head, could well be inserted a little way into a child's external genitalia, causing pain and trauma but no injuries.

Dr. MacMillan said his physical findings were compatible with the children being abused by hand, with bananas and with birds. Asked if he found such allegations of bizarre abuse difficult to accept, the doctor somberly told the court, "I have been quite disillusioned by what I find human beings capable of doing. Anything living or dead has been put into the sexual parts of children. I find it all hard to accept."

Other psychiatric professionals called by the CAS were Dr. Gail Beck, who examined the foster mother, and two other psychiatrists who contributed assessments of Sharon and Gordon Wells. Dr. Eva Gede, who examined Sharon, was a small, efficient woman with a somewhat abrupt and aggressive manner. She was asked to do the assessment because she was a specialist in the psychosocial disorders of women, and had a special interest in multiple personality disorders, a problem that it had been felt Sharon might be suffering from. She did not in fact find that Sharon had multiple personalities, but did conclude that she was suffering from another form of mental illness, a borderline personality disorder.

In interviews with the psychiatrist Sharon said the allegations were gross, that she had never heard of such stuff or even imagined it in her wildest dreams. Sharon said she thought it must all have come from the foster mother, and that Mrs. McInnis must be "sick." She said, "I want to get my kids back and find out what the hell went on with them, who did what with them and why. I know it's not me."

Sharon confided in the psychiatrist that she didn't trust adults, felt safe with kids and dreamed of opening a day-care center. She said, "All men have ever done in my life is complicate it." She admitted that she was not the best housekeeper in the world, or the most stable of people, but said she tried to be strong and do what was right for her children. She said the allegations had destroyed her relationship with Gary Evans. "He loved kids, that's what attracted me to him," she said.

"It's destroyed something so beautiful and wonderful that we all had, all of us. It hurts because I know how much love there was. He blames me for what's happened, because I got weak and I wasn't strong. He says if I would have been stronger this would not have happened. And he's right. He says I wrecked his life. I think that this has destroyed a perfectly happy family that we could have been."

"It sounds as if he wants your kids more than he wants you," said Dr. Gede.

"We love each other a lot and there was a great family reunion in love between all of us," Sharon said.

Dr. Gede confronted Sharon in her interviews, suggesting that the woman's life was moving from crisis to crisis, that she wasn't able to cope with her problems and that she was looking to her children to give her the kind of nurture and emotional support that she was unable to give them herself. She said that the mother did not know what it takes to be independent: "You wouldn't be here if you did."

"I wouldn't be here if the damn CAS didn't have my kids," Sharon replied.

The psychiatrist told Sharon that she seemed to have made the same mistakes over and over again in her life, to which the young woman replied, "I never made the same mistakes. They were always different mistakes.

"My kids give me a lot of security because my life is dedicated to them," Sharon said. "They're why I'm going on. They're why I'm facing things."

She said she had learned through her experience with the CAS to be stronger, and that they will never get another chance to take her kids again. She pointed out that she had put the children in foster care in the first place: "I could have kept them home. I could have beat them. Who the hell would have known what I did to my kids?

"I just feel like all my life I have had to defend myself," Sharon told the psychiatrist. "This is not a problem. This is a major catastrophe. This could wreck so many lives. I'm accused of child molesting, killing. You tell me what company is going to hire me if this ever gets out, and it's getting out like wildfire. So many people are finding out. If you were a day-care-center person and you found out about these allegations, are you going to hire me? No. Do you see what this has done? I wanted to go back to school. I wanted to work with kids."

Dr. Gede said, "You need a lot from your children."

"Is that so wrong?" Sharon asked passionately.

"A parent is not supposed to need," said the psychiatrist.

"Who says that? It's not as if I sit there and cry every detail out to them. It's just that I feel strong when they're there like that. I don't think it's wrong."

The mother said she felt betrayed because she had thought that the psychiatrist was just going to be determining whether or not she was crazy, not analyzing her whole life. Dr. Gede told her, "You're definitely not crazy. You're not psychotic."

"You've got to be psycho or crazy to be in a cult to kill children," Sharon said, repeating that she had no idea how her children could be saying such things about her.

"There's no smoke where there's no fire. That's the problem," said Dr. Gede.

Dr. Gede observed as a result of this interview that Sharon's "insight into emotionally threatening issues is limited." She said, "I have a gut feeling that Mrs. Wells thinks that, if she gets her children back, Gary will return to her. Their relationship was very much inclusive of the children. She regards competent parenting as providing the absolute basics. She openly admits she needs children, from whom she derives strength, comfort, et cetera. . . . Her dream to own a day-care center, where she would never run out of children, I think, was quite unrealistic. When asked about emotionally uncomfortable or conflicting material, her memory gets hazy. It's also possible that she may be trying to withhold information that would put her in a bad light."

Sharon was asked to undergo a psychological test, which consisted of a long multiple-choice questionnaire known as the Minnesota Multiphasic Personality Inventory (MMPI). This is a standard tool psychologists use to evaluate personality. The psychologist who analyzed Sharon Wells's test results noted that the woman "was capable of some pretty bizarre behavior." The psychologist said, "Traditional psychotherapies with persons with a similar profile is extremely difficult because of their almost total inability to accept responsibility for their actions. This is not a healthy profile, and this person is in need of major psychosocial intervention, but it is unlikely she would agree."

Dr. Gede also analyzed Sharon's hospital records, noting that she had apparently been treated three times for drug overdoses. The psychiatrist put some stress on the fact that during one of these hospital admissions she was described as hostile and paranoid and was treated with an antipsychotic drug. Psychosis is a more serious stage of mental illness where a patient loses contact with reality, and has delusions and, sometimes, hallucinations. Dr. Gede did not conclude that Sharon was psychotic, however, but that she suffered from a borderline personality disorder.

"Her knowledge of stability and security is limited. Her ability to relate to adults is seriously impaired. She is dependent and very needy and unable to have her needs met. She can be impulsive in a destructive and self-destructive manner. She can probably control people who back off from her anger fairly effectively because she is not easy to take on. Her ability to understand children's emotional needs is limited, her relationship with them is self-centered and self-serving. She exploits children emotionally, and does not even know it," said the psychiatrist.

Dr. Gede concluded, "Her capacity for insight and judgment into her own problems is poor. Her psychological defenses include denial, projection and distortion. These defenses are characteristic of the psychotic mental illness and of the most severe personality disorders. . . . She does have a mental disorder that can, at times, produce brief periods of psychosis. With lots of support and counseling she may be able to get by, somehow, from crisis to crisis, as she has done in the past. Since she doesn't have insight into what her problems are, her prognosis is very guarded."

Another assessment of Sharon was done by a psychiatrist hired on her behalf and called as a defense witness. His conclusions about her mental state were similar to Dr. Gede's, though he tried to present them in a better light and was more optimistic about the prospects of successful therapy.

Dr. Naomi Rae-Grant did an assessment of Gordon Wells and concluded that he showed no evidence of a psychotic or neurotic disorder. A psychologist said the father's personality profile was "not a particularly healthy profile." Tests revealed mild disturbance in thinking, with poor concentration, vagueness and some difficulty in relations with authority figures.

Dr. Rae-Grant stated in her report, "His description of his interaction with his estranged wife suggests a pathological relationship in terms of the degree of anger and dyscontrol which he feels Sharon was able to arouse in him. The history of violent, aggressive episodes suggests the possibility of an intermittent, explosive disorder, but further assessment would be necessary to confirm this impression. Mr. Well's description of his interactions with Janis and Linda suggests genuine concern for and attachment to the children."

The father told the psychiatrist that he had left school at 15 because "they weren't teaching me anything." He said he did not associate much with his family because he had too many arguments with them, and too many things had gone wrong. He said he had a job, and spent his time working, partying and fending for himself: "When you get street-wise, you get out there and take care of things." He said his hobbies were martial arts, weight lifting, art and photography.

Gordon described himself as a man who likes to resolve problems simply: "I should walk in there, bang, bang, bang, get the right answer. I hate problems that drag on. It starts to irritate me. Sometimes I get up and go. I can be in a rotten mood, and don't like to be around anybody. I sit in my room, draw or write until something's done about it, or I can solve it myself."

With Sharon, Gordon said, "I would say, 'Quit bothering me, or something's going to happen.' I lost control a couple of times, quite a few times. She used to bait me all the time, until I would turn around with no warning and do something. She used to say, 'You don't like fighting,' and call me chicken. She would call me a maniac. I used to warn her, 'Don't do it,' or I would be out of control. I didn't want to hit her. I would rather hit the wall than hit her. If somebody bugs me too much, I warn them. Then it's in their own hands. Everyone knows to leave me alone. Don't bait me. Just back off."

Dr. Rae-Grant did not take the confrontational approach that Dr. Gede had adopted in her interview with Sharon.

Gordon said he was now glad to be away from his ex-wife. He said she would not back down in confrontations with him and "used to get a thrill out of seeing me explode." He said, "She could be pleasant as hell, a great actor when she wants to be . . . I seen her in action, lying, she does a good job. I don't trust her. She's too crafty for what she wants."

He described a conversation with Sharon after he heard about the children's allegations. "I've told my wife, 'If it's true, God help you,' 'cause I told her a long time ago that I put the kids on earth to turn around and raise them up and have a life of their own, not for two screwballs to come along and screw it up. And she said, 'Do you think I could do that?' I said, 'I really don't know.' I said, 'Between you and Gary, I don't know. You've gone so far, now, because of your relationship with him, that half the time I don't think you care about the kids.'

"She put so much junk into their heads," he told the psychiatrist. "As far as I'm concerned I'm glad it's all coming out.

"The kids said I was supposed to eliminate the foster mother. I laughed at that one. The kids are so bollixed up because of being pumped too much. I said, 'I'm trying to fight for my kids, not screw them up.'"

Gordon described Sharon before her first psychiatric hospital admission. He said he found her "in the storage closet with the lights turned out, curled up. She said, 'I don't want to hurt the kids.' It was like she was a six-year-old again. Fast forward picture. She went through her whole childhood. You could see the stages she was going through, coming back up to when she was 22."

He said his ex-wife was always a very lousy housekeeper. He said the relationship was "okay till the end. It sort of went downhill. When I switched over to not hitting the kids, she started hitting them for every little thing going."

The children, he said, were looking better when he saw them in May: "They were getting fed better. Linda filled out more. I don't like the fact Sharon put them in there, but they were looking better."

The psychiatrist asked him why he had threatened Lesley Morgan when he talked to her on the phone, and he said he had merely responded to a question she asked by saying, "Do yourself a favor. It will be the first and last time you ask me that question, if you value anything [meaning her job]."

Asked about the so-called picture of the devil, Gordon said, "I drew a picture ten to fifteen years ago as the devil. I went to a show one night, seen it and re-created it. It meant nothing, just something I drew. I'm an artist and I drew it. Everybody's been calling it the devil. Call it what you want. The cop thought it was a big joke. People want to destroy it, and all it is is a picture. It's got nothing to do with satanism or anything else."

Dr. Rae-Grant noted that, during Mr. Wells's videotaped visit with the children, Linda frequently clung to him, hugged him and kissed him, while Janis was ambivalent, extremely angry and resentful, but with some warm feelings. She said the child punched him, pummeled him and took his car keys, but he maintained a calm, caring attitude.

Gordon told the psychiatrist that his children "need to be back with me and a normal home life."

Gary Evans was given an opportunity to be assessed by either Dr. Gede or Dr. Rae-Grant. He talked to them both, but did not show up for the assessments. He later claimed that this was because he thought they would be biased against him. Gary was subsequently assessed by Dr. Clive Chamberlain, a psychiatrist commissioned by Gary's lawyer. Dr. Chamberlain testified as a defense witness. Although Dr. Gede and Dr. Rae-Grant were called as CAS witnesses at the hearing, there was no suggestion that their assessments of the two parents were in any way biased or unprofessional.

As the CAS began to piece together the results of all these assessments, the children's allegations of abuse appeared more credible than the parents' total denial that anything untoward had ever taken place.

CHAPTER 13
THE ASSESSMENT TEAM

The analysis of the children's credibility conducted by the assessment team from the Hospital for Sick Children was an important new development in child sexual abuse investigation. Their report presented a technique for analyzing the credibility of children's prior statements without conducting further interviews with the children. Since it is generally recognized that it is bad for children to have to repeat allegations several times to different people, this method provided a useful new analytical tool. Its use in a court case where the children were not going to be required to testify also promised to open up new possibilities in child welfare law.

This ground-breaking study was first conceived in a meeting on June 25, 1985, at which the case was discussed and Catherine McInnis was asked to read some excerpts from her notes. In attendance were the CAS representatives, Sgt. Broom and two psychiatrists and a social worker from the Hospital for Sick Children. After discussing the case with CAS representatives and hearing Mrs. McInnis's presentation, the hospital team decided not to interview Janis and Linda. They felt they had sufficient data in the notes of the foster mother and transcripts of other interviews with the children. They concluded that further interviews could be disruptive to the

159

girls' therapy, and might be counterproductive, as they could frighten the children into recanting their allegations.

Halina Klajner-Diamond, the social worker from the Toronto hospital, had been involved in about 550 cases of child abuse during her four years at the hospital's Suspected Child Abuse and Neglect Unit. Describing the meeting to the court she said, "Mrs. McInnis came across as very sincere, committed, credible and concerned about the welfare of the children. She was upset and talked about the pressure she was under. She said that people would think she was a kook. My own feelings were, 'This is incredible. I don't want to believe this. I can't believe it.' I kept listening to the details, and became really prepared to believe we should look into this. It shouldn't be dismissed just because I don't want to listen to it."

Dr. Paul Steinhauer, senior staff psychiatrist at the Hospital for Sick Children, said that he went to the meeting with "a bias that this couldn't be true." He described himself as being highly suspicious of the claims of some of his colleagues in the profession, who seem to maintain that anything children say is true.

"At first I was reluctant to listen. It was extremely hard to take, very upsetting," said Dr. Steinhauer. "We have a natural human tendency not to believe those things could go on, to think, 'It can't be true. Nobody could treat children in this way. Things this horrendous couldn't have happened.' I went in with the feeling that, if it did go on, we have a responsibility to help the kids, and not to support the allegations if they are untrue. As the meeting went on I became increasingly sure that there was substantial truth and I spent part of the meeting trying to figure out where that feeling was coming from. So, I was partly listening and I was partly trying to analyze this new thing, what it was that was making me think that this is truthful."

At the end of the meeting Dr. Steinhauer told the CAS representatives, "I think I can analyze those notes in a way that will demonstrate that there are enough factors supporting validity and reliability that I think they may be of some support to your case."

The defense lawyers would later point to this statement as evidence that the hospital team did not approach their analysis of the children's statements from an objective scientific standpoint, but began by believing that the children were telling the truth, and then tried to find evidence to support this belief. This criticism perhaps failed to do justice to the rigor of the analysis that Dr. Steinhauer subsequently undertook. It also displayed some misunderstanding of the scientific method, as even the most objective study must begin with theories and observations.

The argument turned out to be irrelevant to the judge's final decision, as Judge Beckett neatly defused what might have become the most controversial legal issue to arise from the case by stating in his judgment that he gave no weight to the psychiatrists' report. The judge said he was impressed by the report, and did not question the credibility or thoroughness of the psychiatrists' evidence. But he said it was his job, not that of expert witnesses, to decide whether or not the children were telling the truth. This was a shrewd decision because the defense lawyers had vigorously tried to introduce evidence from witnesses who would challenge this report. Judge Beckett had deemed the evidence they wished to call inadmissible because he didn't consider their witnesses to be expert enough to testify. By saying that he was not considering the hospital report, Judge Beckett removed one very strong basis on which his final ruling might be appealed.

In coming to the same conclusion as the assessment team, Judge Beckett gave strikingly similar reasons. He simply observed that analyzing credibility may be a new field for psychiatrists but judges have been doing it for generations and using the same criteria: consistency, detail, inappropriate knowledge of sexual matters and emotional and physical reactions while witnesses related their stories. What the report and the psychiatrists' evidence did for the judge was organize the children's allegations and the factors supporting their credibility in such a way that it was possible for him to examine them for himself and reach the same conclusion about the girls' sincerity.

While the assessment of credibility is an age-old responsibility for judges, it is a comparatively new task for psychiatrists. In treatment situations psychiatrists generally do not concern themselves with whether or not their patients are telling the truth, since their concern is more with the individual's subjective interpretation of reality. What patients have to say is often seen as a symptom of their disturbance, rather than as a description of what has happened to them. According to many child abuse experts, the tendency of psychiatrists not to take what their patients say at face value has prevented the high incidence of incest from being recognized in the past because complaints have always been dismissed as father fixations and infantile sexual fantasies.

The recognition that child sexual abuse is a widespread problem, and the fact that children's disclosures are often the only evidence for this abuse, has made it necessary for psychiatrists and child care workers to find ways of determining when children should be believed. In reaction to the centuries of disbelief in this phenomenon, some professionals maintain that children never lie about parental sexual abuse, but studies and court cases have shown this not to be the case. In all the public controversy that has surrounded the recent increase in concern and litigation about child sexual abuse, how to determine when children are telling the truth is one of the most central and sensitive issues.

The study that the team from the Hospital for Sick Children conducted on the allegations of Janis and Linda has since been discussed in workshops, conferences and articles submitted for publication in psychiatric journals. The study and the subsequent research that came out of it are expected to have a lasting impact on the development of methods for the assessment of children's credibility.

Dr. Steinhauer told the court, "I can't conceive of a case that has been looked at more thoroughly than this one has. We went beyond anything anyone else has done to develop criteria to allow us to look critically at what children were saying." He said the study applied "the most rigorous set of criteria that we know of."

Although the judge felt the criteria were similar to those normally used in court cases, they also involved the application of psychiatric insights into children's behavior. All of the information was subjected to a more scientific analysis than that usually undertaken by a court. Various repeated elements of the children's statements, such as the references to the bird, or eating "poo," were isolated and codified. Then each reference was recorded in a way that details of the girls' accounts and accompanying symptoms could be compared.

Ms. Klajner-Diamond told the court that the team concluded on the basis of the study that "there is no doubt sexual abuse occurred, probably much as depicted. Despite some confusion due to insufficient detail, lack of clarity, there is enough likelihood that the murders and cannibalism have basis in fact that a vigorous investigation should be undertaken.

On the basis of this we believe that Linda and Janis were talking to Mrs. McInnis of experiences they have been participants in or observed, that there is no other credible explanation for what the girls have been saying and for their associated behaviors."

When the social worker and the two psychiatrists were later presented with further evidence of additional statements made by the children, they said they became more confident that the murders and rituals actually took place as the girls described them. Dr. Steinhauer testified, "There is no way these kids were not involved in rituals along the lines of those described. I am convinced people were being killed, that they were forced to stick knives in victims. As to whether the flesh they ate was human or not, there is a possibility for error. We found nothing that allowed me to draw any conclusion other than the fact that what the children described was actually experienced."

Dr. William Wehrspann, the second psychiatrist on the team, explained that the psychiatric symptoms of distress that the children displayed when telling their stories were particularly convincing: "There's no way to coach this. In cases proven to be fictitious, they are not present. We're talking real primitive stuff here. These kids literally had the crap scared out of them."

Dr. Steinhauer said the children's stories were consistent with one another over a long period of time, and contained the kind of detail, described from a child's eye view, "that they just couldn't have imagined, or couldn't have been led to say by too-aggressive questioning." He said he was also convinced by the "embedded responses," by which some external stimulus reminded the children of something that their memories had suppressed. Dr. Wehrspann elaborated on this phenomenon by saying, "Nobody's setting this up. They go to a funeral and ask if someone's been killed. They've got killing on the brain."

The psychiatrists noted that the conversations between the children, where Janis tried to get Linda to retract her statements, also served to confirm that the allegations were true. "There is not one denial by Janis where the reader does not end up being more convinced of the truth of material being denied," Dr. Steinhauer observed. He added that the children's apparent ambivalence in their feelings towards their parents and the extreme conflict they showed in making their disclosures are not seen in children who are confabulating: "There's a real conflict going on in the souls of these little girls."

The team from the Hospital for Sick Children did consider in their report the possibility that Mrs. McInnis might have fabricated her accounts of the children's conversations and concluded that she had not.

Dr. Wehrspann, an American who often entertained the court with his colorful turn of phrase, said, "If Catherine McInnis is making this up she's Tennessee Williams, she's Shakespeare. The characters are wonderful.

"This woman is a really good reporter, a very good observer. It's very good quality description. I was impressed with the way she delivered under pressure. When I read over Catherine McInnis's notes, I sat there nauseated with a headache. I don't think you can be human and not read through these notes and have a violent reaction," said Dr. Wehrspann.

The psychiatrist observed that this kind of material would be particularly hard for someone to listen to once they became convinced that what was being described was something that really happened. He explained that it is only to be expected that the foster mother should have started to show symptoms of distress, and that her reports should become blemished with such things as editorial comments and coded references: "Nobody wants to see this, and it's hard to look at this. This weird stuff is really bothering her. She gets a threat to her life and family. She doesn't think the police are willing to support and protect her. It is a very, very traumatic experience. It would be traumatic for any of us. It's important to realize the magnitude of this event in someone's life. We thought she was real upset for legitimate reasons."

Dr. Steinhauer said he was impressed by the foster mother's vigilance, perceptivity and sensitivity to subverbal communication. "Her natural reserve causes considerable discomfort with lurid outpourings of sexual data," he said. "Her indignation and repugnance made it difficult to cope with material which clearly she found morally repulsive. She struggled to overcome a tendency to be judgmental. Basically I find her a very fine foster mother. I have enormous respect for her compassion and strength."

In his court testimony, Dr. Steinhauer said, "I am repelled and discomforted by this material. It was difficult for me. Just the reopening of the thing [in preparation for his testimony] was sufficiently upsetting that I woke up at 3 A.M. and couldn't get back to sleep. She was dealing with this repugnant material on a daily basis. At the Hospital for Sick Kids' meeting I was feeling a bit nauseous at the end of the meeting."

After reviewing the evidence about the second pair of children that Mrs. McInnis had in her home, Dr. Wehrspann said, "Catherine McInnis has overinvested in those stories being true. The children deliver their stories to other people in the same style, with the same characters, giving references to details of where they live, who their friends were. It would be difficult for Catherine McInnis to know these things."

He said he was satisfied that the children were not parroting what Mrs. McInnis had told them, or being coached by her, in making these other reports. He added, "I am very sensitive about how hard it is to get people to change. If people could get people to behave in a way they want so easily, being a psychiatrist or parent would be much easier."

The Sick Children's Hospital report also considered whether the details in the story could be based on a dream or an extended fantasy shared by Janis and Linda, or an attempt to please adults with material they suspected that the adults wanted to hear. The team concluded that, although the children sometimes tried to disguise their descriptions as a dream, the detail and their physical and emotional reactions indicated that they were talking about real experiences. A lack of motive on the part of either the children or the foster mother to fabricate material, and the apparent authenticity of the material, as indicated by their structural analysis, led the team to conclude that it was unlikely that the foster mother had done anything but faithfully record what the children had said. This was also the conclusion that Judge Beckett would eventually reach.

Dr. Steinhauer noted that the conversation about plucking or fucking a chicken was "the sort of thing that people don't make up." He said the girls' descriptions were replete with details that normal children would not make up. For example, he said the description of being lowered into an open grave had "a quality of detail, a quality of horror. You get it from what she sees and what she smells.

"Either these girls have the most unbelievable imaginations, an unbelievable ability to make up these incredibly lurid stories, or they are talking about something that happened to them," said Dr. Steinhauer.

When Arthur Brown cross-examined Dr. Steinhauer about some inconsistencies in the children's stories, such as a certain ambiguity about whether it was their father or mother who had murdered little Elizabeth, the psychiatrist replied, "If you happen to be a small child, and are exposed to multiple murders in the middle of the night, and tell a dozen different people, and people are wearing masks and costumes, you may be confused as to who murdered whom.

"Regardless of what happened," Dr. Steinhauer added, "these are very disturbed girls, and the relationship with their parents and Gary is very much related to the source of their disturbance." He said it would be disastrous to allow these people to have access to the children, when they deny the allegations and inspire the girls with fear. Seeing these people would be "upsetting and traumatic, beyond these children's ability to cope," he said. "One of the biggest tragedies, often worse than abuse, is the efforts by parents in a position of trust to distort children's reality by denying what happened. As long as that much fear is associated with the parents, as long as parents continue to take no responsibility for anything that has happened, it undermines any chance of anyone working successfully with them to change anything."

On the future of the children, Dr. Wehrspann said, "Can you imagine what these children would have to go through before they can trust somebody else? It's going to take a big effort on some adult's part to stick with these children. They started trusting Catherine, and then the threat came and they never saw Catherine again."

Observing that Sharon Wells did at times seek help for herself and her children, Dr. Steinhauer said, "It is possible that this woman is very torn, one part of her wanting the girls to re-experience what she went through, the other part trying to protect them. I would have great concern about Mrs. Wells being any more able to parent another infant more successfully than she has those two children. There is nothing here to suggest optimism that it wouldn't just be a repeat of the same thing."

Michael O'Neail, Gary Evans's lawyer, asked Dr. Steinhauer, "Other than allegations of sexual abuse, have you a basis for assessing the parenting capacity of Gary?"

The doctor responded, "That's like saying 'Other than cancer, what's wrong with the patient?'"

At a meeting on July 29, 1985, the Hospital for Sick Children team presented their preliminary report, which indicated that they believed the sexual abuse allegations and felt that there was enough credibility to the murder allegations to warrant a vigorous investigation. Sgt. Broom and Sgt. Bowen were present but did not appear to be impressed with these findings.

Dr. Steinhauer told the court, "In the first interview, the younger man was reasonably open and hadn't reached any conclusions. In the second meeting the young man didn't open his mouth. The older man seemed to have his mind made up. He was radiating disbelief and disrespect. He took no part in the meeting, except to mutter under his breath. He wasn't interested in what we had to say. I had the feeling that, because these were children, the police tended to dismiss what they were saying as inconsequential. We were giving a highly technical, state-of-the-art analysis, adding to it confirmation from a number of other sources. Bowen was saying, 'We're really not interested in what you are saying.' The police had never seen any of our material at all."

Sgt. Bowen testified that he had tried not to "show an attitude" at the meeting, but was very tired because he had been on night duty. He said he was bothered by a comment made by Dr. Wehrspann, who had told him, he said, that lots of charges had been laid with less evidence than this. Sgt. Bowen said that the psychiatrist suggested that the CAS should see the judge in chambers before the defense lawyers were involved, and try to make him sympathetic to the case.

Dr. Steinhauer contrasted the police unwillingness to believe the children, or to even listen to people who did believe their stories, with the courage displayed by Mrs. McInnis in speaking up on the children's behalf even though she was afraid of ridicule, and eventually began to be afraid for her safety. He was asked if he felt the foster mother was being paranoid in her response to the alleged plot to kill her family, and he responded, "There are times when we, perhaps inappropriately, have felt anxiety about our involvement in so terrible a business.

"I wonder whether in the past things like this have gone on, where people haven't had the courage to bring the information forward," Dr. Steinhauer said.

PART FOUR
THE TRIAL

CHAPTER 14

CHILD WELFARE AND THE COURTS

There is perhaps no subject on which so many people in our society would agree as the need to protect and care for children. While there may be bitter disputes about issues such as abortion, day-care and education, the basic premise that children should receive adequate care and be protected from injury and molestation is universally accepted, irrespective of other social, political or religious beliefs. Even among the most hardened criminals, the child abuser is an object of hatred and contempt.

This universal respect for the basic rights of children is something comparatively new in society. The notion that children are more than the property of their parents, have a distinct status and need special protection in law developed in the 19th century. It was inspired in part by the Romantic movement, which tended to sanctify and sometimes sentimentalize the child, placing particular emphasis on education and the spiritual or emotional growth of the individual. Industrial development began to require an educated workforce and public education programs constituted a first step towards recognizing that the state should play a role in children's lives. The brutal excesses of early industrial society and the breakup of traditional communities led to flagrant cases of cruelty and exploitation of children, and more humane and progressive elements in society responded to this by shaping new child welfare laws and institutions.

While criminal and most civil law has evolved through decrees, statutes and precedents for more than a thousand years, child welfare law is mostly new, and still in a state of flux. When it first developed in the 19th century, the emphasis was on saving children from unsavory backgrounds by placing them in institutions. Institutions were eventually found to be inadequate to serve children's emotional needs, and foster care was seen as a more desirable alternative. Now it is recognized, and in fact stated as a principle in Ontario's new *Child and Family Services Act*, that the best place for a child to be, if at all possible, is in his or her own home. Instead of saving children from the unfit home, social agencies now devote a lot of energy to trying to make the home fit for the child, giving support to the family through therapy, public health nurses, homemakers and other social or educational programs.

The first principle of Ontario's child welfare laws remains, however, the best interests and protection of children. The law provides that, when it is found that children cannot be protected in their own homes, they can be made wards of the Crown, their parents can, if necessary, be deprived of access and all other parental rights, and the children can be kept in foster care, institutional care or put out for adoption. To make such an order, a judge must be satisfied through a hearing that the children are in need of protection, and that this protection can only be insured by separating them from their parents or guardians.

Child welfare proceedings, which are directed to the protection of children, are not governed by the same rules as criminal trials. There is no question here of guilt or innocence, and the judge is mandated to achieve a solution that is in the best interests of the child. Society has decided that in criminal cases the risk of punishing an innocent person is far graver than that of letting a guilty one go free, and has therefore evolved very stringent standards of proof and a series of laws and precedents that protect individual rights and freedoms. But the risk of leaving children unprotected in an abusive home is considered just as serious as that of unjustly depriving parents of their rights.

The judge in a child welfare hearing does not have to

make a finding that is beyond any reasonable doubt, but must weigh the evidence and make a ruling based on the balance of probabilities. In a criminal trial, hearsay evidence, second-hand reports of what other people said, is generally excluded. Hearsay evidence, and even expert opinion based on such hearsay, may be admitted in a child welfare hearing, where the children are often considered too young to testify. The emphasis is not on proving that certain specific acts were perpetrated, but on making a decision based on all the circumstances affecting a child's life.

The Hamilton-Wentworth Children's Aid Society was anxious that the police do a full investigation of Janis's and Linda's allegations, and was clearly anticipating some kind of criminal prosecution. Having failed to find strong corroborating evidence that they could take to court, the police and the Crown attorney decided not to lay any charges. In a criminal trial it would have been necessary to rely on the children's evidence. Even if it had been decided that the children were fit to endure the traumatic experience of testifying in court, under legislation in place in 1985 it would have been necessary first to prove that they were competent to testify, and then have additional corroborating evidence, since the law did not consider a child's testimony to be as reliable as that of an adult.

Legislation passed in 1987 has made it easier for children to testify and have their evidence given the same consideration as adult witnesses'. This involves removing the requirements that children face a special competency test, and that their evidence must be corroborated. They still have to satisfy a judge and jury that they can communicate, and that they understand that they have to tell the truth. Child welfare advocates are hoping that the courts will liberally interpret the meaning of the word "communicate" so that Anatomically Correct dolls and other such aids can be used by very young witnesses. The most important consequence of these changes is that children will not face an initial predisposition, which has hitherto been enshrined in law, not to trust children's evidence.

The peculiar problem that children present to the justice system is illustrated by the fact that, while there is a movement towards giving the same credibility to children's evidence as that of adults', it is also being recognized that it is necessary to make special arrangements, such as the use of videotapes or closed circuit television, to save children from the ordeal of actually appearing in a courtroom. Although some jurisdictions in the United States do allow hearsay evidence in special circumstances, this is not accepted in criminal proceedings in Canada. In criminal trials in Canada children, who are easily intimidated and usually have conflicting feelings about disclosing parental abuse, must still face cross-examination from lawyers representing their parents, the people they usually most love and most fear.

The new criminal legislation allows the use in court of statements made by children before the trial, providing these were videotaped and made within a reasonable time after the alleged abuse occurred. This is only permitted if the child is to be available in court for cross-examination. Child welfare advocates are hoping that this will avoid the necessity of children testifying in many cases, and that in practice defense lawyers will often refrain from cross-examining the children.

Judge Beckett was most insistent that Janis and Linda should not be forced to testify or be cross-examined at the Crown wardship hearing. Their therapist stated that it would be extremely damaging for them to be forced to dredge up their traumatic memories again. When Arthur Brown, the mother's lawyer, suggested calling the girls as witnesses, the judge flew into a rage and told the lawyer that taking such a step would be tantamount to subjecting the children to "ritual torture."

In the Hamilton case videotapes were shown to avoid calling the children as witnesses. These videotapes were of therapy sessions rather than investigative interviews and by viewing that kind of material the court was breaking new ground. The judge used the tapes to see for himself what the emotional state of the children was and to have a better basis on which to assess the opinions of their therapist.

The main problem encountered in this novel use of videotapes was that it took a long time for the court to view them. Almost a month at the beginning of the trial was occupied with the court watching play-therapy sessions. It was not until the therapist testified nine months later that the judge was given an insight on the significance of the interactions he had observed on tape.

Another reason for the extreme length of the Hamilton hearing was that the approach the Children's Aid Society took to the case involved presenting every piece of evidence that could conceivably be relevant. The CAS feared that defense lawyers would make a determined effort to discredit the more bizarre and less substantial aspects of the children's stories. The agency therefore sought to prove that, even if the children's allegations were found to be lacking in credibility, there were grounds for making them wards of the Crown on the basis of the violence, abuse and neglect that they had been exposed to in their home environment. Arthur Brown, Sharon's lawyer, consented to the admission of most of the evidence that the CAS proposed to call, on the condition that all other evidence that could have a bearing on the case be introduced. Sixty-one people were called as witnesses.

By the time Mrs. McInnis completed her testimony it was the end of January, 1986, and the hearing had been underway for four months. Some of that time had been taken up with preliminary matters, delays while reports were filed and studied, and short recesses caused by holidays and scheduling problems. The court had heard the evidence of social workers, teachers and day-care staff, as well as that of the foster mother.

Sharon Wells, who had been more than four months pregnant when the hearing began, was due to give birth at the beginning of February, so the court went into recess to await this event. Just days after her baby girl was born, the Children's Aid Society obtained a warrant to apprehend the infant and take her into care. The agency sought to have the baby declared a ward of the Crown on the basis of the abuse and neglect suffered by her two halfsisters. Sharon instructed her lawyer, Arthur Brown, to oppose this. The baby's father, Gary Evans, who had left Sharon shortly after he made her pregnant, retained Michael O'Neail to oppose the wardship application on his behalf.

Since the CAS was relying on the allegations regarding the older children to make its case for guardianship of the baby, it was agreed by all lawyers that the best way to proceed would be to join the trial of the baby's case to the hearing that was already underway. The addition of the new baby to the case complicated the proceedings somewhat from a legal point of view, as new legislation had come into effect since the case of Janis and Linda began. Fortunately for all concerned, although there are several significant differences between the old *Child Welfare Act* and the new *Child and Family Services Act*, they did not have much bearing on the conduct of this case. The new act states as a matter of principle that, while the best interest of children is its paramount objective, support should be given where possible to the autonomy and integrity of the family unit, and that the course of action chosen to protect the child should be the least disruptive one available.

The new statute also leaves less to the discretion of the judge by defining more clearly the grounds that can be used to find that children are in need of protection. The basis for deciding whether or not Janis and Linda were judged to be "children in need of protection" was the *Child Welfare Act* of Ontario, 1980, section 19 (b) xi: "a child whose life, health or morals may be endangered by the conduct of the person whose charge the child is." The *Child and Family Services Act*, 1984, spells out the circumstances under which such a finding can be made. It cites physical harm and sexual abuse, or the risk that either of these will happen in the future, as possible grounds for finding that the children need protection. It also states that a judge may base a finding on the child having suffered or being at risk of suffering "emotional harm, demonstrated by severe anxiety, depression, withdrawal, or self-destructive or aggressive behavior." To make a finding on the basis of emotional harm, the judge must be satisfied that the child's parent or caretaker does not provide, refuses or is unable to consent to services or treatment to remedy or alleviate the harm.

Also spelled out in the act are some of the things that the judge may take into consideration when deciding what is in the best interests of the child. These considerations include the child's physical, mental and emotional needs, and the appropriate care or treatment to meet those needs. The statute cites: "The importance for the child's development of a positive relationship with a parent and a secure place as a member of a family.

"The child's views and wishes, if they can be reasonably ascertained," is another item to be considered by the judge. This was a controversial issue at the trial, as the children clearly indicated that, in spite of all the harm they said they had suffered, they wanted to go home. The lawyers representing the children argued, however, that in spite of this natural, though unrealistic, desire, the children should be made wards of the Crown without any access from their parents.

Although much of the evidence at the hearing and the interest that surrounded it focused on the allegations of ritual abuse, it was by no means solely on this sensational material that the judge's final decision was to be reached. Judge Beckett underlined that point by stating in his final judgment, "It must not be forgotten that this is not a murder case, nor is it a case about cannibalism or satanic cults. It is a case about child abuse and whether these children were subjected to abuse or neglect such as to support a finding that they are in need of protection."

CHAPTER 15

THE CHILDREN'S "TESTIMONY" IN COURT

Watching the children on videotape was a haunting experience. More than 20 hours of taped therapy sessions were shown to the court in order to give the judge an opportunity to see the children without putting them through the ordeal of testifying in court. For day after day, the small group of people who crowded into the stuffy courtroom strained their eyes and their necks as they concentrated on a television screen on a stand beside the judge's bench, just a little too far away for anyone but Judge Beckett to watch with any degree of comfort. Not that anyone could feel at all comfortable watching two very likable little girls display their intense anguish in tormented play, as they struggled with their nightmarish memories. Judge Beckett certainly was not at ease as he leaned forward on the bench and peered at the screen with an intensely pained expression on his pale face.

The children's psychiatrist, Alice Oliviera, had chosen to use a technique known as play-therapy. As Dr. Oliviera later explained, this type of therapy involves letting children play, sometimes joining in their games, and using the themes
178

that come out of this play to help them revise any disturbed and distorted mental constructs they might have about how life is, or how people are. Since the defense lawyers had insisted that the tapes be viewed in full or not at all, the court spent many tedious hours watching the children playing with Play-Doh, dancing, screaming and running around the hospital playroom, or engaging their patient, gentle therapist in games of make-believe.

Janis and Linda appeared on the videotapes as neatly dressed, well-groomed children, boisterous and sometimes unruly, but considerate and affectionate, both to one another and to Dr. Oliviera, with whom they gradually developed a warm relationship. This bond with the therapist was a curious one, at the same time loving, guarded and formal. They never called her by her first name, and clearly regarded her as a figure of authority, yet one who was exceptionally tolerant and permissive. She was a slim, refined-looking middle-aged woman, with a warm rich voice, who entered the children's games without inhibition, and clearly had an easy knack of juggling her attention between the two girls.

They sometimes competed quite strongly for her affection, and would often want to be hugged. Like any normal girl they loved to play house, but the themes of these games were a frightening departure from domesticity. They would pretend that people in the household were being kidnapped and killed. Games that began with pretending to cook a family meal would end in enactments of death and destruction. They liked to pretend to be babies, which gave them an opportunity to cling to Dr. Oliviera and cry despondently. Then they would tell her that the babies were in danger of being killed or kidnapped, scream for her to rescue them and sob hysterically in her arms.

In one session, the girls pretended to be babies who were being cooked in ovens. They climbed into cupboards and screamed for Dr. Oliviera to rescue them. Janis said, "I got cooked up." As the court was shown the tape of the children screaming and swinging on a metal bar inside the cupboard, Sharon Wells watched, anxiously shaking her head and reaching out with her hands as if to try to catch her children. Later in the same session, Janis pretended to phone the police to tell them, "There's this lady that stabs people. This is so impossible I can't even believe it." She smashed the toy phone down and began banging it against the furniture, screaming, "The cop said I don't want to talk to you again." Then she picked up the phone again and shouted, "When are you coming, you stupid cop."

Linda told Dr. Oliviera that her mother and father and Gary had stuck their fingers in her. Janis interrupted to say that her dad didn't do it. She said it was awful and didn't want to talk about it. The girls both evaded any attempt that the therapist made to get them to talk about the bad things that had happened to them. She later testified, "The children only spoke of traumatic events by blurting them out, or in response to a demand perceived from me, always with intense conflict."

Dr. Oliviera noted that Janis was attached to her mother and wished to return to her. The doctor thought it unusual that Linda did not seem to want to go home to her mother. The psychiatrist said, "Janis was carrying a constant conflict between wanting to deal with these terrible events, and knowing that to talk about them would jeopardize her chance of returning to her mother."

These conflicts became particularly acute when the children had supervised visits from both parents. The girls seemed ambivalent during these sessions, which were conducted as part of an assessment of Sharon's and Gordon's parenting capacities. Eight days after the visit with their mother, Janis made her first statements in therapy concerning the allegations she had earlier made to other people. "Okay, I'll talk now," she said. "My mom sticked her finger in us. How's that? That's enough."

The therapist said she understood that this was a hard thing to say, as she understood how much Janis loved her mother. She explained to the child that she was worried that it might happen again.

"That's why you're not taking us home, right?" said Janis, who then told the therapist, "Well, we went to Channel 11 and they stuck their fingers in us."

Dr. Oliviera asked the child if she had seen the people sticking their fingers in at Channel 11. Janis responded, "If you guys understand one little bit, it would be nice and easy for us."

"Little by little, we'll try to figure it out," the therapist told the child.

"No, you gotta figure it out by tomorrow, or today," Janis

demanded. When she was later asked if there were other bad things that happened to her, Janis said, "We saw everything that we can . . . I feel like crying right now, but I can't cry."

Janis continued to talk to Dr. Oliviera until she was interrupted by Linda, who said, "Something's going to happen to somebody if you don't stop talking. . . . Somebody will come in this room and take somebody away from somebody else."

"Nobody will do that," said Janis.

"Yes, they will," insisted Linda. "We need all of us in the family. We don't need somebody taken away." The child began to shout angrily, and said she was mad, "because I realize everything . . . everything is happening . . . I'm in trouble . . . everything is wrong."

After another little argument with Janis, Linda said, "And my mom sticked her fingers in us and our dad sticked a couple of fingers in us."

"Dad did? And what about Gary?" asked Dr. Oliviera.

"He did too. And my mommy did it. But nothing is wrong. But something is wrong."

During the next session Dr. Oliviera and Lesley Morgan questioned the children more about their stories, and Janis told them, "It's sad all the things that happened. But you guys never saw it. So that's why you're asking us. You guys should already know by now."

"But, Janis, one of the things that I wondered is how often does it come into your mind now, the bad things that happened?" said the psychiatrist.

"Really often."

"Really often? Like every day, or every week, or . . ."

"Maybe every Saturday or Sunday, but the only thing I want to know is . . . how did it happen?" said Janis. When Dr. Oliviera questioned her further on this concern, she said, "Okay. Now I'll tell you once more. Okay? Okay, I am really apositive that some of these things I should have said no, but they would still do it. And now, what we really want to know is how they done it, and how they started it."

Dr. Oliviera asked Janis if she ever thought of saying no. "I think I said no. Okay," Janis snapped testily, "but we can't stop it, from doing it."

Linda said, "My dad can stop it. He can get his knife out and stick it up."

"And say, 'I am the power of Greyskull,'" said Janis.

"Yeah, with the knife. He can say 'The power of Greyskull.'"

"And do you think that might stop Mom and Gary from doing bad things to you girls?" asked Dr. Oliviera.

"No," said Janis.

"No, it wouldn't stop them?" the therapist repeated.

"Yes, that would," insisted Linda.

"Yes, I think it would, yeah," said Janis.

"Did Daddy know about the bad things?" Dr. Oliviera asked.

"Yes, 'cause he saw," Linda replied, but Janis interrupted saying that this was not true. She told her sister, "We better not say that he done it, 'cause we're not going to talk about it."

In distress, Linda talked about things that were happening to her that were "rude." Dr. Oliviera told her reassuringly, "Sometimes little girls think it's their own fault, what's happened."

"It ain't our fault, dingbat," Linda replied.

"I felt my hypothesis about Linda's feeling guilty was disconfirmed," Dr. Oliviera later testified.

Janis, who had been appearing increasingly disturbed during this exchange, climbed into the closet they had gone into when they played at babies being cooked in ovens. "My mom sticked her fingers in us, but I think that she never knowed us," she said in an hysterical voice, which changed into something like a song or a chant, as she added, "My dad done it too. My dad done it too. My dad, dad done it too."

"Janis, we can't blame our dad," said Linda urgently.

"Why not?" asked Dr. Oliviera.

"And Gary done it too," intoned Janis, still in the cupboard.

"He didn't do it. He didn't. Dad didn't do it, Janis," screamed Linda.

Linda began to sing, "Something's going on. It won't happen. I mean something's going on, and it won't happen. Something's going on and it will happen."

"But Mom sticked her fingers in us," said Janis.

"I'm making cookies. I'm making cookies," said Linda, picking up the Play-Doh, and engaging in one of her favorite make-believe games.

The psychiatrist and the social worker had agreed in a

meeting before this session that they should give the children some explanation that they could understand about why their mother might have done what she did to them. They agreed that the best way to explain it was to say that the girls' mother was sick, which they believed was the case. Lesley Morgan spoke to Janis, who was still hiding in the cupboard, "Remember, Janis, when you first came into foster care, and we said Mommy was sick?"

"Yeah."

"Do you remember you said, at one time, I think you said that she was getting better?"

"Yeah."

"Well, we sort of think that maybe Mommy is still sick, and that's why she did those things to you and Linda."

As this videotape was played in court, Sharon had been looking more and more despondent. She had been shaking her head and muttering to herself. At one point, she said, "Shit," dropped her head to her knees with a violent movement and sat for a long time with her head in her hands. When she heard the social worker tell the child she was sick, Sharon got up, waving her hands and shouting at the court, "I wasn't sick like that. She's making it all up. I don't want to listen to that. She's saying to my kids that I'm sick."

Sharon stormed out of the courtroom, and the tape was wound back to Lesley Morgan's explanation, and Janis's response, which was quite similar to her mother's. "I'm not going to listen to any more. Okay? That's enough, okay?" the child said.

"You don't like to hear that your mommy's sick," said Dr. Oliviera.

"She's better," said Janis.

"She's better, is she?" asked Lesley Morgan.

"Yes," Janis replied.

"No, she isn't," said Linda. "She isn't. She's not better."

"If she says she won't do it, can we go home?" asked Janis.

Dr. Oliviera replied, "It's a very hard decision because we know you love her very much."

"Yeah, but if I just told her not to do it, can we?"

"Mommy won't say that she did all those bad things to you, and I think it's hard for us to know that she won't do them again," said the therapist.

"She will. She will," screamed Linda.

"Yeah, we think she will, too," said Dr. Oliviera.

"I wish we can go home, but we can't," said Linda, hugging Dr. Oliviera, who then realized that the child had wet herself in her distress.

Linda looked very upset when the girls arrived for their next session with Dr. Oliviera a week later. "Can we talk?" she asked the doctor.

As was so often the case when one child wanted to talk, her sister tried to disrupt. "I'm going to be the baby, but we're not going to talk about anything right yet," said Janis. She played at being a very unhappy, demanding baby until Lesley took her out of the room, so that Linda would have a chance to talk to Dr. Oliviera alone.

"Something was bothering you on the way here. What were you thinking about, when you were coming here? Were you worrying about your mommy?" Dr. Oliviera asked. The child did not answer and the psychiatrist continued, "Last time we were talking about how hard it is to understand that Mommy loves you and you love Mommy, but Mommy did some bad things."

"She didn't. It was a lie," said Linda.

"Is that right? When did you decide that, Linda? Did someone tell you to say that? Who told you to say it was a lie?"

"My mom."

"Oh, when did she tell you that?"

"When we were with her the other day."

"Did she say you mustn't talk to me?"

"That's right."

"Did Mom say that something bad would happen if you talked to me about all these things?"

"Yeah, something really bad."

"What would happen? What did she say would happen if you talked to me about all these things?"

"Really bad," Linda repeated.

"Yeah?"

"She'll stick another one in us. Another birdie."

"Into you?"

"That's what I said. A black birdie."

"She said she'd stick another black birdie into you?"

"Yeah, and its white wings, and its black head," said Linda, whose fear seemed to subside somewhat until she suddenly pointed to a picture of a bird on the wall of the playroom, and said in a state of extreme agitation, "See that thing, that bird right there. That's what she's gonna stick in us, if I tell you."

It was a very somber group of people who watched these videos in the court. Journalists who are used to encountering all kinds of horror with professional detachment would sit brooding over their coffee during the breaks, and would find the image of these tormented children returning to them at night. For the women, particularly, the references to the bird conjured up unbearably painful images, and it was almost impossible not to identify with these little girls, who tried to drown their traumatic memories in old familiar childhood games.

Arthur Brown, in his closing arguments at the hearing, noted that people who saw the children tended to believe their stories, while people who did not see them remained skeptical. This was an odd argument for the mother's lawyer to advance, and it would appear that the point that he was trying to make was that it was easy to be taken in by these little girls. But Harper, the CAS lawyer, saw this observation as simply underscoring a point that he also had wanted to make, that one only had to see the children on video to realize that the trauma and anguish they showed when they talked about what had happened to them were not things that could be either fabricated or coached.

Lee Coleman, the psychiatrist who has challenged the techniques of therapists and interviewers in many of the American child abuse cases, has stated that one only has to look at tapes of therapy sessions to see how children are manipulated. He said that if the media had been allowed to see these tapes they would have instantly recognized that the children's allegations were phony. All of the journalists who saw the tapes in the Hamilton case, which were shown early in the hearing, started out being highly skeptical of the children's allegations. After watching the children through 20 hours of therapy sessions, they were all prepared to accept that the children could be telling the truth, and that certainly there had been some horrendous disturbance in these young girls' lives.

In the next session that was shown to the court, Linda again talked about the bird, and about being forced to eat "poo" and drink "pee." She said Gary had told her "it was good, when it wasn't." She went on to say, "My dad killed three people, Elizabeth, little Elizabeth." The therapist asked her who the other people were, and Linda said, "They're little children like us, like Janis and me."

Linda appeared relieved that she had talked about these things, but Janis was extremely upset and did everything she could to disrupt her little sister's communications. Dr. Oliviera did not press the children after this session to disclose more of what was obviously so painful and difficult for them to talk about. She concentrated more on helping them to work on their feelings through play and their interaction with her.

In a session on November 1, Dr. Oliviera saw each child separately, and asked them, "What's Halloween like for kids?" Linda talked about kidnapping, and Janis talked about murder.

While Janis played she would occasionally let out what Dr. Oliviera described as "blood-curdling screams, ear-shattering screams." The therapist said she had never heard a child scream like that before, and it suggested to her that "this little girl has a lot inside to scream about."

Dr. Oliviera noted that, although Janis had evidently been exposed to a horrendous family interaction, she was still very attached to her father and mother, and that is what one would expect to see, even in badly physically, sexually and mentally abused children. She testified that the children were told that their father and mother would visit them over the Christmas holiday, and Janis said, "Please, pretty please, I want to go stay one night with Mom and Dad because I miss them. I'll give you a house. First I want to see Daddy and then Mommy. I want to stay one night."

The Christmas visits by the parents were authorized by Judge Beckett. A court order of May 28, 1985, terminated the parents' access rights and since then they had been allowed to see the children only once, shortly before the trial commenced. The purpose of that earlier visit was to allow the psychiatrists who were assessing them to make some observations about their behavior with the children.

The psychiatrist said she found it unusual that Linda didn't want to see her father. She said Linda told her that her father had forbidden her to speak, and she was afraid he would kill her with a knife to the neck because she had seen her father make that threat to her mother.

When Sharon visited with them she demonstrated that she was able to play well with them, and showed a lot of love for them, but was also quite manipulative. When she talked to the girls about visiting their relatives, the children started talking about death and showed a great dislike of all their relatives. Linda said, "I don't like Uncle Fred, because he says you got to eat poo."

"Do you eat poo?" Sharon asked, in a theatrical tone.

Linda and Janis laughed as they gave the negative answer that was clearly expected of them.

Sharon pointed to the bird picture on the wall, to which Linda had referred in the taped therapy session, which Sharon had already seen in court. "Pretty bird, isn't it," the mother remarked. When Linda did not assent to this, Sharon said, "You don't like that bird? Dull colors, eh?"

Sharon told a story about a movie character who shot his eye out. She said this wouldn't have happened if he had listened to his mother, because "mothers always know."

When the therapy sessions resumed after Christmas, Janis told Dr. Oliviera that the visits had been confusing and scary, but added, "My mom didn't hurt me."

In the next session, Dr. Oliviera showed the children a videotape called *Feeling Yes, Feeling No*, designed to help school children deal with sexual advances and assaults by adults. Janis was enthralled and watched it avidly with her mouth open. She wanted to see it a second time and then reenacted two of the scenes. She said, "This is very important to me."

When she arrived for the next meeting a week later, Janis went straight to the video and put it on. As she watched it she said, "What if someone is touching you and you like it?" Dr. Oliviera told her it is wrong, and Janis replied, "If this happens, children are put in a foster home."

Linda said she was afraid it would happen again if she returned home. The two girls argued about whether it would happen again. Janis was very sad, and sang, "Yucky things in the home, but everything is all right, and God will look after you."

Although she did not feel that her therapeutic goals had been achieved with the children, Dr. Oliviera decided to put their therapy on hold because she thought that the degree of pain and conflict that they were experiencing was irresolvable. Janis knew perfectly well that if she talked, she confirmed reasons not to go home to her mother. The therapist felt it was too difficult for the child to deal with this issue while her fate was in limbo.

Dr. Oliviera told the court that she concluded from the 26 therapy sessions she had with the children that they were describing things that they had experienced, and that they witnessed events that they interpreted as murders. She said the children's stories could not be interpreted as fantasies. She noted that Janis and Linda were "unusually unimaginative children," and said that, even when children have very active, rich fantasy lives, they are generally able to distinguish between what is fantasy and what is reality.

The psychiatrist said she could draw some conclusions on the nature of the children's relationships with their parents and Gary Evans on the basis of the fact that the children made these allegations, irrespective of whether or not they were true: "For children to make these statements about their caretaking figures, the relationships must be grotesquely and bizarrely distorted. It just doesn't happen otherwise that children would say these things about their principal caretakers.

"I feel these children have some very disturbed mental constructs. Our responsibility as a society is to help them revise them so they can lead healthy lives. I feel strongly they should have more therapy," Dr. Oliviera told the court.

She said that such therapy would be impossible as long as the children have any contact with their mother and father or Gary Evans: "The children described experiencing sexual abuse at the hands of these three parenting figures, but had never received any acknowledgment or confirmation from these people that validated their own experience or enabled them to deal with it or understand why it happened, or have any reassurance that it would not happen again, which both had some doubts about; Janis hoping it wouldn't and Linda feeling surely it would. They both understood that there was a prohibition from either mother or father against discussing these issues, and so it was impossible for me to see how they could reach any resolution on these extraordinarily difficult things for a young child to integrate, and move on in their development while in either continual or intermittent contact with people who deny their having happened and prohibit their dealing with these issues."

Michael Hartrick, Gordon Wells's lawyer, asked the therapist if these comments meant that "the father has either got to say, 'Yes, I killed three children,' or he is not going to see his children. If it didn't happen, he's not going to see the children again."

Dr. Oliviera responded, "Something happened. These children believe they saw their father kill children. No explanation at all has been offered which helps the children make sense of their reality. He would have to explain to me why the children would think these things. Either it happened, or something happened, which I could understand that the children could interpret as those events."

Arthur Brown, cross-examining on behalf of the mother, asked whether the children were fit to appear in court to testify. Dr. Oliviera replied, "It is clear that what they said to me was reported in the midst of enormous internal conflict on their part. To have the children in court would be a very frightening experience."

Dr. Oliviera said the children needed a decision on their future soon. The court in fact failed to meet their needs in this respect, as it would be another nine months before Judge Beckett was finally able to deliver his judgment. The therapist said, "The children need as soon as possible to be in a stable living situation which they see as stretching into the future. They need to be able to integrate, and make sense of, the anxiety-provoking, difficult experiences that they report. They need to make sense of the bizarre events in their lives, and to integrate them into a view of themselves as good and lovable children. They have to learn to make sense of the world, its predictability, its benignness."

She warned that if they do not deal with these issues they would have to "seal off an area of experience which had a major impact on them, and is impossible to deal with." She said that in later life these experiences would break through in flashbacks. The consequences of these unresolved childhood traumas would emerge in their own parenting behavior, in an inappropriate interest in sexual experience at too early an age. Their self-esteem, and their sexual and marital relationships would be affected, and young people with such problems are more likely than other people to become prostitutes, Dr. Oliviera said.

Even with treatment, Dr. Oliviera said she was not completely confident that the children would flourish. She told the court: "In the best of circumstances, it is a chillingly large therapeutic task. I still don't know if they will turn out to be okay young women, okay young mothers."

CHAPTER 16

THE MOTHER'S TESTIMONY

In spite of all the shocking and unusual testimony heard during the first 12 months of the trial, no one in the court was prepared for Sharon's dramatic courtroom breakdown while under cross-examination in October, 1986. The scene stunned everyone who saw it, and aroused widespread sympathy and concern among those who read or saw the sensational media accounts. The image of a young mother being wheeled, strapped to a stretcher, from a court where she had spent more than a year fighting for the return of her children became a sharp focus for public debate about the strange process that was unfolding in the Hamilton court, and the bizarre and disturbing phenomenon that it represented.

On the 114th day of the hearing Sharon Wells began her testimony. She looked like a frightened child as she took her place in the chair beside the judge's bench. Her eyes darted around the courtroom. Her whole body was shaking, and her breathing accelerated to the point where she obviously had difficulty speaking. "I waited for this day, and now I'm scared," she said in a tremulous voice.

"Take your time. Catch your breath," Judge Beckett said soothingly.

Sharon seemed to have difficulty remembering where she lived when Arthur Brown asked his first, very basic question. As the lawyer gently led her into an account of her horrific childhood, the woman seemed to lose her self-consciousness, and began to give very moving and vivid testimony about the consequences of abuse and deprivation. At one point she hesitated to answer a question about her mother and looked over at the reporters, who were writing furiously. "Me and my mom are on good terms right now, and if I start cackling about the way she kept her place she might pounce on me. Are they allowed to print everything?" she asked.

"Try to forget the media are here," Brown told her.

She did seem to forget as she went on with her harrowing story, and seemed sometimes to be reliving the anguish that she had suffered throughout her tragic life. It took her more than a day to describe her childhood, her relationship with Janis's natural father, Ross, and her tumultuous marriage to Gordon.

Near the end of her second day of testimony, Brown began questioning Sharon about her use of a videocassette recorder that Gary rented for several months in 1984. She said the girls watched films on it that Gary had got for his little sister. She listed some of the titles of films they saw: *Care Bears, Bedknobs and Broomsticks, Goofy Sports,* and *Purple Rain.* She told the court about a film called *Last House on the Left,* which she said she rented for her brother, Mike. That was the same brother who had been accused of sexually assaulting Janis a few years before. Sharon said she was back on good terms with him, though she did not leave him alone with the girls.

"I didn't watch all that movie. I wanted to get Mike a videotape that I thought he would like. I saw a box with a woman running from a house. I figured the house was full of spooks," she explained. "As he watched it, he just called it a sick movie."

Sharon said that the children were playing in their bedroom while Mike was watching the film in the living room, and she was cooking in the kitchen. She said she wandered in and out of the living room and so did the children. She said she would send the girls back into their bedroom whenever she saw them in the room where the television was on, and also "scooted them out" when Mike told her they were watching it. She said she did not know how much of the film they saw, but they did have an opportunity to see some of it.

Brown told the judge that he wanted the court to see the film, as he felt there was a similarity between its subject matter and some of the allegations made to Catherine McInnis. The judge asked when the movie was shown, and Sharon said it was in 1984, and she would have to try and get a record of when she rented it to pinpoint the exact time. Brown said he had not been able to find such reports. The judge said he had not been told where it was shown.

"If the court is confused . . ." Brown began to say.

The judge responded sharply, "The court is not confused. The court is not informed."

Sharon explained that it was in her apartment in Toronto. The judge said he was still not satisfied that the film that Brown proposed to show was properly identified by Mrs. Wells. The lawyer asked his client to tell the court all that she remembered about the film, which, it soon became apparent, was very little.

"Her memory of it is very vague," said the judge. "No story line, just a few pictures: a raped girl, a finger with a ring."

Sharon said, "The reason I remember it is my brother said to me, it's one of the grossest movies he's ever seen, and my brother's seen a lot of movies."

It was already about 4:30 P.M. and the judge asked the lawyers if the morning would be a more appropriate time to watch a gross movie. Hugh Atwood said, "I have trouble enough handling my coffee in the morning." The court agreed to watch the film, and the judge asked Sharon to leave the courtroom while it was being shown.

After viewing the film, Judge Beckett glared at Brown with a look of extreme disgust, and stumbled as he hurriedly left the darkened courtroom. He later wrote in his final judgment, "I must say that her brother's description of the film as being 'sick and gross' was an understatement. The film depicted brutal scenes of murder and dismemberment of two teenage girls."

The film did not provide an instant explanation for the girls' bizarre statements, but it did give everyone who saw it in the court pause to think about what sick images of violence are readily available in society. It was profoundly shocking to realize that this inartistic, humorless celebration of sadistic sexual violence is readily available at video stores and marketed as popular entertainment.

When she resumed her testimony the next morning, Sharon said she had remembered more details about the film. The judge was very skeptical about her further descriptions of the movie. He noted: "It was apparent that, overnight, she had had a very sudden and almost total recall of details of the film. She even remembered the last scene in the movie, a chainsaw murder, about which she had gone to some trouble the day before to tell me that she had not recalled. She was even able to remember precisely what she had cooked for dinner that night.

"Sharon Wells seemed to offer this film as an explanation for some of the children's allegations of murder and dismemberment. However, she failed to mention this film to anyone previous to her testimony in court; not to the CAS, the police or to her own psychiatrist," said the judge. He stated that he did not believe her testimony about the film, especially after hearing evidence called by the CAS that the video store where she said she rented the film did not even have the film at the time she said she got it, and had no record of her ever taking it out.

Sharon testified that Janis knew how to operate a VCR, and that the children also saw videos at her brothers' and sisters' homes, as well as at Gary's and Gordon's. She said that the other films they saw included *Clash of the Titans* and *The Dark Crystal*. She said that in *The Dark Crystal* animated characters go on a journey through winter and dark spaces, and see witches are stirring something in a pot from which heads pop up. She also mentioned a scene in *Clash of the Titans* where a head is chopped off. She said she let the children watch *Poltergeist* on television, and now believes she was wrong in letting them see it. She said she was very careful not to let the children see programs like "Dynasty," which showed people in bed with each other.

Sharon told the court, "I cannot say I'm 100 percent sure Gary didn't sexually abuse my kids. But I can say I'm 100 percent sure I didn't sexually abuse my kids. As God is my witness, I never sexually abused my kids once. I would never put them through the pain I went through."

She said Gary did have the opportunity to abuse them. She said Gary was very upset when she got pregnant with the new baby, and told her she should have an abortion. She said she prayed, and opened the Bible randomly at "A seed will grow for the next generation." She said she took this as a sign that she should keep the child. Sharon testified that she did not think Gary gave a damn about the child, as he had not even wanted to have pictures of the baby, and had never asked her what the baby looked like. She said Gary asked her, "What am I going to tell my next girlfriend about a kid that I had?"

"I see her for one-and-a-half hours, twice a week. I love her. She's my daughter. She's beautiful. I never thought she'd come out so good. She's just beautiful. We play," Sharon said. "She laughs at me when she sees me. I think she knows who I am. I can't be certain."

Sharon claimed to have seen very little of her ex-husband, Gordon, since the court case began, an assertion that, the judge noted, was not supported by a comment she made about the fact that she had not seen Gordon wearing his knife on his belt since the trial began, but had noticed it in his car.

While Sharon vehemently denied any involvement in a plot to kill the McInnises on the May 1985 long weekend, the judge said he found her account of what she did that weekend "left a lot to be desired" and was "to a degree, at least, fabricated."

"What would I gain from killing her?" Sharon asked, "Sure, I was angry in the beginning. I thought she was sick. I thought she should have a one-way ticket up the mountain with a straitjacket. Now I have a different idea of Mrs. McInnis. I sat through her whole testimony. I can't say I think she's an upright, nasty person. I think she thought she was doing right. I think maybe she exaggerated things the children said. I think she perceived what my kids were saying in a different way from what they said it. Sure they said some things to her. I wasn't there. I can't actually say what was said, what went on. I never ever wished her dead. Say I wanted to do that, would I have any chance of getting my kids back if I blew up the McInnises?

"Gary and Gordon are just as the colors they are, black and white. They hate each other," she said. "For the three of us to get together to kill the McInnises, that's farfetched, if you ask me."

Arthur Brown introduced into evidence numerous pictures and coloring books that had belonged to the children, and among these he solemnly produced two Cabbage Patch dolls. Elizabeth, together with her official adoption papers, and Laura, who, Sharon explained, did not have any papers, were formally entered as exhibits. The court clerk marked them as exhibits 119 and 120, placing little tags on the front of each doll, and carefully sat them side by side on top of a row of paper file folders. Little more was said about the dolls or their significance to Sharon's case, but they sat there through the balance of the hearing, symbolizing, perhaps, the two children, the absent protagonists in this protracted tragedy.

Brown continued to question Sharon through five days. He next asked her if she had ever used a vibrator. She responded with almost theatrical tones of disbelief, "I'd never seen one of those up until a couple of months ago. Me and my mom went to a lingerie party. I thought it would be just nightgowns and such like. They had more than nightgowns there. I was embarrassed. They had vibrators and pants that you can eat. I'm serious, they did. Jelly stuff and two little ball things that woman walk around with in the supermarket. I swear to God, never in my life."

She said the children only saw Gary and her in bed on one occasion: "When I have a relationship, I have it in the bedroom with the door shut." Asked if she discussed the facts of life with the children, she said, "I explained about periods, what I know about them.

"I'm the type of person who doesn't like to look at men down there. When Gordon was finished, he always put on his underwear, and Gary, when he went to the washroom, put a towel on. When it comes to looking at men, I'm very self-conscious," Sharon testified. She said she used to tell the children "their body's their own. Nobody gets to touch it but them. I always used to ask them, 'Can I wash you downstairs.' If they don't want me to, I would let them do it themselves. I wanted to stress to them that their body's their own. Lots of times I'd put cream on Linda, she would say, 'Mommy that hurts.' I would let her do it herself."

She said she thought that perhaps the children got the idea about her sticking things in them from her using a thermometer to check their temperatures. Brown wanted to file a thermometer as an exhibit, but the judge told him testily that he knew what a thermometer looked like.

She gave an explanation, which the judge found "very strange," for the allegations about the bird. She said, "I had put an old couch on the balcony [in Toronto]. There was a hole in the part you sit on. Some birds made a nest in there. I asked Gordon to help me get the birds out of there, and we were to get rid of the couch, and that's what we did with the birds, we took the old blanket that I had, and we put the birds on the blanket and put them beside the door, and the birds died, and we had to throw them out. Like, they didn't live. We would watch them every morning."

Judge Beckett noted that she had said the birds were black, and concluded, "I found this explanation unbelievable, and I do not accept it. I thought it strange that birds would be nesting on the 20th story. No other witness was called to corroborate this evidence. It is significant that at no time Mrs. Wells gave this explanation to the CAS or to the police."

Sharon was very hesitant when she was asked for explanations about the alleged killings and mutilations, and offered the possibility that the girls' stories were inspired by the cutting off of the head in the *Clash of the Titans*. The judge observed, "It's interesting to note that Mrs. Wells made no mention of the *Last House on the Left* at this stage in her evidence."

"When asked about the children's allegations about Channel 11, she seemed very uncomfortable and took a long time to explain her answer," Judge Beckett noted. Sharon explained that they often went by the television studio, but "we only looked in it, we have never ever been right inside of it."

Sharon had no explanation for the children's allegations about graveyards, though she said they did ask her about a graveyard that they used to pass on the bus, and she told them that was where the dead people were. She denied any knowledge of satanism or satanic cults. She described the children being scared by people in masks on Halloween.

Judge Beckett stated in his judgment that during the course of her testimony, "she went through many mood swings, often slumped in the chair, sometimes with her head down, not answering questions for long periods of time, sometimes appearing extremely excited and other times flat and almost disinterested."

Sharon told the court, "I'm not going to stop. These are my children. I know I didn't do nothing to them. I'm going to fight until I can't fight no more, until there's no life in me to fight.

"I think I can take care of them, but I think I'll need help. Teach me better than what I've learned. There's so much to kids that I don't know and that I have to learn. I want my kids back. I love them very much. I want them to get to know me, to remember me again. I don't even know if they talk about me," she said. "I gave the CAS two necklaces to give to my kids, to tell them I still love them and am fighting for them."

She also gave what could be taken as a hint that there were other recourses open to her. She told the court that she knew the identity of the baby's foster mother, and knew her car, "But I'm taking the legal road."

The cross-examinations began gently, in a good-humored tone, as Michael Hartrick questioned Sharon about her ex-husband. He had asked her about Gordon's treatment of the children, and she had told him that he never hit Janis in the face. Then she said, "He kicked her toy one time, and broke it, because she smashed his skull ashtray. He kicked her turtle and broke the foot."

Hartrick responded, "We're dealing with a satanism trial here. Is this something we should be worried about?"

Sharon laughed as she replied, "No, it was made of ashtray stuff."

Hartrick turned to the allegations of marital violence, and said, "I suggest that he did not come at you with the machete, but whacked it into the wall."

"We both have different views of what happened."

"I suggest that if he was trying to strike you with the machete he could have done so."

"Yes, he could have. Just like he could have slit my throat with the knife."

"Was the machete something he used regularly, or only on festive occasions, to trim a tree?" asked Hartrick.

"He used it to trim the tree more than once. Other times only when he would show it to his friends."

When Hartrick asked if Sharon took Gordon's threats seriously, she replied, "When he threatened me, I believed him. Talking to Gordon now, I think he just shoots his mouth off. There's a lot of people that he said he wanted to kill, that he hasn't done anything about. He even threatened to blow up the income tax people when he didn't get a good return. Well, I'm still here."

"And the income tax people are still here, unfortunately," said Hartrick.

Sharon seemed to take some delight in telling stories

about Gordon's exaggerated threats and dramatic acts of violence, and she relaxed under the influence of Hartrick's witty responses.

When the cross-examination resumed again the next morning, she was again highly nervous. Although it was warm in the courtroom, Sharon was shivering, and her teeth were chattering. She put on her coat, folded and unfolded her arms several times and leaned forward, wringing her hands in a frenzied gesture.

The lawyer asked her about her account of the incident where she said Gordon tried to throw her off the 20th story balcony. He suggested that Gordon was in fact trying to stop her from jumping. She replied, "People can see things differently. That's what I've learned from this trial. Even in some of the videos I've seen with the kids, I can see it one way and you can see it another. It's all in the way somebody looks at something. Me and Gordon had a lot of fights. When he throws the machete and misses my head, I figure he's out to kill me."

Judge Beckett noted that, on the whole, during this cross-examination she seemed to downplay the threats that her husband had made to her. The judge observed that she gave a rather strange answer to a question by Hartrick about whether Gordon worshiped the devil. She took a very long time to answer the question and finally said, "Did he worship the devil? No, not that I know of. He, at times, would say that 'I'm going to come back and haunt you,' because there was times when I would get mad at him and I'd say, 'Well, I wish you were dead,' or something like that and he'd say, 'I can't die. I'll come back and haunt you' sort of thing. But that's as far as I can remember."

Sharon looked frightened as John Harper, the lawyer for the Children's Aid Society, began his cross-examination by explaining to her what perjury is, and then launched into a series of questions about the movie, *Last House on the Left*. He pinned her down about when and where she had rented the film, and then told her he would bring evidence to show that it could not have been rented at that time from the store she had named. He showed her the box that contained the film, which had a vivid illustration of a woman with her hand above her head, a man with a knife in front of her, and a man with a chainsaw behind her. Sharon said she did not remember seeing the men, only the girl and the house in the background. She said she didn't read the writing on the box, which described the film as "A story of terror, involving the death of two girls, kidnapped by a gang, an unbearable and brutal climax never before seen."

Harper questioned her aggressively about her memory of the film, suggesting that she was lying when she claimed to have suddenly remembered minute details while the court was viewing the film. "It was what the judge said. I figured I should remember more. That's why I tried to remember more," said Sharon, who stuck to her story that she had seen bits and pieces of the film in 1984 and not viewed it since. "Please don't scream," she asked the lawyer, who was questioning her sharply and rapidly, but in a normal voice.

"When you saw the movie in 1984, were you not sick at the part where the girl was raped in the woods?" asked Harper.

"I don't remember being sick," Sharon replied.

"Were you not sick at the part where one girl's chest was being cut and bleeding? Did it not bother you?" Harper persisted.

"Yes, it bothered me."

"And you told the court the kids were able to see the movie? You didn't think to shut the movie off?"

"I didn't know what the next scene would be."

"You continued to watch it till the end, where the father cut the man with the chainsaw?"

"I didn't know what was in between."

As Harper asked her why she had never mentioned the movie before she testified in court, Sharon's teeth were chattering again. She began exhaling loudly, and screwing up her face in a look of extreme anguish. Harper said, "I notice that you're shivering."

"I'm freezing," she replied, "probably because I just drunk a cold Coke."

The remainder of the day, Sharon's eighth day on the witness stand, was taken up with cross-examination about her childhood, her relationships and her treatment of the children while they were living in Toronto. Harper tried to expose inconsistencies in Sharon's story, points on which she had said things to third parties that differed from what she said in her testimony. He questioned her about the violent incidents with her first boyfriend, Ross Fuller, and asked her if she was sure that he had been jailed for two years as a result of her charging him with assault. She said she was. He suggested that, after

Janis was born, she moved around a lot because she was on the run from the Toronto CAS. He questioned her judgment in allowing her brother Mike to sleep with Janis two nights in a row. He criticized her practice of sending the girls to stay with her mother and stepfather, when she was well aware of her stepfather's perverse interest in children.

For the morning of the next day Harper questioned Sharon further about the children and their injuries while they were in Toronto. He probed the view of Gordon that she had given in her earlier testimony, which was more lenient than that implied by allegations she had made against him in the past. Then in the afternoon he returned to the question he had raised earlier about Ross going to jail. Harper said, "I suggest Ross Fuller was never charged by you, never found guilty of assaulting you. I suggest you lied to this court."

"No sir."

"He was convicted of armed robbery in 1979 and sentenced for two years less a day for armed robbery," said Harper.

"I know he was convicted of holding up a Becker's store. But, yes, I must have got it confused," said Sharon.

"You knew about it?"

"Not until my sister showed me the paper, and laughed in my face about it."

"That was in January, 1979, just a few months after, you say, he was sentenced to two years less a day for assault causing bodily harm," Harper said.

"I know he went to court because I laid charges on him," Sharon replied.

"You said you heard the judge sentencing him?"

"Yes, sir, that's what I thought he said. I know that we went to court because I almost got in contempt of court. Maybe I've got mixed up, sir. Maybe I got them confused. I didn't mean to but I did. Maybe I got confused, but I knew . . . my sister laughed in my face. She said your daughter's father is a milkman bandit."

Sharon began to cry, and continued to repeat, "I know she laughed in my face about it. Maybe I got them confused, but I didn't mean to. But I know I went to court with them."

She controlled her mounting hysteria for a moment, and said, "What happened was, okay, I charged him. Then I got with Gordon. Then I was at my sister's. Then he came there to my place and threatened me with a gun."

She began crying again, and waved her hands frantically, as she shouted, "This whole thing is getting to me. I wake up with nightmares. I can't take it no more. Don't come near me. I can't take it no more."

Sharon got up from her chair, and turned her back on Harper. She was now sobbing and shaking convulsively, and said in a distracted but pleading tone, "I'm so confused about so much. I'm trying to . . . I want to get my kids back. I don't know what's wrong with me."

Brown approached her holding out a paper tissue, but she screamed at him, "Don't touch me, please. Don't hit me."

Her lawyer urged Sharon to walk out of the courtroom, but she was now in a state of total panic. She shouted hysterically, "I can't walk. I can't get my kids back. I want them, and I love them, but I'm not ready. I'm just not ready."

As the judge, lawyers and other people in the court watched in a stunned silence, Sharon slumped down onto the courtroom floor against the wall, in a space between the judge's bench and a stand that held the television set on which the court had earlier watched her children's anguished play. Shaking violently and shrieking, she lay there in a fetal position, while Brown asked for an adjournment and Judge Beckett cleared the court. She continued to yell and scream as an ambulance arrived. A few minutes later she was wheeled out of the courtroom, struggling against the leather straps that bound her to a stretcher.

Judge Beckett later stated, "I must say that I found the episode in court shocking, even frightening. As there was evidence given by Sharon Wells herself that the October 16th episode was similar to breakdowns that she had suffered in the past, and which had been witnessed by her children, there can be no doubt that these breakdowns must have had a stunning and fearful effect on the children."

During the three days that Sharon was recovering in a Hamilton hospital, public concerns were aired about the extreme length of the hearing. At a weekend seminar attended by journalists, lawyers and a family court judge, the wardship hearing became the focal point of a discussion on family court issues. "Was this mother the victim of an abusive legal process?" it was asked, and "Has the Hamilton hearing been allowed to get out of control?" These questions were pursued in newspaper articles, and an editorial in the *Hamilton Spectator* directly criticized the judge for his handling of the case.

Such public speculation about a case in progress, while common in the United States, is almost unheard of in Canada, where strict contempt of court laws restrict such discussion. When the court resumed the following week, the judge and lawyers spent several hours in chambers, apparently reviewing some of the newspaper coverage with these prohibitions in mind. No action was taken by the court on this issue, but Hugh Atwood did make a statement in court deploring the *Spectator* editorial, which seemed to take the position that the judge should somehow clamp down on the hearing in a way that would obviously deny the rights of a full judicial process to all parties involved. After the trial the newspaper published an editorial praising the way the judge handled the case.

When the court resumed the following week, Judge Beckett said he had been informed by Brown that Sharon was ready to continue her testimony. The judge said, "I must tell you I'm very uncomfortable. She may very well be physically and mentally ready to resume. But based on what I saw I have very serious reservations about whether she is in a state ready to resume the witness stand."

Harper said he wanted to make a motion that the court should require her to undergo a psychiatric examination before she continued. Brown asked for a moment to consult with his client, saying, "My client probably doesn't understand what's going on here."

"That's the point, isn't it?" said Judge Beckett. "This is not trial by ordeal."

The lawyers discussed whether the judge had the power to order a psychiatric examination, and Judge Beckett settled the issue by saying, "I'm satisfied I have the power. If I don't have the power, I'm going to exercise it anyway."

When the court next convened, Dr. Emil Zamora, the psychiatrist who had first examined Sharon on her arrival in the hospital after her courtroom collapse, gave his report on his subsequent assessment of the patient. He gave the opinion that she was fit to testify: "I don't feel she had a psychotic breakdown. She had an adjustment reaction to stress. A dissociative reaction can be very short-lived and is not considered a psychotic breakdown, a nervous breakdown *per se*."

Hospital notes that Dr. Zamora brought to the court stated that Sharon described how, when Arthur Brown approached her in the courtroom, she felt that she saw the face of her deceased father. The psychiatrist said this was an illusion, a distortion of something she saw, rather than a true hallucination. The hospital notes also stated that Sharon recalled feeling frightened on the witness stand, but also angry about the length of the trial, her childhood and the stress she was suffering. It was also noted on the records that she cried hysterically on the day after she was admitted to the hospital, saying that she was expecting to get therapy in the hospital, and now she was going to be discharged and nothing had changed. The notes also stated "impaired concentration, memory, fatigue, suicidal thoughts—no plans made, has no supports other than lawyer."

Dr. Zamora testified, "Mrs. Wells seems to have a selective component as far as her memory is concerned. There may be some areas she is either willingly or unwillingly blocking out, usually distressing areas. . . . Her life has been very stressful, parts of her life are a blur to her. In court she felt cornered, didn't know what to do."

The hospital notes stated that Sharon was questioning whether there was another person inside her that could in some way have done the things that she was accused of doing. Dr. Zamora said there was not enough evidence to conclude she was suffering from multiple personalities. He said he believed that the woman would not follow through on the suicidal ideas she had entertained. He said, "She would like this to be over, not to have to go through this. But she does recognize she does have to."

Judge Beckett concluded from Dr. Zamora's evidence that Sharon Wells was mentally and physically capable of resuming her testimony. Looking lost and forlorn, the small, pale woman returned to the seat at the front of the court to continue her ordeal. John Harper, a generally composed and aggressive, but not insensitive, man, also looked uneasy as he prepared to resume his cross-examination.

CHAPTER 17

THE MOTHER'S TESTIMONY CONTINUES

Sharon's fear and confusion were evident as soon as she returned to the witness stand. Her startling testimony during the next few days made it clear that it was not just the court process that frightened her, and not only other people that she was confused about.

"Is there something wrong with your voice?" Harper asked, as Sharon responded to his first few questions in a hoarse whisper.

"I think so, sir, my throat's all dry," she responded timidly.

She was even slower in answering Harper's questions than she had been before, and sometimes repeated the questions several times as if struggling to comprehend them.

She said she had recently met Gordon at her mother's house, where her ex-husband was a frequent visitor. She said he told her, "'I'm going to testify, but I'd better be on and off in four days,' and he went into one of his spastic fits. I didn't want to talk to him about it, because he just goes on and on about this court case. He always takes a fit and rattles on and on."

"You have told us in your previous evidence that Gordon

Wells, since this trial had begun, has threatened Gary Evans?" Harper asked.

"Yes, sir, he has."

"Since this trial began has Gordon Wells threatened anyone else in this courtroom?"

"Yes, sir."

"Who?"

"He has threatened his lawyer; he has threatened you, sir; he has threatened the judge, sir; he has threatened my lawyer, sir; he has threatened me, sir."

"And that was in your presence?"

"The only ones he hasn't threatened is the kids' lawyer and Mr. O'Neail, because he figures Mr. O'Neail shouldn't even be here. But that's the truth, sir, I swear it's the truth."

"When was the last time he said that in your presence?"

"That he has threatened?"

"Yes."

"The weekend past. On the weekend, I don't think he threatened you, sir. He just said he's not going to take a lot of crap from you," said Sharon. She said Gordon threatened the judge on that occasion: "He said that he was going to get him off the bench and going to sue him. He shouldn't be up there."

Sharon looked up at Judge Beckett, and added, "And win a million dollars and pay you off, sir. He said, 'If I have a million dollars I can pay him off.' He threatened at one point he was gonna blow his lawyer away, then me away, then Arthur, then the judge. I said, 'If you're going to blow them away, how can you sue them?' and he said he was going to sue them and then blow them away. He also said he was going to fire his lawyer. He's made a lot of threats like that, but some of them make me laugh. I told him, I said, 'You just have to go in and answer the questions.' You're a lawyer doing a job for your client. But I wouldn't want to blow you or anybody away. I wouldn't go to extremes like that, but Gordon has a different point of view than I do.

"That's the way I remember it, sir," said Sharon, describing how, when her ex-husband makes such threats, "his voice gets really deep and his face gets red. He didn't make these threats all this weekend. The main one he focused on was firing his lawyer, and Arthur. I said, 'You can't fire Arthur.' He said he could."

The judge commented in his judgment: "In observing

the manner in which she answered these questions, and comparing them to the manner in which she had answered previous questions, I believe that she was telling the truth with respect to her statements about Gordon Wells's threats to bring harm to people in the courtroom. I found Mrs. Wells's testimony concerning recent contacts with Gordon Wells to be troubling. Bearing in mind her testimony concerning their violent relationship, there seemed little reason why they should be having any contact since the children have been in care. But during cross-examinations, she admitted to four or perhaps five occasions that she had contact with Wells since she started her testimony."

The judge told Sharon he was confused about what seemed to be a change in her attitude to Gordon. He asked her if anyone had made threats against her that would in any way affect her evidence in court. She appeared upset and frightened, said she was not as afraid of Gordon as she used to be, but added, "He said that he would blow me away. If he has to bring a gun into the courtroom, he'll just blow me away."

"I had the impression he issued this threat to you because of something you already said, or something you might say," said the judge.

"He's also threatened, he'll get me up for perjury," said Sharon. "I talked to him last weekend, when he phoned at my mother's. He said, 'My lawyer said you said too much, and I think you said too much, and I'm going to get you for perjury.'"

"Has it affected your testimony?" asked the judge.

"I just told the truth."

"I want to know if you feel you need protection."

"I must say I've been pretty nervous at times, but I just try and tell the truth the way I see it," Sharon replied. "I've had it up to here with his threats. I'm at the point where, do what you want, I don't care. I guess in a way his threats concern me, but I'm in such a confused state, where I don't give a damn. I want to get this whole thing done and over with, and get some help for myself because I need it. And Gordon's threats don't make it any easier.

"That's all I can say," Sharon told the judge. "Like there are other things I know about Gordon that I haven't said."

The lawyers all had a fresh opportunity to question the witness after the judge had done so, and it was inevitable that this hint would be probed extensively by Harper. Hartrick, the father's lawyer, tried to preempt that by asking about it himself. He asked Sharon if there was anything about Gordon relevant to the case that she hadn't disclosed. She told him about a big meat hook that Gordon kept. "It was very ugly-looking and scary," she said. "I don't know where he got it. It weighs about 15 pounds. When I was pregnant with Linda he said, 'If anyone comes through the door, just hook them with it. I couldn't even lift it—it's not funny, sir. It was after this Paul guy that Gordon knew came over with a bunch of friends and kicked in Mary's place. They came up to our place, and apparently Donald had threatened Paul with a knife. They come up to our place and they made a lot of threats back and forth. It was after that that he had that meat hook. They came over to our place and threatened us. The guy showed us a scar of his having a knife cut.

"I guess I was scared to mention anything like that," she said. "I guess because of the allegations."

"Has Gordon Wells ever told you what to say or what not to say?" asked Hartrick. Sharon was silent for more than a minute, and the lawyer asked her, "What's the problem?"

"I'm just thinking."

"Has he ever told you what to say?"

"Not that I can remember."

"Has Gordon Wells ever told you what not to say to this court?"

After another long pause, Sharon asked, "About anything?"

"About what not to say in your evidence. Has he ever said don't say this?" asked Hartrick. "Are you nervous about something? Look at me. Just answer my question. I'm not trying to cause you a problem, just trying to find out the truth."

The judge interrupted, "Mrs. Wells, I can see from here that you're shaking. Your head is down. Are you afraid to answer this question?"

"I'm trying to answer it. Has he ever told me not to say something? I can't answer that."

The judge said, "I can see from here you're extremely upset. You're not answering the question put by Mr. Hartrick. I'm bound to ask you if that's fear of something, because if it is the court will see to it you have whatever protection is required. Are you afraid?"

"To answer that question? Yes, I am. I'm afraid. I just . . ."

"Are you afraid somebody will hurt you?" asked the judge.

"Yes."

"See that policeman at the back of the courtroom. Why do you think he's there? So that people don't have to be afraid. There's ways and means. I'll make whatever order is necessary to protect you in whatever way is necessary. Now tell the court why you're afraid."

"I'm afraid of what Gordon might do to me," said Sharon, "because I've seen Gordon, now. He's really coming to a breaking point. It's not you people he's going to come after. It's me. He's made threats to other people, but it's always me he's come after. I'm just afraid. I told him I just don't care what he does. I just told him I don't care, because I'm just at a point of my life when I have so much hatred for everything around me, and Gordon threatens me, and that just makes me worse."

The judge noted that Sharon continued to show sheer terror as Hartrick questioned her about what it was that Gordon had said that she was afraid to tell. She said that she had met him at a donut shop in Hamilton to give him some pictures of the children, and they had a conversation in the parking lot: "He said that he's going to shut down this court case, and, if he has to, he'll bring some of his satanic friends to testify. I never knew that he had people like that. I was just shocked because I didn't know he had friends like that. And I'm confused whether he does know people like that, because, if he does, I'm scared."

Sharon repeated Gordon's threat again, and said, "I'm very scared. I never knew he had friends like that. He said if I told anybody he'd kill me. If he does have satanic people like that he knows, I'm sure that he's capable. He said, if I told anybody, he'd kill me. He said, if I told anybody, he'd totally deny it."

Hartrick said, "He didn't want you to give us some kind of notice that these potential witnesses are going to come and testify."

"What I got out of it was not to tell anyone that he knew people like that, satanic people," said Sharon. She said she did not ask who these satanic friends were: "I wasn't going to keep asking him about it. I guess it's because I'm really afraid of the answer that he might give me."

Special police protection was ordered for Sharon. When

the court resumed the following day, there were several plain-clothes policemen outside the courtroom, looking very conspicuous in their light-colored raincoats, and there was a high state of nervousness inside. Hartrick resumed his cross-examination of Sharon by suggesting that her statements the previous day about being afraid of Gordon were in conflict with her earlier testimony.

Judge Beckett said, "The statements are not in conflict. When she said earlier she was not afraid, she could have said parenthetically, 'As long as I don't tell.' The fear arises out of telling yesterday. As long as she didn't tell, she was not in fear. I repeat, I interpret her evidence as: I keep my mouth shut, I have nothing to be afraid of."

"I'm afraid now of Gordon," said Sharon. "If he walked in this room now I'd be afraid of him and what he would do to me. I'm very afraid of him."

Hartrick said, "I would submit that you've been giving us little clues in the last few days, comments about Gary Evans, Gordon Wells, and yourself, inviting questions to be asked."

"Maybe subconsciously I wanted someone to ask me. Maybe that's what I did, because it's been eating me up inside. I want to know if he's got satanic friends. Do you think I'm going to ask him questions about it? Maybe because it's been tearing me apart for a long time now, wondering what I should do. Okay, maybe I was wanting somebody to ask about it."

"Your own lawyer knew about this?"

"He said we were going to sit on this, and see what we're going to do about this."

Hartrick continued to ask her about her delay in revealing this conversation, but the judge interrupted, "What I saw, yesterday, was raw fear from this witness, which amply explains her reluctance, her long delay in telling the story. If you didn't see it, I'm telling you what I saw was trembling, stark fear. I heard her say her life was threatened. I dare say you wouldn't have told if your life was threatened."

"I'm suggesting to this witness that it's baloney," said Hartrick. "The question I had asked was why she had chosen that point to finally tell us all."

Judge Beckett replied, "After a reading of the transcript, I don't think anybody in this courtroom would say she chose that moment. The moment was chosen for her."

Later Sharon told the court, "If he actually knows satanic people, I don't want him to have access to my kids. I don't want him near them. It's good to know finally he's threatening somebody else. Maybe you might know the fear I've faced for years. At least I've got protection."

Harper began questioning Sharon on her allegations, and asked her about Donald, one of the people involved in the meat hook incident. He had been the best man at Sharon's wedding and had stayed at her apartment for a period of time. Sharon said she didn't know his last name. She said she understood that he had since died in a car accident.

Sharon said that Janis had been threatened by the intruders in the incident involving the meat hook. Harper said, "I suggest you hid the fact of the meat hook from the court because it might relate to what the children were saying about the allegations?"

"About killing? Because a meat hook could kill somebody? Because a meat hook is a dangerous thing?" asked Sharon.

"It might go to show that what the children were saying was true," said Harper.

"Maybe it would have related to it. But it doesn't mean it's true."

"You withheld it because of that?"

"To tell the truth, sir, yes," said Sharon.

Harper suggested that Sharon's mother and her brothers were Gordon's friends. Sharon said, "I knew they weren't his satanic friends. That's my family."

"Do you know it as a fact? Do you know none of them were involved in any satanic cults?" asked Harper, who reminded her about the fact that Gordon used to hang around with her brothers in the days when they had their room painted black and decorated with skulls. He reminded her about Gordon's picture of the devil, and comments he made in the past about the devil. Harper asked why she should have been shocked when he spoke of satanic friends.

"I didn't add up everything like you're doing. I'm sorry I just didn't," said Sharon.

"I suggest to you, you withheld this from the court because once again it was too close to the allegations," said Harper.

"No, sir, I deny this, yes, I do."

Sharon later told Brown that Gordon had said, "When he reaches the breaking point he doesn't care if he goes to jail for ten years, he's going to bring someone down with him. I feel I'm the one who's going to get it."

She said, "I do feel I did the right thing in talking in court. Although I'm scared, I feel at peace of mind."

Brown had a few more questions. He asked Sharon if she had experienced blackouts where she couldn't remember things. She said she had, and she described memory lapses where she could only recall "blotches of what happened."

When Harper had questioned her about Gary and the children's allegations, Sharon said she had difficulty remembering some things, and added, "That's why I questioned myself, and said, 'Could I be two people.' There's a lot of things I don't remember about my life. That's why I'm questioning myself. Should I remember everything? Gary did say that to me once, that when I get angry I'm like two people. Last Thursday and before that, I have been questioning me as a person, who I am. And like, I'm wondering is there a possibility that I could be. Like, I don't know if I am. But there is a possibility and I want to rule it right out, and I want to know if I did, 'cause as Sharon Wells, as far as I can remember I did not do anything like that to my kids. But is there a possibility that I could have? That's what I want to know."

Sharon's nervousness and hesitancy was gone at that time, as she became totally absorbed in speaking out about the fears that were tormenting her. "I've had such a hard life," she said, almost choking on her tears. "I'm not asking for sympathy. But people who have such a hard life, like me, could be two people. I'm wondering, could I be? I want therapy. I need therapy. I want to know."

Harper asked her why her children were so terrified, and she replied, "I don't know, sir. I don't know. All I know is I never did that to my kids. I never sexually abused them, never ate people, never committed rituals and that. I'm so torn in so many different directions right now. I don't even know who I am. I wake up in the morning, and leave to come here, and I don't know who I am. I have to accept that the possibility exists that I may be two people.

"When I was a kid, and I got hurted, I laughed. Now I cry. Is that normal? It opened up a lot of things. I'm confused. Now if I got the kids, I'd say to the CAS, 'Please take them, I'm scared. I might hurt them, because I don't know.' Like when I get an anxiety attack, I don't know if I'll hurt them or not. Like I'm scared of me."

Her lawyer watched with a pained expression on his face as Sharon explained, "That's why I cannot get my kids back now, sir, because I want to explore this possibility."

Harper listed all the children's allegations, asking for Sharon's response. She said that she knew that she, Sharon Wells, did not do those things, but speculated again about whether she might be two people. She said she was willing to have "psychiatrists pick at my brain." She said she wished the CAS would compromise, and just agree to keep the children while she found out if she had multiple personalities.

Once again Sharon began to make a tearful speech to the court. Her lawyer looked anguished, but there was no way for him to stop her speaking her mind. She said, "Could any one of you people in this courtroom sit here where I'm sitting, go through what I went through, and not have a doubt in your mind. I want one of you to sit here, and not have a damn doubt in your mind. Thoughts are racing in my mind, feelings racing through me. I don't know why my kids say this stuff. Maybe it got fabricated. I'm sitting here in a chair, fighting for two kids I love very much, and I want to get them back. I know what I'm saying now might have blown my shot to ever have my kids back again. I am willing to explore any possibility, go through anything, to find out who I am. I don't know who I am. If I am another person, and I did do that to my kids, I don't know if I'll be able to live with it, but I'll try."

She paused, and then said that if she found out that she did those things she wouldn't want the children back. She said she would tell the CAS, "Keep them, raise them, love them, because I know the hurt.

"You have to sit where I am sitting, be where I am, to know what I'm feeling," she told the court. "I feel the CAS should give me the chance, and not stop me seeing my kids for the rest of my life, or the rest of theirs. They're there to help people. It's not easy for me to sit up here and say this. I want to feel secure in my heart and mind that I am not two people."

CHAPTER 18

THE FATHER'S TESTIMONY

The court awaited the appearance of Gordon Wells with nervous anticipation. On the day he had been expected to testify he did not show up. His lawyer, Michael Hartrick, had not been able to get hold of him by phone. Hartrick said he would contact him in person, a task that he did not appear to relish because the father had allegedly threatened both to fire him and to "blow him away." Judge Beckett and Hartrick joked about these threats in court when the judge made reference to the possibility that the lawyer might be replaced. "I hope it's *replaced*, your honor," said Hartrick.

However, Gordon was not present when the court next convened, even though he had personally assured the lawyer that he would be there. Hartrick called another witness: Gordon's previous lawyer, Cathy Agnew. She was called to testify about Gordon's picture of the sorcerer, which she said he had given to her but had been lost while she was moving out of her office a year before. She said it was a pencil drawing of a menacing face. It was not a picture of a traditional devil, she said. "I wouldn't be afraid of showing it to my children, but it's not what I would choose to hang on the nursery wall."

Hartrick told the court that he had been informed that his client did not appear in court that morning because he had

213

been arrested the night before for unpaid traffic tickets and had spent the night in jail.

The following day Gordon Wells made his much-heralded appearance. He was a tall man who walked with a slight stoop. As he took his place on the witness stand, he peered nervously about him through dark eyes, deep set in a furrowed brow. Thick wrinkles formed on his forehead as he grinned in response to Hartrick's opening line, "Welcome to Hamilton, Mr. Wells."

Speaking in clipped tones, he gave details of his background. He said he had a grade eleven education, and a good relationship with his parents as he was growing up, though he didn't get on well with his brothers and sisters. He was born in Toronto, and when asked in what part of the city he grew up, replied, "East, west, wherever I was living." He said he had a stable work record, having held one job for eight and a half years. He said he worked up to 13 hours a day at his present job. He talked about his early relationship with Sharon, and how he had adopted Janis, "because her so-called father wanted to take her." He described Janis's natural father as "a meathead." He said his relationship with Sharon was "the pits" because she used to bait him all the time.

Asked about the meat hook, he said, "Nothing to it. I got it from work, used it for towing cars." About the machete, he said, "I got it when I was 14 and had it ever since. I just kept it around." When Hartrick questioned him about Sharon's allegations about the machete, he replied, "I went up to move the rest of the stuff from my premises. She started baiting me. I turned around and swung it in the wall, like, 'Leave me alone, because I don't want to hurt anyone with it.'"

Gordon said his knife was a buck knife, a skinning knife with a four-inch blade, and not a switchblade. He said switchblades are spring-loaded, whereas his knife locks and has to be pulled out manually. He later admitted that he did once possess a switchblade "years ago, when I was a kid." He said the sawed-off shotgun was a pump-action twelve gauge, which never worked: "I got it ten years ago. Something went wrong with it, and it never did fire. Not that I ever fired it. The spring was loose. I'm a gun collector."

"Did you ever assault Sharon Wells with the knife?" asked Hartrick.

"Not that I can recall."

"With the machete?"

"No."

"Did you ever use the knife in an assaultive way?"

"Just to turn around and say, 'Leave me alone.' About three times. She knows how to bait me. I did it to the point to say, 'What you're doing to me is killing me.'"

The judge asked for a brief delay in proceedings while he filled his pen, and Hartrick said, "His honor is loading his weapon, the worst weapon of all." Gordon laughed, and again large wrinkles appeared on his forehead. He was then asked about his disciplining of the children, and he said he would tap them on the hand or the butt. He admitted that he once put Janis up against the wall, but "if I done it like the way she said, she would have gone through the wall."

He said that, after their move to the new apartment complex, his relationship with Sharon went "downhill all the way. . . . Sharon knows my pressure points. Sometimes I'm not the easiest person to live with." After their separation he said they would often try to make up, but "it seemed to backfire. She'd push me into a corner until I naturally blew up."

Asked if there were good times, he started to talk about Christmas, and then said, "A couple of Christmastimes I was there and at four in the morning her boyfriend phoned and said he was coming over—not Gary, some other guy she was seeing. And she wanted to throw me out. It destroyed my Christmas and the kids'."

He described an incident that occurred soon after they were married: "I hit her but I didn't know I hit her. I punched her out, when she woke me in a half-and-half sleep." He was asked if he had hit her on other occasions, and he explained that, if you hit a woman you should slap her, rather than "hauling off, and drive her one between the eyes." When this prompted some laughter in court, Gordon grinned and added, "Well, you asked me. I done it to her just once. But I didn't know it was her I was doing it to."

Asked about Sharon's relationship with Gary, he said, "I figured it was a wild-goose chase." Hartrick asked him to explain that comment, and he replied, "In my own words? If I did they wouldn't record it. He was just after her for her, and that was it." He said he met Gary on the street after he heard about the children's allegations, and told him, "I didn't exactly appreciate hearing the allegations of what they were supposed to have done to the kids. If that was true, that was it."

"Meaning?"

"He would get what is coming to him."

Gordon said the allegations were "all B.S." Hartrick asked him about his tattoos, and he showed his "little devil" tattoo to the judge. Judge Beckett examined it and described it for the court record: "Almost like a little cherub-type character, a childlike cartoon head, what appears to be two emerging horns, perhaps pointed ears, a three-pronged pitchfork over the right shoulder, red pants or diaper, a tail with a forked prong on the end." The judge asked if anyone else wanted to look at it.

"To them I charge," said Gordon. "It's just a little devil, Hot Stuff, a cartoon character that was popular back then. Janis liked the tattoos."

On the subject of recent contacts with his ex-wife, he said, "Since the trial started we got together. The last five years of our life hasn't been a dream boat. If I got the children, or Sharon, they don't need to come back to see us arguing again. We wanted to get our differences sorted out before." He said he did not have any satanic friends: "I haven't had any connections like that in my life. The only thing I told her is that the courtroom is all wrong. It's gone on way too long, and should be shut down and started again properly. A year-and-a-half to two years to straighten out a simple problem has gone too far."

Gordon told Brown that he had dismantled the shotgun and thrown it away, because "with all the stuff that's gone down, you wouldn't exactly keep a few of them around, would you?" He said he used to keep it in the apartment in Toronto for protection after "we had a little bit of discussion around the premises," and the lives of Sharon and the children were threatened. He said the fact that the gun did not work was irrelevant, since "if no one knows you, and you walk up to a door and someone sticks a gun in your face, whether it works or not, they ain't gonna stick around and ask questions; they're just gonna leave."

Judge Beckett later observed, "I found that to be an amazing answer by Mr. Wells. I certainly do not believe him when he says that the gun was inoperative. It was he who had cut the gun down. A sawed-off shotgun can only have one function, and that is as an anti-personnel weapon."

"Do you open the door with a gun?" Brown asked Gordon.

"If I know what's coming down. I had it around in case anything did happen. I don't want any harm coming to my family. I had shells around, 12-gauge shotgun shells, but they didn't belong to the gun."

Brown asked him if he ever put the gun to Sharon's head, and he replied, "That's her story. As far as I know nothing like that transpired. I may have done a lot of stuff, but that I didn't do."

The mother's lawyer asked Gordon if he recalled seeing a skull suspended from the ceiling of Sharon's brothers' room during the days when he and Sharon's brothers used to be best friends. He said he did not recall ever seeing anything like that.

Gordon said he had lost a $30,000-a-year job because of the case. "It was mind straining. It had a very physical impact on me. You can't run heavy equipment and keep your mind on the job when something like this is going on," he said. "I told the boss. On the one hand he understood. On the other hand he didn't give a shit and fired me."

He said he had found it hard to separate from his wife, because he loved her. He said he was concerned about the effect of their violent scenes on the children, but "certain things vanish from your mind until you realize things have gone down wrong. I never really lost my temper with anybody else at all. I don't like fighting. I'd rather walk away than do anything." Asked about the holes in the wall, he said, "Let's put it this way. Isn't it better to punch a wall than to lay somebody out, and have criminal charges against you?"

Sharon sat shaking as she listened to Gordon's reply to Brown's question about her "satanic friends" allegation. Gordon said, "I think she's been sitting in the courtroom too long. When she wants to get her way she'll turn around and lie through her teeth. Somebody's going to believe her. If she goes in bawling her eyes out, the judge is going to believe her. She's been putting on an act for two years. She'd been saying, 'Let's work together to get the kids back,' then comes out with this idiotic story. She's been sitting in this courtroom too long, listening to the B.S. that's shoveled in this courtroom. If she bubbles her eyes out long enough she's going to get the kids back. That's a lot of bull. I'm an artist trying to raise my kids. You bring this on my doorstep. I'm not involved in anything like that. As far as I'm concerned this is a simple custody hearing. McInnis is the one that brought that out. You tell me she's sane? You tell me we're crazy?"

He denied threatening people in the court: "I wish I could win the lottery. But I didn't say the other half." When O'Neail asked him if he had referred to Gary as "a fucking black bastard," he said, "I've referred to a lot of people in a lot of ways." As to whether he said "That nigger should be shot," he responded, "If this court case comes out the right way, and he's done things to my kids, what do you think should be done to him? It's got nothing to do with him being black."

"Are you suggesting Sharon Wells was putting on a big act to this court?" asked Harper.

"Yeah, Sharon's noted for a lot of stuff to get what she wants. It wouldn't be the first time she pulled it on me. She lied like hell in family court. She's trying to use every ways and means for me not to get the kids if she doesn't get them.

"She doesn't like what I call open sex. But I don't have to turn around and force someone to do it. I'd wreck my own furniture. It was better than hurting her. I put my fist through walls, but it's better than hitting her," Gordon said.

Gordon said he had no contact with Sharon and the children for two-and-a-half months after they moved to Hamilton in the fall of 1984, following Gordon's allegations about the sexual abuse of Linda and Janis's allegations about the man at the baby-sitter's apartment. Harper asked him why he had failed to check on the children's welfare during this period. He replied, "If you complain and nobody listens to you, you get fed up after a while . . . . I did my part. The police in Toronto and the CAS in Toronto neglected to do theirs. What am I supposed to do, stay on the phone 24 hours and lose my job?"

When Sharon did finally get in touch with him, and let him see the children, Gordon did not try to find out where they lived. He said this was because if he had turned up on her doorstep it would have caused trouble. "She left me, figuring getting away from me. She would have had the police on my back. I don't need any hassle with the police. All I wanted to do was see my kids. I don't care what my wife does. Me and her aren't important any more. It's the kids. That's what I've been trying to punch into her head for the last two years."

As Gordon began to get upset about being questioned on the children's allegations, his brows furrowed with anger. The large wrinkles on his forehead accentuated the look of menace in his eyes. He said he had not attended the court hearing because of his work and because "this court case has got a lot of junk. It's all garbage. I don't need to listen to stuff like that." He asked, "Who put the devil part into their heads? Who put the picture into their heads? I never heard the kids say that. They used to like my tattoos."

When questioned further about the picture of the devil, Gordon said, "I don't draw to scare the shit out of anybody. It's art—nothing more."

Gordon told Harper sharply that he was "dead wrong" in his suggestion that Sharon visited on the long weekend. Harper said, "I suggest you were so angry with Catherine McInnis that you threatened their lives and the children heard you."

"Why would I be that mad at the McInnises, when the judge gave me access? I went in and had conversations with them? Don't you think that's a little absurd? I already had access to my kids. Why should I be mad at the McInnises? Why should I turn around and plot anything?" Gordon said. "No one knows what goes on behind the closed doors at the foster parents. She's the one who watches movies about satanism. She's the one that has bars on her windows. Mrs. McInnis is a nut case. You have an outside psychiatrist examine her and you might find out. She's supposed to be a churchgoer and she watches devil pictures on TV. She needs a straitjacket. They brainwashed those kids so bad, they'd come out with anything."

"Is that your answer to the allegations?"

"You got it."

Atwood read Gordon details of the sexual abuse allegations, and the father said, "How are they supposed to know about it? Between Gary and Sharon and the foster parents themselves, something had to go on. Janis and Linda, even if they were looking at *Penthouse*, wouldn't have known what they were looking at. It'd be just a bright picture. They have got to be guilty, or somebody's got to be guilty. They got to get it from some place."

He said he hadn't followed the trial because "I hear enough of this. I sit there and read the junk in the paper. I just get sick of it. I read about it now and again." During a break, however, he did warn the newspaper reporters in a menacing voice, louder and harsher than he had sounded during his testimony, that he would be keeping a sharp eye on what they wrote about him.

"No one can actually say she done it or not. But she put the children in the CAS. I'm saying she shouldn't have them, because she doesn't deserve them," said Gordon. He told Atwood that his own view on child sexual abuse was that "if you turn around and do that to a child, you've got no rights to live."

Atwood asked Gordon about a statement he had made earlier about the Toronto apartment building having a reputation for kiddy porn. He replied, "I know of the building, and what came down in it. Certain things like that were going on in there. Sharon said people in the building told her. A cop at the station said he knew the building because he patrolled it for violence in the building."

Judge Beckett asked the father for his explanation of the children's allegations, and he replied, "The kids were saying something in confidence. Then Catherine McInnis and Lesley Morgan took the whole thing and blown it out of proportion."

"With what motive?" asked the judge.

"Who knows. You can't say things haven't been greatly fabricated in this court case. They have. The Children's Aid can't afford to lose this court case, because they'd lose face. The girls wouldn't know what satanism meant, wouldn't know what a dead body looked like unless somebody showed it to them."

The judge asked, "You've said that Mrs. McInnis has bars on her windows. How did you know that?"

"Through the grapevine. Certain parties told me. They turned around and went by the place, and seen bars in the windows."

"Who told you?"

"Sharon did. A long time ago."

"When?"

"Seven or eight months ago. Somewhere in there."

"Where?"

"Probably over the phone."

"I get the impression that you talk to each other from time to time. Sharon Wells testified she had four, possibly five contacts with you during the time she testified."

"Could be."

"You're a gun collector?" the judge then asked.

"I was."

"The pump-action shotgun, what make was it?"

"I can't remember."

"Why cut it down? Did you have any knowledge that is not lawful?"

"I did. But I did not use it. Most of the time it was in the trunk of my car."

"I'm curious as to why it was in the trunk."

"Because for a time most of my stuff was in the trunk. I'm the type of person that packs something away and forgets it's there. It must have been in the trunk of my car for years. It never really dawned on me. I just did it for the hell of it."

"I'm curious as to why you would mutilate a shotgun. What purpose would it then have?"

"Most people say, if you cut the barrel, it's better known as a scatter gun. It's just something that I did, then I got rid of it."

"For what purpose."

"No purpose at all. Just something to do at the time. I turned around and seen what it looks like. That's it."

"It wouldn't have any sporting purpose? You wouldn't go shooting with it?"

"There's a spread, so whatever you fire at, if it was birds, instead of getting one bird, probably you'd get two or three different ones."

"Did you ever intend to go hunting birds?"

"My brother was hunting and that. I was going to get into it."

When court resumed, Brown asked Gordon why he believed that the children couldn't have completely made up the allegations. He replied, "It's very simple. When a kid's first born they don't know nothing. When they go to school, they have to be told what's going down. They have to be shown, told, what things mean. That's what's called education.

"Satanism? Cannibalism? Why would Lesley Morgan and Catherine McInnis keep playing on that? Kids don't know anything about that," Gordon added.

Sharon, who had been looking scared and upset through most of Gordon's testimony, started laughing when the next witness appeared, and continued to giggle throughout her brief testimony. The witness was Gordon's mother, a large woman with dyed blond hair, who was wearing a big fur hat, a fur coat and a pink dress, the effect of which was slightly marred by what looked like a coffee stain on the back.

The woman testified that Gordon had been a very good boy, and had attended Sunday school every week. She said his shotgun didn't work and he didn't have any satanic friends. "My son is not evil. He is not a violent person," she said.

The court had earlier heard from Ann and Neil Murphy, the friends with whom Gordon had lived for several years after separating from Sharon. They had actually been called as Sharon's witnesses to testify about the condition of the children on the May, 1985, visits to their father. But the judge concluded that their evidence was perjured. This was significant because Ann was one of the people named by the children as being present at the graveyard rituals. The judge rejected their clumsy attempts to offer an explanation for statements by the children about Ann wearing a mask at the graveyard. This, combined with Gordon's unconvincing denial of the "satanic friends" remark, and the lack of any credible innocent explanation for the children's allegations, created a distinctly sinister impression of Gordon and his associates.

Judge Beckett stated in his judgment: "I found Gordon Wells to be an unreliable and unbelievable witness. I had the opportunity of observing him carefully for a period of three days in the witness stand and was not impressed by him. The fact that he lied to this court on several issues, especially about the statement to Sharon about his 'satanic friends' is, in my view, very significant."

CHAPTER 19

THE BOYFRIEND'S TESTIMONY

Gary Evans was a slightly built, shy, soft-spoken young man, who completely denied all the allegations against him, maintaining that he was not "that kind of person." He offered no explanation for why the girls would fabricate such graphic and detailed accounts of sexual abuse at his hand. He presented a picture of them as normal, healthy little girls, and of Sharon's home as clean and tidy, which conflicted with all other evidence in the case.

It was hard to imagine, if he did not have a sexual interest in Sharon's children or some even more sinister involvement with her, why this well-bred university graduate would form a relationship with this disturbed, hostile, uneducated and distinctly unattractive young mother.

Judge Beckett clearly did not accept his story, and concluded: "I observed Evans closely during his testimony. I have since reviewed his testimony, and have come to the conclusion that he was not telling the truth when he denied sexually abusing Janis and Linda."

A psychologist and a psychiatrist who testified on Gary's behalf did not find any evidence of a propensity to sexually abuse children, but neither could say that they were confident that he had not committed such acts. Ronald Langevin, senior research psychologist at the Clarke Institute of Psychiatry, testified that Evans had not shown any abnormalities while undergoing an impressive battery of tests, including a phalometric test to measure his erotic responses. The psychologist then admitted that it was possible to fake responses to such tests, and that they are, anyway, subject to a high rate of error. Psychiatrist Clive Chamberlain testified that Gary Evans seemed to be a normal, well-adjusted person, but then conceded that apparently normal people can commit horrendous crimes and that he could not really give an opinion about whether the young man did what was alleged without knowing about other facets of the case.

Dr. Langevin's evidence precipitated a wrangle over the admissibility of expert testimony, and an angry outburst from Judge Beckett. The defense lawyers were desperate to get an expert opinion that challenged the report of the Hospital for Sick Children. Langevin was apparently willing to offer some criticisms of the report, but the problem was that he was not a psychiatrist, and had no experience working directly with sexually abused children.

O'Neail, Gary Evans's lawyer, tried to argue that the psychologist, as an expert in testing and research design, could comment on the structure and the scientific basis of the hospital report. Harper said that the design of psychological tests and research projects is a totally different field to the analysis of children's statements.

Judge Beckett said, "I would welcome an expert with a great deal of clinical experience in dealing with abused children, but in his CV there is nothing that relates to that."

Atwood, representative of the Ontario Official Guardian, said the psychologist might just as well apply his expertise in test design to structural engineering. "He can psychologically test nuts and bolts as much as he wants, but he's not going to make them talk."

After Judge Beckett ruled that the witness was not qualified to give expert opinion on the children's credibility, Brown and Hartrick persisted in trying to get him to answer questions on this issue. The judge eventually became angry with this tactic and said, "I am not going to allow this trial to be turned into some kind of parody, a travesty of the way trials should be run. It seems to me like we're playing scrub ball here, getting witnesses as we go along."

In the testimony about Gary Evans that the psychologist was allowed to give, he said, "My impression is he is a naive man, inexperienced, candid, I believe, in his responses to me. I believe he was being honest."

Atwood, who was displaying some skepticism about Dr. Langevin's conclusions, drew the judge's attention to the fact that one of the questionnaires administered to Gary began by asking, "Have you ever been aroused by inanimate things?"

Gary Evans's mother testified that he had been brought up as an Anglican, had gone to Sunday school and still goes to church. She said there was never any problem between Gary and his younger sisters.

She described to Brown how her house was visited by police, who told her they had permission to search Gary's room: "I asked, 'For what?' They said dead birds, dead bodies, dead kids and things like that. They just destroyed the whole thing. They watched tapes on the VCR in the basement. Daytime soap operas. Three big men sat in there and watched them."

"Were there any religious programs?"

"No, just soap operas."

Mrs. Evans told Harper that her son now has a new girlfriend, but was reticent about telling her name. Harper asked her when Gary had returned the VCR that he and Sharon had subleased from his father. Mrs. Evans became hysterical. "God in heaven give me grace, because I never come in a place like this before, never been in a court," she said. "Don't try to put words in my mouth. I don't know what you're trying to do to my brain. I don't know, I don't know. If I say, I'd be lying."

Gary Evans testified that he had lived with his family near Toronto since coming to Canada from Barbados as a child. He said that he had a B.A. and was now doing postgraduate studies. He said he had held a number of summer jobs while he was in high school, and worked as an ice cream salesman when he was 15. In the fall of 1984, he was completing university in Hamilton, he said, and looking for work. He said he only lived with Sharon for about two weeks, but would look after the children, while she was working, until he found a job in December with a company that did out-of-town contract work.

Gary said his hobbies and interests were sports, track and field, soccer, basketball and photography. He said he took pictures of sports events and would usually take his camera when he went traveling.

He described Linda and Janis as "really nice little kids, playful, just nice kids. They weren't rude or anything, well-mannered, well-behaved." About the condition of the apartment and the children in Toronto, he said, "As far as I'm concerned it was decent living. The kids' rooms were always kept clean. She made their beds, kept them neat, prepared good meals for the kids all the time, made sure they always ate. Their clothes were kept clean. She was always wiping their faces."

Asked about the allegations made in the anonymous phone calls that Gordon had received, he said, "It was all false. I never struck a woman in my life. I'm not that type of person. I never abused children in my life. I'm not that type of person. I never made a woman pregnant before."

Gary said the reason he sometimes did not take Linda to school when he was looking after her was that he was looking for a job, and it was easier to take her with him, or drop her off at his mother's house, than to have to drive back to Hamilton to fetch her from school.

He said he was "totally shocked" when he was told about the children's allegations in March 1985. They were all false, he said. He denied each allegation in turn as O'Neail listed them out to him. He described some of them as very sickening and disgusting, explaining that he was "not brought up in that type of manner." He shook his head when O'Neail asked him about satanism, and said, "I was brought up a good Christian. That's false." And on the question of cannibalism, he said, "I wouldn't eat a person if I had to to survive. That's gross. It turns my stomach.

"It's so unbelievable. The only thing I can see is these kids been misled, and they misinterpreted some things the children said. They never gave us a chance, never talked to us. They took the kids, and said they've been abused and that was that. I'd play with the kids. If I pushed the kids playing, they might say Gary pushed me. They were just two healthy normal kids, healthy, bright, energetic kids. There was nothing wrong with them."

Sharon gasped loudly as Gary testified that, when she became pregnant, she had not told him that she was no longer using birth control, and that the only reason he suggested an abortion was that he knew that the CAS would try to take the child away. He said he would like to have access to the baby, but would not be able to take custody yet because of his work and study commitments. He spoke very fervently about his desire to clear his name from a list of known sexual abusers that is kept by the provincial government: "My name is on the sexual abuse register for these false allegations. I don't want to have to plan my life around these false allegations . . . if I have a child in Ontario, they're just going to snatch her. It's ridiculous. I just want to get these accusations removed from my record. They're false and there's no truth to them."

Brown asked him why he was attracted to Sharon, and he replied, "I saw the person she was inside. A very caring person. A very loving person. The fact she had two kids didn't matter to me. It was her."

"Did you have an interest in her so you would have two vulnerable little girls that you could abuse?" asked Brown.

"Not at all. Never in my life. I'm not that kind of person."

"You were naive in sexual matters, a late bloomer. Was your first physical relationship with a lady with Sharon?"

"Yes, it was."

Brown asked if they had discussed child abuse, and Gary replied, "She said she'd never be able to live with me, if I did that. I told her, 'I'm not like that. I've got sisters myself. I wouldn't want any harm to come to them. I would never harm your kids in any way.'"

Harper asked him why he refused to talk to the police. He replied, "I told them I hadn't obtained counsel. The allegations were false. I felt in my best interests to tell them the allegations were false, and, until I obtained counsel, not talk to them." He agreed with Harper that he had an opportunity to talk to Eva Gede, the psychiatrist who assessed Sharon, but he said he felt she was "not an unbiased person." He said he made arrangements to talk to Dr. Rae-Grant, but cancelled them when he decided that "she had me convicted before we sat down."

Judge Beckett noted that this, and other evidence before the court, was in conflict with his claim that he never had a chance to tell his story to the CAS.

Harper questioned Gary's assertion that the foster mother could have got the children to make false allegations against him within three weeks of their coming into her care. He responded, "You can put things into kids' minds very easily. They've messed up these kids. It all started out in the foster care home, and I would say that they have taken the kids and they have, sort of, you know, twisted what the kids might have said, and gotten the kids believing it; got the kids so confused that the kids are actually believing it, and then the kids got to the point where they are saying it, and they don't know what they are saying, and that is the honest truth. These kids have been misinterpreted and they have been messed up."

Judge Beckett quoted this statement in his judgment, and commented, "Gary Evans's recourse to the explanation given above was totally unsupported by any evidence in a situation which cried out for some kind of an explanation. In my opinion it was unacceptable."

Responding to questions from the judge, Gary said he did not remember birds ever nesting on Sharon's balcony, that he had never heard of the movie *Last House on the Left*, and that he had never been told the children were exposed to any kind of movie that they shouldn't have seen.

Dr. Chamberlain, a child psychiatrist experienced in doing court assessments, said he found it hazardous to do an assessment for a child welfare hearing without having a chance to see all parties involved. He said he agreed to do a partial assessment of Gary Evans because he had been told that there had been no comprehensive assessment in the case, and that Evans had not seen a psychiatrist. Later, in response to questions from Harper, he said he had not been made aware of several of the assessments and reports that were done on the case, and had not seen transcripts of evidence that was presented to the court.

As a result of his examination of Gary Evans, he said, "My impression is that of a well-adjusted young male, somewhat unsophisticated and late in developing sexually, but certainly within normal limits. He does not fit any personality pattern of men who initiate sexual activity with children, or who are likely to be aggressive physically or verbally. His moral standards, as far as I can know them within the limitation of this assessment, should preclude involvement, even passively, in activities such as have been alleged."

He added, "It is possible he was concealing his behavior and not telling the truth. There is no way I can assure myself people are telling the truth, particularly in circumstances like these. I can't read minds. I conducted a very limited investigation. I would have preferred to have talked to a large number of people, all the protagonists, and fit them into the mosaic. I am left with a question in my mind. How can this person, as I see him, become involved in behavior which I've heard happened?" Dr. Chamberlain said.

The psychiatrist said that, having seen Lesley Morgan's assessment of the case and the Hospital for Sick Children report, he felt at a loss as to how he could fit that together with his knowledge of Evans: "Either I have to change my notion of the person I've seen, or change my notion of the validity of the reports, or find some other way to understand it." He said, "I am left then, much like one of the proverbial blind men, touching part of an elephant. My part does not fit reports from others."

Asked about the report from the Hospital for Sick Children, he said, "I have never seen one as carefully crafted and thoughtfully put together. I have no quarrel with it whatsoever." He added, "If the conclusions are that the events reported by the children all happened, I would not draw that conclusion." He said he would have wanted to do a more expanded inquiry before reaching that conclusion.

Brown asked if notes taken by an unsophisticated interviewer were an adequate basis for forming an opinion on children's credibility. Judge Beckett said, "I don't mind telling you now. I wish the whole thing were televised. I'm sure there are better methods. But that didn't happen."

Dr. Chamberlain said, "As I understand it, the assessment was an effort to correct through analysis inconsistencies that were occasioned by an inexperienced interviewer, compensating for an inexperienced interviewer by a fairly sophisticated technique."

He told Brown that he would have liked to have seen the children, but said he recognized that "part of the agony of trying to come to terms with this issue is you've already got children at risk who have suffered a great deal. To have another stranger come in creates problems. I am not a wizard. There's nothing special about me." When Harper told him that the therapist testified that it would be harmful for the children to be interviewed, Dr. Chamberlain said, "I would want the therapist to convince me she was right. Dr. Oliviera is a well-known and excellent therapist. I would certainly be impressed by what she had to say."

In response to a further question from Brown, he said, "It is a mistake to assume that children always tell the truth or that they will lie. I've seen many children represent different realities depending on who they are with. Children say what they say for all sorts of reasons, logical reasons, to feel safe and comfortable. Lying or telling the truth is an adult notion that perhaps shouldn't be applied to children."

"Children tend to be susceptible?"

"People are susceptible."

In a section of Dr. Chamberlain's report read to the court by O'Neail, he stated that he found that Gary Evans did not fit into the two types of personalities who sexually abuse children. But Harper quoted a further sentence that O'Neail had not read: "It goes without saying that normal people can behave in ways different from normal disposition given a situation different from their normal context." Harper asked him, "Are there, in fact, three types?"

Dr. Chamberlain replied, "Sure. Normal people. That is, clinically normal people. All one has to do is reflect on what happened in Germany before and during the Second World War. Quite clinically sound people do unimaginable things under unusual circumstances."

CHAPTER 20

THE JUDGE'S DECISION

Gordon Wells believed Judge Beckett released a written judgment on the case, and did not come into court to give oral reasons for his final decision, because the judge was "chicken." Others who reviewed the 106-page ruling saw it as a fine mixture of caution and toughness.

It did not come as a surprise to many of the people who had followed the case to find that the judge ruled that the two girls and their baby halfsister were in need of protection, or that he had come to the very hard conclusion that their parents should not have any access to them. Nor had anyone expected him to go out on a limb and state that he emphatically believed everything that Janis and Linda had said, concluding that the children definitely had witnessed murders and were the victims of a satanic cult. The evidence to support that kind of finding had not been presented.

The judge might well have concluded that he did not believe any of the children's more bizarre allegations, and still decided to make them wards of the Crown, solely on the basis of the evidence of neglect, psychological damage and sexual abuse. He could have simply dismissed the most troubling aspects of the case as being irrelevant to his ruling. The fact that he did not do this made the judgment an intriguing one. Judge Beckett was cautious in not trying to reach conclusions for which he had insufficient factual basis, but he did pose all of the tough questions that arose from the evidence that was presented to him. His judgment would force those who read it to seriously ponder the almost unthinkable possibilities suggested by the children's strange stories.

It was not that the judge was anxious to delve into this material, which he described as "almost beyond human comprehension." Referring to what he characterized as "a virtual flood of the most lurid, gruesome, bloodthirsty stories that any person could possibly imagine," Judge Beckett said, "the court heard allegations of murder, of cannibalism, of graveyard rituals and acts of bestiality, allegations so horrible, so gruesome, so loathsome that no one, including myself, wanted to believe any of it. In fact I wanted very much to believe that none of the allegations made by Janis and Linda could be true."

Judge Beckett said that the reluctance of the police to believe the allegations was understandable and reflected "the natural abhorrence of any normal person at the very thought that children in our community could possibly be involved in such matters." He said he did not intend the hearing to become a forum into the adequacy of the police investigation of the case, and, while recognizing that they did not find evidence to support the children's more "florid" allegations, he stated, "That is not to say, of course, that any of these events did not occur: it is only to say that the police found no evidence of it." He said this lack of evidence could not prove either that the children did not have experiences that "prompted childlike misinterpretations or distortions of fact that resulted in their stories.

"We may never know for certain to what extent the so-called 'florid' allegations are based on fact, or what occurrences or experiences the children had that could have prompted them to say such things," Judge Beckett said.

The "rich detail" of the children's stories impressed the judge, "as well as the fact that they related them with obvious reluctance and fear." He said he was struck by the signs of distress that they showed when telling their stories, particularly such symptoms as soiling, wetting, trembling and shaking. He said, "Most particularly, I was impressed with the age-inappropriate knowledge they have, especially of sexual matters.

"The CAS called no evidence with respect to 'satanic cults' and the court does not intend to take any judicial notice of the practices and rites of any such cults," the judgment stated. "Nonetheless, the descriptions of midnight graveyard scenes with dancing and singing, of people with masks, of opening of graves and coffins together with gross sexual activities suggests cult activities."

Judge Beckett said he certainly found many things that the children said difficult to resolve or accept. For example, he said, the evidence about the Channel 11 television studio made him conclude that it had probably not been used for pornography sessions, such as the children described. But, he said, one has to wonder why Janis described the interior so accurately and why she was so frightened when being driven by it.

"Why did the children refer to the number 666—a symbol we know is a biblical reference to the 'beast or the devil'?" Judge Beckett asked. He noted that it had been suggested during the hearing that this reference arose from the fact that one of the children's relatives lived at an apartment building with the street number 666. But the children did not refer to the number in connection with this, the judge said. "On the contrary they connected it with graveyard activities." He also asked, "What experience did the children have to enable them to speak such horrors and why did Janis persistently draw pictures of graveyards? Why were the minds of these children dominated by thoughts of death and of characters like 'the Blob'? Why do they speak of their father with such fear and say that he had killed people, and think they could engage him to kill Gary Evans?"

In posing these questions, the judge remarked that some of the things the children spoke of turned out to be proven later. He said "the man with half a face," for example, turned out to be a real person, and their father did, in fact, have a picture of "the devil" in his room. "Were Sharon Wells, Gary Evans or Gordon Wells involved in cult activities?" Judge Beckett asked. "Clearly on the evidence, I cannot find that they were. But what of the fact that Gordon Wells spoke to Sharon Wells in October, 1986, of his 'satanic friends'? The fact that he would make such a remark does little to allay the suspicions raised by the children's allegations."

On the issue of the children's allegations about a plot to kill the foster parents, the judge observed that evidence indicated that Gordon Wells was prone to making threats of violence, and that it is not difficult to infer that the children might have overheard statements that they interpreted as a plot. Judge Beckett said he was not convinced by the evidence that Gordon Wells was violently antagonistic to both Sharon and Gary, which had been advanced by defense lawyers as proof of the absurdity of the children's story of the alleged plot.

"I am left with the question of where the 'florid' allegations originated," the judge stated. "Was it fantasy? Were the children lying? If the children were fantasizing or lying, the question arises as to where the children got the material to produce their so-called lies or fantasies. I cannot accept that two little children of this age could possibly describe the matters I have described above without some knowledge or some experience in order to create the lies or the fantasies. Such matters surely cannot come out of the minds of young children as native or original thought. But is not the fact that they said such things, that such horrors were in their minds, evidence of a very bizarrely disturbed relationship with their caretakers? Was this not evidence of brutal trauma to their psyche, just as would bruises and broken bones be evidence of physical abuse to their bodies?"

The judge went on to comment: "The world of small children is a narrow one: it is mother, it is father and their families, their school and their playmates. It is in this milieu that a child's mental constructs are molded. What experiences did these children have, while in the care of the adults involved, that would cause them to say what they said and to say it with such fear and terror? To say that they 'lied' or that it was 'fantasy' falls far short of explaining how such things could have been in their minds. It also should not be forgotten that statements by small children must always be viewed from the perspective of a child—what a child says may not be truth but that does not mean it is a lie or fantasy. What may not, in reality, be truth, may be interpreted as truth by a child. For example, a child told to eat meat, which is in reality raw chicken, but is represented to the child by his caretaker as human flesh, would not be 'lying' if he said that he had eaten human flesh; he would just be mistaken.

"But does it really matter, for the purposes of this case, whether the children saw murder or something that they interpreted as being murder? Whether they ate human flesh or ate something they thought was human flesh, whether they were in Channel 11 Telecenter, or whether they were in some place that they believed to be the Telecenter? It is really unimportant in reality as to which it was," Judge Beckett concluded.

The judge had no difficulty, however, in concluding that the children had been sexually abused by all three adults. He said, "I was particularly impressed by the fact that the children did not tell their stories with any degree of pleasure or satisfaction. Quite the contrary—they did not want to tell and often attempted to interfere with each other when one was disclosing. In the telling of these stories, there was far more than consistency that compels me to believe the allegations of sexual abuse, especially the use of graphic detail about sexual matters children of this age could not possibly know otherwise. Young children of this age might indeed find a sexual aid such as a vibrator in their parent's premises, but how would a child know how such an instrument is used? How would a child know that it is necessary to use Vaseline in order to achieve the purpose of the instrument? Where would children get notions of oral sex, not only as between their mother and Gary Evans, but as between those two individuals and the children? How could they describe such events unless somehow it had been part of their experiences?"

Judge Beckett said it was impossible to see how the children could be mistaken in presenting such graphic descriptions, or how such explicit statements could possibly have been misinterpreted. While he said that the girls might have a motive for lying about Gary's involvement in such things, he found it difficult to imagine why the children would make false allegations against their parents, when they loved their parents and knew these allegations were the reason for their not being returned to their home.

With apparent discomfort the judge concluded, "The graphic description of the children being forced to eat feces has a distinct ring of truth about it, loathsome as that thought might be. The children's descriptions of oral sex, particularly with Gary Evans, contain detail and descriptions of sensation and tastes that could not possibly come out of the imaginations of children. As much as I did not and do not want to believe these children were forced into such loathsome activities, I find it impossible on the basis of what these children have said over the past two years to come to any other conclusion."

Judge Beckett found that Gary Evans had grossly and sexually abused the children on numerous occasions. He described Sharon's explanations for the allegations as "somewhat bizarre," and rejected them as "at best, hopeful speculation, and, at worst, a deliberate resort to fabrication in an attempt to deceive the court." He concluded that she too had sexually abused the girls over an extended period of time. The allegations of sexual abuse against Gordon Wells had not been that extensive, but Judge Beckett found that the children had clearly accused their father of sexually abusing them, not only in statements to Mrs. McInnis, but also to Lesley Morgan and Sgt. Elwood. He also noted that Linda had talked in a therapy session about her fear that her father would kill her with a knife to the neck. The judge made the finding that the father had sexually abused the girls, and that, anyway, they needed to be protected from this man, because they saw him as a figure of fear and violence.

"The allegations that these children made cried out for some reasonable and rational explanation from Sharon Wells, Gary Evans or Gordon Wells. None was forthcoming," said the judge. He agreed with Dr. Oliviera that, unless these people were able to either validate or satisfactorily explain the children's belief that the statements they made are true, further contact with these adults could be harmful to the children.

The judgment had taken more than two months to prepare, and the judge made frequent reference to the difficulty he had been faced with. He said, "Perhaps in the history of such cases in Canada, no judge has been faced with such an overwhelming volume of evidence." He referred several times to his extreme personal distaste for dealing with the repulsive subject matter of much of the evidence. He described the decision that he was faced with as "an awesome responsibility for any one person to have." He went on to say, "I can think of no order that any judge could possibly make that can so profoundly affect the lives of the people involved; to take someone's children from them is a power that a judge must exercise only with the highest degree of caution, only on the basis of compelling evidence, and only after a careful examination of possible alternative remedies.

"Certainly no one can derive any pleasure or satisfaction from the order that I have made," Judge Beckett said, "but by the same token, society cannot tolerate young children being exposed to the abuses that Janis and Linda have suffered, and that the baby would likely suffer if left in the care of their parents."

Judge Beckett's ruling ended with a compassionate statement about the woman who had played such a tragic role during the 18 months that the case was before the court. "Sadly, life has dealt Sharon Wells little happiness, but much sadness and brutality," he said. "She is a pathetic woman who desperately needs help and one can only hope that the system will now turn its attention to her as well, in an attempt to mitigate the horrible experiences of her past and the devastating effect of the order that I have been forced to make."

EPILOGUE

Do children lie? This question was put to almost every expert witness at the hearing, and would almost always come up whenever interested outsiders discussed the case. People continued to ask the question long after the clear and emphatic answer was given by Judge Beckett and most of the witnesses. That answer is "yes, of course children lie. And they can easily be confused, deceived or mistaken."

Adults also lie. Some people, including child abusers, pornographers and members of secretive cults, are especially practiced and skillful at concealing the truth. History has proven over and over again that people are also easily confused and misled, especially if the truth is something that would be troubling to accept. Adult lies and myths are much more complex and impenetrable than children's deceptions. The important thing is to be able to distinguish between lies and falsehood whether they are coming from children or adults.

The question that the Hamilton wardship hearing posed was not whether children in general can lie, but whether Janis and Linda were lying or mistaken when they made a series of detailed, consistent and explicit allegations against adults whom they loved and feared. The answer that came out of more than a year of evidence was that they were not lying, and, though they may have been mistaken about some things, their allegations were apparently based on real experiences. It was never proven exactly what those experiences were, beyond the fact that they were certainly exposed to gross sexual abuse and degradation, but the judge noted that the children's statements suggested that they were involved in cult activities.

Even the least distressing explanation for the children's allegations confronts us with unsettling truths about the nature of our society, and presents us with grave concerns about whether children are receiving adequate protection. The explanation that would be least anxiety-provoking for the average parent would be that the children's more bizarre allegations were fantasies generated by an appallingly horrific history of abuse. If this is the case, all we have to worry about is trying to improve child protection services and watching out for these unnamed perpetrators, and perhaps many similarly dangerous individuals, who may be living in our neighborhood. Perhaps we would want to go further and look for cures for the underlying sickness in society that generates such aberrations, but we would at least be assured that the evil we have already recognized is the evil that we are dealing with—and to some extent learned to live with.

However, evidence does not tend to support the idea that the Hamilton case was a unique aberration. The girls' allegations in this case were remarkably similar to those made by many hundreds of children all over North America. No theories have yet been advanced to adequately show how even the most horrendous forms of sexual abuse might lead children to relate convincing and detailed accounts of ritualistic violence. These accounts almost all involve references to the same specific acts of violence and abuse, and often refer to elements of satanic symbolism, presumably outside the experience of the average seven- or eight-year-old. Most of the children's statements also refer to the use of cameras. In the absence of other credible explanations, we cannot afford to dismiss the possibility that these allegations point to the activities of groups engaged in satanic ritual, or pornography, or both, and that there may be some communication or connection between such groups.

The response of many individuals and agencies who do not want to pursue this line of investigation has been to ask, "Where are the bodies? Where are the pornographic materials that were produced by such groups?" Some people, including police investigators, who believe that human sacrifice is being practiced, respond to the first question with statistics about missing children, and explanations about how skillful these cult groups apparently are at completely destroying all evidence. A more easily acceptable answer is that, if children are being manipulated, terrorized and used as pornographic subjects in rituals involving animals and simulated human sacrifice, there would be no bodies. There have been numerous discoveries of animal remains in conjunction with evidence of rituals. The fact that pornographic materials have not been recovered in connection with individual cases may only be a reflection of how difficult it is to investigate a sophisticated pornography operation.

Roland Summit told a Florida state commission on pornography in November, 1985, "There are thousands of pictures without known children. And there are thousands of photographed children without known pictures. Far from establishing credibility, these two opposing clues tend to nullify one another. Obscene pictures of anonymous children provoke only helplessness, while children who report being photographed in the midst of sexual exploitation trigger a single-minded pursuit of the photographic evidence. The almost inevitable failure to find identifiable photos tends to discredit other aspects of the child's story. Every unproved allegation seems to encourage the hope that nothing the child is saying is true."

The motivations and the practices of cult groups are radically different from conventional criminal activity, and completely outside the experience of most police forces. Police investigators and others who have seriously looked at the problem of child pornography and the phenomenon of ritual abuse all agree that these are areas in which traditional police methods are inadequate. Professional pornography rings are highly sophisticated operations, and their investigation requires large-scale co-ordination of information from many different sources. Evidence is difficult to find and, if this evidence involves ritual material, one must first have the specialized knowledge required to interpret it. Infiltration is either impossible or unethical when it involves dealing with groups that require its members to engage in acts of violence or child exploitation. For the same reason one is unlikely to find informants from within such groups, who would necessarily incriminate themselves by what they disclose. Investigators must therefore rely a lot on victims' accounts together with surveillance and exhaustive checks into suspects and their contacts.

Although the Hamilton hearing certainly did not provide proof that the children were forced to participate in a satanic cult or a professional pornography ring, the suggestions that such organized child exploitation was involved were strong enough that I believe we have to take them seriously. We need more investigation in this area, and we have to provide the police with funds for training and the establishment of special units for this type of investigation.

Any surveillance operation is expensive and labor-intensive, and is not likely to be entered into without credible witnesses. The question of assessing the credibility of child witnesses is therefore crucial. It is extremely difficult not because children are particularly prone to lying, but because there are several factors (such as fear, love, dependency and insecurity) that may cause them to withhold the truth in certain situations, disclose it in others, and often retract an earlier allegation or denial. Studies such as those done in connection with the Hamilton case are helping psychiatrists and social workers to evolve better methods of assessing credibility, and conducting interviews that encourage children to speak without fear but do not contaminate their disclosures with leading questions. Police investigators in this field need to co-operate closely with child care professionals in order to comprehend these sensitive issues.

The polarization of opinions on the issues concerning children's credibility led investigators in many of the cases in the United States first to rely too much on disclosures by child witnesses, and then to completely discount their stories. In Jordan, Minnesota, particularly, it appears that arrests were made too hastily, without adequate research and surveillance, and a multiplicity of interviews with the same children by several different people resulted in some of the children changing their stories and the evidence of others being so contaminated by the investigatory process that it was unusable in court. Several of the defendants in the Jordan case, against whom charges were dropped, attempted to sue police, prosecutors and therapists for allegedly conspiring to fabricate evidence of a sex ring in order to further the career of the Scott County attorney. The United States Court of Appeals for the Eighth Circuit, which dismissed this suit in February, 1987, clearly found that the conspiracy theory was absurd, but also noted that there were reasonable grounds for arresting the suspects.

The senior judge of the court expressed misgivings about the handling of the case, and stated, "The children's accounts are so startling and egregious, however, that it is difficult to accept the prosecutor's dismissal of the charges against the parents and the other parties charged . . . . The children's accusations, if true, demand the prosecution of the guilty parties. The prosecutor's action in dismissing the charges leaves this shocking and abusive affair in limbo." The judge went on to say that accused people may have been dealt with unjustly and, expressing concern over the difficulty in ascertaining what did happen in Jordan, urged that such perplexing cases be handled cautiously, keeping in mind the rights of both children and parents.

The investigation of the Hamilton case was also impeded by conflicts between the police and social workers over the children's credibility, and a lack of surveillance, research and timely searches. The hearing exposed inadequate communication between different agencies and professionals in Toronto. Such problems could be eliminated, or at least minimized, by better training and education programs for all professionals who deal with children, and the provision of financing for services that would co-ordinate the work of different agencies in the field. There is also a need to clarify the mandates of the police and the Children's Aid Societies in child abuse cases. The CASs now rely on police to do much of the investigation, but police forces do not consider themselves responsible for following up on child welfare cases that do not look as if they will result in criminal charges.

The length of time it took to reach a determination of the children's future raised concerns that their rights and those of their parents were being eroded. The public was also concerned over the million-dollar cost of the court hearing, in which all the lawyers were either financed by Legal Aid or represented public agencies. The case did provide a full examination of the evidence and issues involved, and achieved its aim of giving the children the protection they sadly needed. Having sat through every day of the 18-month hearing, I was not left with the feeling that anyone was to blame for the slow progress of the case. The novelty and extreme complexity of the issues required careful consideration, and the legal system rightly allows all parties to present and question all evidence that may be helpful to their case.

The lawyers involved in the case all agreed that ways have to be found to deal with such cases more quickly in the future. The many legal rulings that were made during the course of the hearing after lengthy arguments will perhaps result in quicker resolution of similar issues in other cases, while lawyers and judges will certainly study the way that evidence was presented in the Hamilton hearing in the hope of finding more efficient ways of handling such material.

The bizarre allegations and the sensational nature of the parents' evidence resulted in the hearing attracting a level of public attention quite unprecedented for a child welfare case. Not only has the case helped to alert the public to the need for more research and investigation into the perplexing issue of ritual abuse, but it has also served to promote awareness about child sexual abuse in general, a problem of epidemic proportions, of which ritual abuse is an alarming new mutation. Protecting children is something that most people in our society see as a high priority. For this reason politicians have placed it high on the public agenda. While members of the public are concerned about such issues, they do not usually trouble themselves much over the details. This is what enables politicians to practice a sleight-of-hand by which they can pay lip service to the public's concern by means of rhetoric and impressively tough legislation, but avoid the commitment of resources that will enable professionals working in the field to insure that the intent of the legislation is fulfilled.

I believe that a realistic response to ritual abuse and other forms of exploitation of children requires financing of innovative investigation and research—at the very least, a commitment by government to give child protection agencies the money they need to do their jobs properly. While reports of child sexual abuse have increased all over the country in the past few years by as much as 300 percent a year in some regions, there has been virtually no corresponding increase in the number of child welfare workers, Crown attorneys and police officers. The new legislation, which could make it easier to prosecute sexual abuse cases, will be of little value unless governments also provide agencies with the staff they need to investigate and take cases to court.

Judge Beckett's decision protected Janis and Linda from further abuse, but not before they had suffered potentially irreparable psychological damage. Their therapy, suspended in the spring of 1986, was resumed after a few months when it became clear that the hearing would continue well into 1987. Their psychiatrist was not optimistic about their prospects of growing up to be happy, well-adjusted adults, breaking the cycle of abuse by protecting their own children from the kind of suffering they and their mother have endured. "They are going to need a great deal of support," Sylvio Mainville, the executive director of the Hamilton-Wentworth Children's Aid Society, said in an interview. "We can only hope and pray to God that they are going to come out of this in a way that they can lead meaningful lives as adults."

The problems that tainted the lives of Janis and Linda have their roots far in the past, and are continuing to grow. The sickness that they suffer from has such a strong hold on our society that it is hard to see how it can be eradicated without a fundamental change in our priorities. The problem is partly one of economics and social policy. It is often argued that child sexual abuse is something that transcends class barriers. Gary and Sharon are an example of that, in that they came from such vastly different economic, cultural and social backgrounds; it seemed that almost the only thing they had in common was an inclination to sexually abuse children. However, it is not true that there is no relationship between child abuse and social class. Concerns mentioned during the hearing about the prevalence of sexual abuse in the Toronto public housing complex where Sharon lived are underscored by the Badgley Commission *Report on Sexual Offenses Against Children And Youths*, which stated that 47 percent of the girls and 33 percent of boys sexually assaulted in metro Toronto between 1979 and 1981 lived in public housing. The report stated: "Public housing units appear to constitute an easily visible target where a large number of children live in the same location."

Child abuse expert David Finkelhor noted in a 1986 book: "Although abuse is certainly not limited to the lower classes, as the stereotype might suggest, to most researchers it makes sense that the frustrations of poverty, joblessness, lack of education, and inadequate housing contribute to the conditions that increase violence toward children."[14] Finkelhor goes on to make the point that this may not be the case with sexual abuse, as with physical violence towards children. He states that studies and incidence reports do show a higher prevalence of child sexual abuse among low-income families, but this may be because such abuse is more likely to be detected by social agencies that work more with poorer people.

Certainly it would be naive to assume that Sharon's children would have been safe from abuse if she had been housed in a decent building, which was not depressing and inconvenient, rife with violence and criminal activity and crawling with cockroaches—but it might have helped, especially if she received a family allowance that gave her financial independence from the men who had such a devastating impact on her and her children's lives. It would also have been beneficial to her if she lived somewhere close to a day-care center and a mental health center, and if the social worker who was responsible for monitoring the family felt she could make regular visits without risking her own life.

Sharon had been trapped all her life in a cycle of poverty and dependence. She had been brought up to think of herself as a victim, and she was vulnerable to any form of exploitation. Gordon came from a similar environment. One would have no difficulty in characterizing him as "a frustrated, hostile, but powerless figure, who lacks legitimate means of striking back at supposed aggressors." As a description of Gordon, this could be peculiarly apt, since the words are taken from a sociological study of members of a satanist group.[15] This study describes such individuals as not necessarily poor, but usually marginal, deviant people, who desire success but do not understand how they can legitimately achieve it: "A great many of the satanists whom I interviewed reported childhoods marred by strife: they spoke of broken homes, drunken parents, aggressive and hostile siblings."

This corresponds with the observations of Louise Edwards, a British Columbia therapist, who has become increasingly concerned about the relationship between satanic cults and child abuse. She said in an interview that, while satanic cults appear to have memberships that include affluent professional people, they seek to involve alienated individuals whose only power is physical violence. She says such people make perfect victims in that they are often regarded as "low-life, expendable people: who keeps track of them? Nobody ever complains when anything happens to them."

There can be no doubt that the influence of satanism in society is alarmingly high, and the hold that it has on many young people through heavy metal music is a disturbing

trend. Again the connection between powerlessness, aliena-
tion and a craving to make an impact through magic, ritual
and violence can be seen in this form of teenage pop satanism.
In this phenomenon can be seen, perhaps, another form of
child abuse—the commercial exploitation of young people by
a music industry that profits from the sale of images of horror
and despair. This is not because there is any satanist conspiracy or particularly evil intent on the part of the people who
make and sell these records. It is simply that the image of evil
has become a highly marketable commodity. The same form
of exploitation caters to the popularity among young people of
horror films that feature graphic portrayals of sadistic sexual
violence, usually inflicted on teenage girls. *Last House on the
Left*, which shocked everyone who saw it in court, is a fairly
typical example of these films, which regularly attract large
line-ups at movie theaters and are among the most popular
items for rental in video stores.

Child sexual abuse is just one of many frightening realities that it would be more comfortable to ignore. There is overwhelming proof of its pervasiveness, but many people work
very hard at denying the seriousness of the problem, in the
same way the threats to the environment and the survival of
the species are ignored or made light of. In this context, it is
not surprising that few people would want to believe young
children's bizarre stories of cannibalism and ritual murder.

Ellen Bass wrote in an introduction to a book of writings
by survivors of child sexual abuse: "The sexual abuse of children is part of a culture in which violence to life is condoned.
Our forests, our rivers, our oceans, our air, our Earth, this
entire biosphere, all are invaded with poison—raped, just as
our children are raped. It is very possible that in 50 years or
less, life as we know it will not exist on Earth. Nuclear war
could kill us all. Even without an explosion, the radiation
emitted in the various phases of mining, milling, and con-
structing nuclear power plants and weapons is already so
abundant that the continuation of our species is in grave danger. It is not odd that men whose desire for profit has super-
seded their own instinct for survival should so abuse their
young."[16]

A police investigator concerned about satanism stated
that the phenomenon is frightening because of the all-
encompassing motive behind the abuse that is practiced on its
victims. He saw this motive as a desire to distort the values and

change the thinking of a future generation. We will not know until we have done some further investigation of the allegations of satanic cult involvement in ritual child abuse if this is paranoia or a realistic fear. In looking at the documented cases of child exploitation that surround us, in observing the images of violence and dehumanized sexuality that are part of our everyday cultural landscape, it is not that hard to believe that, conspiracy or no conspiracy, the satanists' goal could easily be achieved without much effort on their part.

In one of her most poignant statements, Janis told her foster mother, "Most people are bad." In about ten years' time, she and her sister will be young adults trying to make their way in society. It would be comforting to believe that by that time some changes will have taken place that will have encouraged her to revise her view of humanity.

AFTERWORD

On July 21, 1987, four months after Judge Beckett delivered his final judgment in the case, an appeals court received some poignant evidence about the children's response to the judge's decision. This was presented to an Ontario Supreme Court judge, who was considering an application from Sharon Wells for interim access to her children pending an appeal of the judgment.

The court was told that when the judgment was first explained to the children on April 3, 1987, Linda said, "I wished on a wishbone and I got my wish. It came true. It came true."

The children's therapist Alice Oliviera described in an affidavit how delighted the two girls appeared upon hearing the news, and hugged their foster parents, Stan and Helen Kovaks. Dr. Oliviera said that, as the children snuggled up to Mrs. Kovaks resting their heads on her bosom, Linda said, "My mom told the judge she didn't do bad things and it was a lie. She did do bad things."

The children told the therapist that they would like the Kovakses to adopt them. Janis said that she would like to buy land next door to the Kovakses home so that she could build a house and always live beside Aunt Helen. Linda said she would even live in the ditch next door.

The Supreme Court judge was clearly so convinced by Dr. Oliviera's affidavit and other written material submitted to him that he dismissed the mother's application for access without asking to hear arguments from the lawyers representing the Children's Aid Society and the Ontario Official Guardian. The judge also ruled that it would not be in the best interest of the 16-month-old baby to be visited by her natural mother. Sharon had been allowed to visit her baby twice a week during the trial, but these visits were terminated when Judge Beckett made his final decision. The appeal court considered the opinions of a social worker who had observed the mother's visits. The social worker said that the baby seemed mildly distressed whenever she was taken to see Sharon, and would cling to her foster mother for one or two hours after the visits. The social worker observed that Sharon would speak to the infant in high-pitched baby talk, and would often refer to herself as "Mom," which, the judge was told, would tend to be confusing to a child who regarded her foster parent as her mother.

Dr. Oliviera stated in her affidavit that the Kovakses provided Janis and Linda with a loving, secure and stable environment. She said it would be "utterly cruel" and "terribly, terribly abusive" to throw them into the limbo of insecurity again. "The most vital need in the world for these two children is to know that they belong to adults that will take care of them for an extended period of time, adults who will protect, nurture them, let them feel they are worthwhile and lovable," the therapist said.

Dr. Oliviera said she told the girls on March 6, 1987, that the judge was very close to making a decision, and both children said that they wanted more than anything else to stay with "Auntie Helen and Uncle Stan." When the therapist asked them how they felt about the possibility that they might not be able to stay with the foster parents, Janis replied that she would kill herself.

After the judge's decision was handed down, the children were told that they could have one last visit with their mother, or else write a goodbye letter. Janis said she would rather write a letter, and she and her sister decided that it would be a good idea to get the letters written right away. But, realizing that the judgment would be appealed and not knowing how else to convey this concept to the girls, the social workers told them that their mother was not yet ready to say good-bye as she had not yet accepted the judge's decision.

"No, she's probably still arguing," said Linda. "But it's no use. Her time is up. It's no use still arguing. The judge believed she did those bad things to us. She did bad things when she was mad. She has no more chances. Her time has run out."

Janis said, "I don't feel sad about Mom because of the things she done. She lied. She's a liar. You can tell the judge that."

Linda said she was afraid that the judges would "change their minds," and she said that if they did she would run away and hide.

When a representative of the Official Guardian later interviewed the children in order to determine what their wishes were with respect to the appeal, they again repeated their desire to stay with the Kovakses and told the lawyer to ask the judge if they could have their old toys back.

Janis wrote a letter to Dr. Oliviera, saying that she would be sad if she had to go back to live with her mother or father. The letter, which was presented as an exhibit to the appeal court, had all the untidiness and errors in spelling and grammar that one would expect from a child who was not yet ten years old. But Janis also showed a sophisticated understanding that belied her age as she wrote, "If we won't see Mom or Dad, then they can make a new life. Then we can make a new life too."

The determination with which the children appeared to be grasping this opportunity to make a new life gives some cause to hope that their harrowing story may have a happy ending.

NOTES

1. Florence Rush, *The Best Kept Secret* (1980, McGraw Hill, New York)

2. Ambroise Tardieu, quoted in Jeffrey Masson, *The Assault on Truth* (1984, Farrar, Straus and Giroux, New York), page 15.

3. Quoted in Florence Rush, op. cit., page 2.

4. Ellen Bass in Ellen Bass and Louise Thornton (eds.), *I Never Told Anyone* (1983, Harper & Row, New York), page 38.

5. Quoted in Jeffrey Masson, *A Dark Secret* (1986, Farrar, Straus and Giroux, New York), page 25.

6. Ann Wolbert Burgess, *Child Pornography and Sex Rings* (1984, D C Heath & Co., Lexington, Massachusetts), page 25.

7. Jeffrey Russell, *A History of Witchcraft* (1981, Thames and Hudson, London).

8. See: Gerhard Zacharias, *The Satanic Cult* (1980, George Allen & Unwin, London), page 114.

9. Norman Cohn, quoted in Margot Adler, *Drawing Down the Moon* (1981, Beacon Press, Boston), page 30.

10. Quoted in Masson, *Assault on Truth*, page 104.

11. William Bainbridge, *Satan's Power: A Deviant Psychotherapy Cult* (1978, University of California Press, Los Angeles).

12. J. Gordon Melton, *The Encyclopedia of American Religions* (1978, McGrath Publishing Co., Wilmington, North Carolina), page 301.

13. Coleman is quoted in Paul and Shirley Eberle, *The Politics of Child Abuse* (1986, Lyle Stuart, Inc., Secaucus, New Jersey). Details of the Miami case are given in Jan Hollingsworth, *Unspeakable Acts* (1986, Congdon and Weed, New York).

14. David Finkelhor, *A Sourcebook on Child Sexual Abuse* (1986, Sage Publications, Inc., Beverly Hills, California), page 67.

15. Edward J. Moody in Irving Zaretsky and Mark Leone (eds.), *Religious Movements in Contemporary America* (1974, Princeton University Press, Princeton, New Jersey), page 360.

16. Ellen Bass, op. cit., page 43.

ABOUT THE AUTHOR

Kevin Marron was born in London, England, in 1947 and spent his formative years in Egypt, Bahrain, South Wales and the west of England. After completing secondary school, he taught for a year in Algeria under a voluntary service program. In 1970, he graduated from Cambridge University with an honours BA in English, and came to Canada to do postgraduate studies at McMaster University.

Now a Canadian citizen and living in Hamilton, Ont., Marron has worked as a freelance reporter for the *Globe and Mail* since 1978. Before that he taught at a free school, helped run an alternate community newspaper in Brantford, and edited a weekly newspaper in Dundas. He is now preparing a book about occult groups in Canada.

SEAL BOOKS

Offers you a list of outstanding fiction, non-fiction, and classics of Canadian literature in paperback by Canadian authors, available at all good bookstores throughout Canada.

The Mark of Canadian Bestsellers